THE KINDERGARTEN

REPORTS OF THE COMMITTEE OF NINETEEN ON THE THEORY AND PRACTICE OF THE KINDERGARTEN

AUTHORIZED BY THE INTERNATIONAL
KINDERGARTEN UNION

BOSTON NEW YORK CHICAGO
HOUGHTON MIFFLIN COMPANY
The Riverside Press Cambridge

CONTENTS

CONTENTS

PREFACE

THE Committee of Nineteen was originally formed in response to a demand on the part of educators and the general public to know what kindergarten is and what the modern kindergarten does.

A restatement of Froebelian principles seemed to be necessary in the light of the recent contributions of biology, sociology, and modern psychology to the science of education.

During the thirty years in which the kindergarten has existed in this country, its ideal has been more clearly defined and its practice modified to conform to a better understanding of its educational instrumentalities and aims. The fundamental principles of the system are accepted by all; but as truth permits many angles of vision, variations in methods have arisen. It was therefore impossible to harmonize all views at once and issue a unified report.

The reports now submitted are the result of much discussion of the psychologic foundations of the kindergarten and of comparison of methods in the use of the Froebelian materials and other means of education. They present from three viewpoints the underlying theories which control the practice of the kindergarten of to-day and illuminate that practice by concrete illustrations.

The Committee sends forth this volume in the hope that it may help to clarify and vivify the work of the kindergartner and to extend the educational influence of the great apostle of childhood.

LUCY WHEELOCK,
Chairman of Editing Committee.

INTRODUCTION

BY

ANNIE LAWS

INTRODUCTION

AT the tenth annual meeting of the International Kindergarten Union, held at Pittsburgh, April 14–17, 1903, it was decided to appoint a Committee of Three, namely, Miss Susan E. Blow, Mrs. Alice H. Putnam, at that time president of the Union, and Miss Lucy Wheelock, these three to select a Committee of Fifteen, including themselves, "to formulate contemporary kindergarten thought" with a view to more clearly defining the points of agreement and points of difference in theory and practice in existing kindergarten centers.

The original Committee consisted of Miss Blow, chairman, Mrs. Maria Kraus-Boelté, Mrs. Alice H. Putnam, Miss Lucy Wheelock, Miss Elizabeth Harrison, Miss Caroline T. Haven, Miss Patty S. Hill, Miss Caroline M. C. Hart, Miss Laura Fisher, Mrs. Mary B. Page, Dr. Jenny B. Merrill, Miss Harriet Niel, Miss Nora Smith, Miss Fanniebelle Curtis, and Miss Annie Laws.

To these were afterwards added Mrs. James L. Hughes, Miss Mary C. McCulloch, Miss Alice C. Fitts, and Miss Nina C. Vandewalker, making a Committee of Nineteen instead of the original Fifteen. Miss Smith resigning later, her place was filled by Miss Stovall, who also resigned, and Mrs. M. B. B. Langzettel was elected to fill the vacant place.

Miss Blow called the first meeting of the Committee

at Rochester in 1904, at which time the Committee
organized by making Miss Wheelock chairman and
Miss Curtis secretary. Later, at Buffalo, in 1909, Miss
Wheelock resigned from the chairmanship on account
of ill health, and the present chairman was elected to
fill the vacancy.

The Committee has held nine sessions at the same
time and place as the annual meetings of the Union,
namely, Rochester, Toronto, Milwaukee, New York,
New Orleans, Buffalo, St. Louis, Cincinnati, and Des
Moines, and two special sessions, in December, 1904,
and December, 1911, in New York City. Each session
has consisted of several meetings. The session held at
the Hotel Westminster, New York, December 28–30,
1904, is noticeable as having a complete attendance of
the Committee, with exception of Miss Stovall, who
sent her resignation, finding the distance from San
Francisco prohibitive so far as attendance at meetings
was concerned.

At the second New York session, 1907, all were
present but Miss Harrison, and at the third New York
session, in December, 1911, all were present but five,
making the New York sessions the most largely attended of the eleven.

The first selection of topics for consideration was
under the following headings: —

      I. Plans of Work.
     II. Materials and Methods.
    III. Psychology.
    IV. Symbolism.

The Committee resolved itself into three subdivis-
ions with the following leaders, Miss Blow, Mrs. Page,

and Miss Laws, for the purpose of formulating statements for discussion.

The question of self-activity aroused a very spirited discussion in one of the large meetings. The philosophic and psychologic basis of practice; the place of imagination in the life of the child, its growth and culture through constructive and æsthetic occupations, fairy tales, and games, and its relation to the formation of ideals, were also topics under consideration.

Plans of work formed the bases of many discussions, with the object of gaining comparative views of lines of work as followed in different localities, which might be of practical value to kindergartners. The annual conferences of training teachers and supervisors frequently enjoyed the fruits of many of these discussions.

One result was undoubtedly a better understanding among Committee members, not only of working principles and practice, but of one another, and the acquisition of more definiteness in the formulation of ideas and principles. While diversity of opinion undoubtedly existed, there was evident a unity of spirit and a common desire to reach the best and see the best in the work of others.

In order to meet the desire on the part of kindergartners and educators generally for such a statement as not only should embody the principles which have been accepted from the beginning, but should suggest the present trend of the movement as far as it could be determined and account for some of the variations of practice, the Committee selected as a culminating topic the following: —

"Fundamental differences between the so-called schools of kindergarten; — essential differences in the varying interpretations of Froebel's theory."

This formed the basis of discussions at the Milwaukee and New Orleans meetings.

After each member had expressed briefly her views, it was finally decided to assign to three leaders the presentation of the various standpoints classified under the headings of Conservative, Liberal, and Conservative-Liberal or Third Report; Miss Blow to present the first, Miss Vandewalker the second, and Miss Wheelock the third point of view.

The three authorized reports were submitted, carefully read and discussed, and signed respectively by members of the Committee according as they best represented their attitude of thought.

The following preamble to the reports was discussed and arranged by the Committee in session: —

"In thus presenting three distinct reports, the signers desire to state that this indicates no lack of harmony on the part of members of the Committee, but an earnest endeavor to present clearly differing points of view brought out in the deliberations of the Committee.'

"The discussions which have culminated in these reports have resulted in giving to the members clearer insight and an increasing appreciation and respect for differing points of view, and the hope is expressed that in this honest presentation of view the whole body of kindergartners may be stimulated to more alert thought and earnest study which may lead eventually to a larger synthesis."

These reports were presented at the business meeting of the International Kindergarten Union in Buffalo, April 29, 1909, accepted by the Union, and ordered printed in the *Proceedings of the Sixteenth Annual Meeting,* which were distributed among members and branches of the Union, and copies of which are still available.

The Committee was continued by order of the Union, and the following two meetings were held at St. Louis and Cincinnati respectively.

At the former the following resolutions were presented to the Union by the Committee: —

"WHEREAS the kindergarten cause throughout the United States has suffered an inestimable loss in the death of Dr. William T. Harris:

"*Resolved:* That the Committee of Nineteen of the International Kindergarten Union express its sincere appreciation of the debt which all kindergartners owe to Dr. Harris for the invaluable services, the stanch support, and the wise counsel which he gave to the cause, especially in its early history.

"*Resolved:* That the Committee also recognizes that in his intellectual greatness, philosophic insight, and unwavering allegiance are found the influences which more than any other have given the kindergarten its high place in American education.

"*Resolved:* That a copy of these Resolutions be sent to the family, also presented to the International Kindergarten Union, with the request that it be spread upon the minutes and published in the Annual Report."

This was signed by all members of the Committee,

and a copy appeared in the Seventeenth Annual Report.

At the Cincinnati meeting in April, 1910, it was decided to gather together all past papers and material for presentation, but not for publication.

Headings for final report were arranged as follows:—

I. Statement of type of program preferred.

II. Principles underlying program making.

III. Process of program making.

IV. Concrete illustrations.

Miss Blow, Miss Hill, and Miss Harrison were selected to present three papers along these lines at a session to be held in New York in December, 1911.

Miss Blow and Miss Hill presented reports, and Miss Harrison, who was unable to be present, presented her report later at Des Moines, in April, 1912.

Copies of these reports were placed in the hands of the following Advisory Committee of Men who had consented to give the benefit of their views on the questions presented: Professor Henry W. Holmes, Dr. John A. McVannel, Dr. John Dewey, Mr. James L. Hughes, Dr. Angell.

The presentation of the completed report of the Committee to the Union at the Des Moines meeting and the arrangements for final form of publication were placed in the hands of a Committee of Five, consisting of Miss Blow, Miss Hill, Miss Wheelock, and the Chairman and the Secretary *ex-officio*.

It was decided to eliminate former headings of reports, and designate them simply as First, Second, and Third Reports.

A letter from Mrs. Kraus-Boelté contained a rendering of an old fable which seemed such an apt illustration of some of the present conditions in the kindergarten that it was decided to include the following abstract in the final report.[1]

In bringing the work of the Committee of Nineteen to a culmination in the presentation of its final report, the hope is expressed by the members of the Committee that one result of the valuable experiences gained through these conferences may be the formation in the International Kindergarten Union of a Department of Training Teachers and Supervisors in which members of the Committee may find opportunity to continue on a broader scale and with greater numbers the dis-

---

[1] "A father had three sons whom he loved equally well. This father owned a precious Ring — said to be endowed with power to bring highest blessings to its owner. Each one of the three sons asked the father to bestow the Ring on him after the father's death. The father, in his great love for his sons, promised the Ring to each one. In his old age, the father sent for a jeweler and asked him to make two rings exactly like the precious Ring owned by him. The jeweler assented, and after a while he brought the three rings to the father, who could not distinguish the precious Ring from the other two, so well were they made. When the time came that the father died, he called each of his sons separately to him, blessed him, and gave him a ring. After the father's burial, the three brothers met, and each one claimed the birthright and the ownership of the genuine Ring. Finally, when they could not decide which was the original one, they went to a Judge, who gave the decision in the form of advice, viz., 'As the true Ring is said to have the magic power of making the owner beloved and esteemed by God and man, and as each of you three brothers believes his Ring to be the genuine or original one, so let each one, untouched by his prejudice, strive to reveal the power of the Ring in his life by loving peaceableness, and by charity and sincere devotion to God; and when in later generations the power of the true Ring reveals itself, I will call upon you again, before the "seat of Judgment." A wiser man than I am may be there and speak.'"

cussions and conferences which they have found productive of so much interest and value to themselves and through them to others.

The Chairman desires to express her appreciation of the able manner in which the Committee was organized by her predecessor, Miss Wheelock, thus greatly simplifying her work; and also her sincere thanks to all of the members of the Committee and especially to the efficient secretary, Miss Curtis, for their hearty coöperation. She congratulates herself that she was present at the Pittsburgh meeting when the Committee was formed and has been able to attend all of the eleven sessions.[1]

ANNIE LAWS, *Chairman,*
Committee of Nineteen, International Kindergarten Union.

[1] Since the completion of the final report of the Committee of Nineteen, Miss Caroline T. Haven has been called from among us.

Miss Haven was one of the founders of the International Kindergarten Union. She served it first as corresponding secretary, then as vice-president, again as secretary, and in 1898 was elected president; and this position she filled a second time. She was long on the Advisory Committee, and from the formation of the Committee of Nineteen she was one of its most honored members. Miss Haven attended the last meeting of the Committee at the Hotel Marseilles in New York, in December, 1912, knowing full well that the hand of the angel was stretched out to her. But her attitude was always one of fearless courage. A few months previous, when, as Chairman of the Nominating Committee of the International Kindergarten Union, she had been cautioned by a friend because of the labor involved, she had replied, "As this is in all probability my last bit of service for the International Kindergarten Union, I want it to represent my best effort at any cost."

No tribute that we can accord Caroline T. Haven is too great. She was the rugged, sincere, invigorating friend, yet withal most gracious and kindly; and these remembrances of her are the lasting and dear possession of each member of the Committee of Nineteen.

FIRST REPORT

SUSAN E. BLOW

PART I

THE CONCEPTION OF THE GLIEDGANZES

THE kindergarten is one phase of the general educational process and will be differently conceived as that process is differently understood. In other words, our conception of the kindergarten will depend ultimately upon our definition of education.

Definitions of education may be more or less comprehensive. Thus education may be broadly conceived as a process of interaction between the individual, the social whole, and the natural environment. In a still wider sense history may be conceived as an educative process and defined as a series of interactions continued through centuries, and extended from limited to larger physical and social environments.

Thus far there is quite general agreement as to the nature of the educative process. It seems to be further agreed that in a more specific sense education is "the conscious control and direction of the process of interaction";[1] that it involves the influence of a relatively mature person over a person relatively immature; that the standard for determining educational values is the civilization into which the pupil is born, and that in the psychical powers and attitudes of the pupil must be sought the basis for educational method.

The perplexing questions of education arise within

[1] See *Kindergarten Problems*, pp. 3-6. Columbia University Press.

the limits of these large agreements. The recognized values of life are not all equally valuable. No consensus of opinion has been reached as to their relative values. From this lack of agreement as to relative values spring differences of opinion as to emphasis upon language, literature, history, and art on the one side and the natural sciences and industries on the other. Even more fundamental than this contrasted emphasis, is the contrasted emphasis upon the ethical and intellectual values. Finally, besides the problems relating to relative emphasis upon different values, must be mentioned the very serious problems arising from the attempts to discriminate the specific contribution of different educational agencies to the general process of education. The family, the kindergarten, the economic organization, the state, and the church, all exercise some conscious control and direction over the general process of interaction between the individual, the social whole, and the physical environment. It is in drawing the boundary lines between these several spheres of influence that educational theory confronts some of its gravest problems, and educational practice some of its most serious difficulties. Shall the teaching of religion be relegated entirely to the family and the church, or shall any portion of such teaching be given in the kindergarten and the school? How far shall the common school prepare for the industries and arts, and how much may it do to capacitate its pupils for citizenship? To what extent shall the kindergarten assume responsibilities hitherto conceived as belonging exclusively to the family? What dangers are incident to the assumption by one educational institution of duties belonging primarily to another? These questions suggest some of the more serious problems with which thoughtful educators are constantly wrestling.

The various perplexities suggested in the preceding questions are concerned with educational values and agencies. Another series of perplexities arises when we devote our attention to educational method, for, while there is general agreement as to the fact that its basis must be psychological, there is the widest divergence of opinion as to the interpretation of psychological data, and the relative accent to be placed upon different psychical capacities and attitudes.

Two great educational documents, "The Report of the Committee of Ten" and "The Report of the Committee of Fifteen," have made all students of education aware of a contrasted emphasis upon the rational type of mankind, and the native tendencies of particular human beings which deviate from that type. The Report of the Committee of Ten "proceeds upon the view that each peculiar and individual expression of the common human nature is the one fact of truly cardinal value"; the Report of the Committee of Fifteen, "upon the view that the supreme consideration must be the type characteristically human, not private and peculiar, but public, generic, and above all historic."[1]

The kindergarten is an attempt to mediate these contrasting views. It holds with the latter view that the supreme consideration is the type characteristically human, but it calls attention to the fact that this

[1] Prof. W. G. Howison, *The Correlation of Elementary Studies,* University of California.

type itself has not been adequately realized. "One
generation does not follow another in facsimile. Each
generation is a step in human progress and each
new birth an unprecedented experiment." Therefore,
while insisting upon the "rational authority of the
human type historically developed and tested and
warranted," the kindergarten demands ample opportunity for that individual initiative, through which
the type may be more completely revealed and
embodied.[1]

No less fundamental than the contrasting appreciations of educational values and the contrasting accents
of educational methods, are the contrasting convictions with regard to the goal of the educational process.
It is held by some thinkers that the sufficient aim of
education is to make men ethical. Critics of this view
contend that it is one-sided because it ignores the
intellect and places all its stress upon the will, and they
offer as a more adequate definition of the goal of education that it is "development of the theoretical and
practical reason in the individual." This latter con-

[1] "Man, *humanity in man*, as an external manifestation should
be looked upon, not as fixed and stationary, but as steadily and
progressively growing in a state of ever living development, ever
ascending from one stage of culture towards its aim, which partakes
of the infinite and eternal.

"It is unspeakably pernicious to look upon the development of
humanity as stationary and completed and to see in its present
phases simply repetitions and greater generalizations of itself. For
the child as well as every successive generation becomes thereby
exclusively imitative, an external copy, as it were a cast of the
preceding one, and not a living ideal for its stage of development,
which it has attained in human development considered as a whole,
to serve future generations in all time to come." *Education of Man*,
pp. 17–18.

ception is in accord with the ideal of Froebel as expressed in the following statement: "By education, then, the divine essence of man should be unfolded, brought out, lifted into consciousness, and man himself raised into free, conscious obedience to the divine principle that lives in him, and to a free representation of this principle in his life."[1]

Differing appreciations of educational values, differing interpretations of psychologic data, and differing conceptions of the goal towards which education should move are finally to be explained through differing world-views, whether such views be the mystical presuppositions of religion, or the consciously defined and organized presuppositions of philosophy. The norms of Oriental civilization differ from those of Occidental civilization, because the two civilizations are based upon contrasting world-views. The world-view consciously or unconsciously adopted by each particular educator colors all his thinking and biases all his practical activity. Defining the educative process in its larger sense, as one of mutual adjustment between the individual and his social environment, we become aware that, in our country and age, both change so rapidly that we are threatened with educational anarchy. Furthermore, the immature individual is often subjected to a bewildering variety of educational environments. The child of Hebrew parentage, sent to a Christian kindergarten, promoted to a school whose teachers have inwardly renounced Christianity in favor of scientific materialism, and graduating from a university whose professors are under the spell of

[1] *Education of Man*, p. 4.

pragmatism, will have lived through a series of adjustments and readjustments with manifestly problematic outcome.

In what has thus far been said there has been an effort to suggest the necessity for some conscious standard by which the goal of education may be determined, the several educational values appraised, and the psychical capacities and attitudes interpreted. For the disciple of Froebel such a standard is provided in the conception of man as *Gliedganzes*.

The signers of this report hold that the conception of the Gliedganzes embodies final truth which may be dialectically demonstrated. In claiming for it the mark of finality they mean, not that it leaves nothing new to be discovered, but that all new discoveries of truth will make explicit some of its as yet undefined implications.

While the word Gliedganzes was coined by Froebel, the conception it embodies did not originate with him. It is mystically divined by the Christian consciousness, and mystically stated in Christian creeds. As a philosophic insight it has been attained by a heroic struggle with the implications of self-activity. The everlasting foundation of philosophy was laid when Plato announced his insight into the self-moved. To Aristotle it became clear that the self-movement demanded was most adequately realized in the thinking activity or reason. The doctrine of the Gliedganzes is simply a statement of the necessary implications of a completely realized thinking activity. These implications have been more adequately developed by Hegel than by any other philosopher. Finally, one essential phase of the idea overlooked by Hegel has been pointed out by Dr. Harris. The truth of the doctrine of the Gliedganzes can be apprehended by any person who will go through the necessary mental discipline. This report presupposes the Gliedganzes as true, and limits itself to a description, as opposed to a justification, of the insight.

The word Gliedganzes means the member of a whole who is potentially commensurate with the whole to which as member he belongs, but who can make this potentiality actual, only in and through active membership. Each individual human being is an incarnate paradox. He is an integral member of humanity. He is also ideally coextensive with humanity. Throughout the vegetable and animal world there is a bridgeless chasm between the individual and the species. Hence nature presents the tragic spectacle of generic energies which are always seeking, but never finding, their adequate embodiment. No rose can be all roses, and no dog all dogs. As a physical being man is subject to the same limitation, and the human species falls apart into races, these into tribes, and tribes into mutually excluding individuals. Spiritual humanity, on the contrary, is not a whole composed of parts, but a whole composed of wholes, a totality wherein each individual is also total. As an intellectual and volitional being each man is ideally capable of reproducing the human species within himself. He can assimilate all human experience, and order his life in free obedience to the ideals which are its distilled result. The final outcome of this intellectually and morally assimilated experience is the development of impulses accordant with its ideals.

The conception of man as Gliedganzes is not fully apprehended when it is conceived as relating only to the relationship between the individual human being and the human species. It contains three distinct implications, all of which must be clearly seized before the doctrine itself can be adequately understood. The first of these implications is that "that which is generic or the reproducer of the species in lower forms of life, becomes the Ego in man," and that it is because in each man humanity is implicit that from each man it may be evolved. The second implication is that this generic Ego or universal self is not only the ideal human, but the divine; the God immanent in man, yet transcendent of him. The third and final implication is that this immanent-transcendent God is one with the absolute first principle through which nature is given its being.

No student of contemporary philosophy can fail to be aware that, in all its varieties, it tends towards denial of the theses which the doctrine of the Gliedganzes asserts. Its general tendency is to minimize the significance of human self-consciousness. The accent of thought is upon will, or self-determining activity conceived in detachment from self-consciousness, or awareness of this self-determining activity by itself. The result is an ominous one. In proportion as self-consciousness is minimized, self-determination or will is finitized, and in proportion as will is finitized, mankind is lost in men.

The general tendency above described shows itself in different forms in the several systems of philosophy most in vogue. Contemporary naturalism discredits self-consciousness altogether as a regrettable by-product of evolution, and hence looks upon humanity as a mere transition towards a higher race. Pragmatism denies an absolute subject, active in nature, and immanent in man as the transcendental self. Hence it knows no eternal values, and its adventurous universe is without a chart to guide its uncertain course. Contemporary gnosticism accepts an absolute first principle, but looks upon nature as a finite conscious life; conceives humanity as a specification of this life and interprets the relationship of individual man to the human species after the biologic analogy. Finally, contemporary mysticism in all its varieties denies to conscious intellect ability to ratify and interpret the occult divinations of the subconscious self, and therefore tends perpetually to fall into agnosticism.

In opposition to all these philosophies, the doctrine of the Gliedganzes presupposes a completely realized self-consciousness as the absolute first principle of the universe, asserts the participation of humanity in this principle, declares that all valid ideals are its approximate definitions, recognizes that all creations of art express its form, and defines the aim of education as its more perfect realization in all individuals.

The object of the foregoing discussion has been to describe the conception of man as Gliedganzes, and to suggest that it implies in each individual participation in that aboriginal self-determining energy which achieves in self-consciousness its ideal form. Only a self-conscious being could be a Gliedganzes, because only in self-consciousness does a generic energy duplicate itself in its product. Humanity is implicit in

each individual of the race. This implicit humanity
is divine. To make the implicit divine explicit is the
goal of education. It can become explicit only in self-
consciousness. Hence, says Froebel, "To become conscious of itself is the first task in the life of a child as
it is the task of the whole life of man."

Manifestly the realization of self-consciousness
through the reproduction of the genus within the
individual is a goal which education can never reach.
It is none the less a goal towards which education
must always move.

From what has been said it should be evident that
the educational ideal implicit in the conception of man
as Gliedganzes is most inadequately defined when it
is limited to education for the purpose of social
efficiency. The conception of man as Gliedganzes implies, indeed, that the individual shall act as a worthy
member of a social whole, but it also induces modesty
by its insistence that only in and through active membership can the individual either realize or know himself. "Educate your child in this manner," writes
Froebel, "and at the goal of his education he will
recognize himself as the living member of a living
whole, and will know that his life mirrors the life of
his family, his people, humanity, the being and life of
God who works in all and through all. Having attained to a clear vision of the universal life, his conscious aim will be to manifest it in his feeling and
thought, in his relationships and his deeds. Through
the self-consecration begotten of this lofty ideal he
will learn to understand nature, human experience,
and the prescient yearnings of his own soul. His

individual life will flow with the currents of nature and of humanity, and move towards a realization of the divine ideal immanent in both." [1]

In his preface to *Symbolic Education*, Dr. Harris calls attention to the several facts that the first statement of the doctrine of the Gliedganzes is to be found in the *Metaphysics* of Aristotle; that this doctrine is an explication of the constitution of mind; and that the constitution of mind, as we know it in ourselves, points towards a completely realized Gliedganzes as divine first principle of the universe. "It is interesting to note," he writes, "that Hegel found this thought in the famous seventh chapter of the seventh book of Aristotle's *Metaphysics*, where he speaks of the intelligible as being the 'co-element' ($\sigma\upsilon\sigma\tau o\iota\chi\acute{\iota}a$) of the thinking activity or reason ($\nu o\hat{\upsilon}s$). He exclaims, on quoting this passage, 'One can scarce believe his eyes,' at finding this thought in Aristotle; and proceeds to explain the word $\sigma\upsilon\sigma\tau o\iota\chi\acute{\iota}a$ (which is often translated *series*) as sometimes signifying 'an element which is itself its own element, and is always self-determined' — that is to say, it is a member of itself and thus a whole and a part at the same time. The reach of this thought is noteworthy as explaining the constitution of mind or consciousness (which is subject and object — co-elements — and at the same time a whole including both; the subject and object are likewise wholes as well as co-elements). Here we have a Gliedganzes. But what man is as personality, he is also in his institutions; he is a citizen of a state; the parent or the child of the family; a member of any

[1] *Mottoes and Commentaries*, p. 60.

coöperative community. This, too, is expressed in the highest thought man has reached, that of the Invisible Church celebrated in St. John's Revelation, wherein each person, inspired by the missionary spirit of self-sacrifice for others, becomes a member of an infinite choir or congregation, and at the same time he is an individual self-active whole in himself. Indeed, is not the mystery of the Holy Trinity the supreme exemplar of this independence in the midst of perfect unity with others?"[1]

The nature of man as a potential Gliedganzes is not understood until it is illuminated by the conception of God as an actual Gliedganzes. The Christian doctrine of a triune God is a mystical statement of the divine first principle as a completely realized Gliedganzes. The supreme achievement of philosophy has been the transfiguration of this mystic intuition into a compelling insight which may be actively reproduced by each individual thinker. The Froebelian ideal of education consciously posits this coercive insight as its goal. The individual shall know God as an actual, and man as a potential, Gliedganzes, and his deeds and impulses shall be accordant with this knowledge.

[1] *Symbolic Education*, Editor's Preface, pp. xiv–xv.

PART II

THE DEFINITION AND ORDER OF
EDUCATIONAL VALUES

HAVING defined the goal of education as determined by the standard of the Gliedganzes, we must next apply the same criterion to the definition and ordering of the several educational values. These values may be summarily included under the heads of Religion, Ethics, Language, Literature, History, the Fine Arts and Industries, Mathematics, and Natural Science. It is to be understood that our discussion of these values is independent of the questions of educational methods and agencies. We are not asking how, or by whom, the several values shall be developed, but simply discussing these values in and for themselves. Our reason for preceding the consideration of a kindergarten program by a discussion of educational values is, that we believe each value must be conceived in its entire scope, and in its relation to all other values, in order that, from the beginning, it may be rightly developed.

THE FIRST GREAT EDUCATIONAL VALUE: RELIGION

In the order of educational values for the Occidental world, the Christian religion ranks first, because in the form of a mystic experience it is the primary revelation of God as an actual, and man as a potential Gliedganzes. The root of religion is the feeling of community with invisible beings, or with one transcendent invisible being—God. There may, however, be different conceptions of God. Christianity is that religion which conceives God as transcendent, immanent, and incarnate. He is primarily the self-subsistent and transcendent Unity — God over all. He gives himself to all things in so far as they are able to receive Him, and is therefore immanent in nature and in humanity. The goal of immanence is incarnation, and the Christian God is conceived as incarnate potentially in all men, and actually in one historic individual, who in virtue of this incarnation becomes the concrete revelation of what God is, and man ought to be.

The Christian religion teaches that what is true of Christ is true of God.[1] The supreme revelation of Christ's divine human life is made in the Cross, and the final import of the Cross is that the historic sacrifice upon Calvary adumbrates that perpetual sacrifice through which a God of perfect love communicates Himself to and realizes Himself in and through his creatures. Unless there be, indeed, an eternal reality corresponding to the historic event, all the light of sacred story gathers in vain around the Cross, and that law of sacrifice which is the law of life remains a ghastly and intimidating mystery. The eternal Cross is God's eternal plight of love, and it is the increasing penetration of God's world by God's spirit which explains the sacrifice of the bird for its nestling, of the

---

[1] Philip saith unto him, Lord, show us the Father, and it sufficeth us. Jesus saith unto him, Have I been so long time with you, and dost thou not know me, Philip? He that hath seen me hath seen the Father; how sayest thou, Show us the Father? John xiv, 8-9.

human mother for her child, of the patriot for his country, of the hero for his cause, of the missionary for the cannibal, of Jesus for the world.

It should be evident to any thoughtful person that this summarized statement of Christianity relates only to the most fundamental facts of the Christian consciousness, and ignores the more or less adequate interpretations of that consciousness as bodied forth in the varying creeds of Christendom. All Christian churches accept in some form the dogmas of transcendence, immanence, and incarnation, and all recognize, though in differing degrees, the authority of one divine human life. The substance of the definition given is the common experience which discriminates the Christian from the non-Christian world, and since this experience is the chief norm of Occidental civilization, it seems not only reasonable, but imperative that its influence should pervade all phases of education. In other words, while it is the duty and privilege of each Christian church to give its specific interpretation of the Christian consciousness, that consciousness itself should be presupposed by and clarified through all education, direct and indirect, given by the family, the school, the community, the economic organization, and the state. The location of any point on the earth's surface is accurately fixed only when it is referred to as the projection of a corresponding point of the celestial sphere. So each great human value is accurately defined only when conceived as the projection of a corresponding eternal value.

Since religion belongs to the realm of the subconscious, and embodies a mystic experience, it becomes

of primary importance to discriminate between different varieties of this experience. The tendency of contemporary mysticism is to assert the divinity of the
subconscious. It would be quite as true to assert its
diabolism. The subconscious as such has no character;
it is simply a name which we give to that part of our
mental life which is beyond our own ken, and it is often
intellectually foolish and morally perverse. A criterion
is necessary by which its divinations may be tested,
and that criterion is the form of self-activity. Since
this form is ours, or, more correctly stated, since we
are this form, it acts in us both as a creative and apperceptive agency. Its definitions are our ideals; its self-
projection creates art; its selective interest directed
towards the phenomena of nature gives birth to science;
and its occult sense of its own divinity is our mystic experience of God transcendent, immanent, and
incarnate. It is not the subconscious which is divine,
but the *eternal form of self-activity* present in the subconscious, and emerging from it, first as feeling, imagination, and conscience, and finally as reason aware of
itself. Testing the dicta of our subconscious selves by
this criterion, we are able to judge which are of God
and which of the devil.

The absolute truth adumbrated in the mystic divinations of the Christian religion is God as completely
objectified self-consciousness, and therefore as completely realized Gliedganzes. To know this true God,
live in communion with Him, and become assimilated
to Him through participation in His eternal life, is the
goal of human existence. It follows that education as
a conscious process should posit the same goal. There-

fore religion, conceived as the mystic experience of God transcendent, immanent, and incarnate, is the supreme educational value, and in maturity this religious experience should consciously define itself as theologic insight. It was this conviction which led Froebel to insist that as the age of Jesus demanded faith, so the present age demands insight, and to declare that not only should the process of education culminate in a conscious world-view, but that from the beginning it should be conducted with reference to this world-view, and break a path towards it.

The conception of religion which has been presented differs alike from the view of those who accept an external revelation of divine reality, and those who either deny the existence of this reality, or challenge man's ability to know it. Traditionalism fails to satisfy man's intelligence. Rationalism, which ignores the heart and imagination, fails to create the religious experience which is the indispensable preliminary of theologic insight. Mysticism, which tacitly or openly denies the competency of the intellect to know truth, and which offers no criterion by which the occult divinations of the subconscious self may be tested, must perpetually relapse into vagueness and self-contradiction. It is necessary, on the one hand, that eternal truth shall be presented in the form of a compelling insight, and on the other, that education shall provide a genetic development of the normative experiences through which to perpetuate the Christian consciousness which that insight defines. In so far as this double requirement is met, we may hope to overcome the present disastrous schism between a traditional creed formally professed, and a secular life rooted in the unregenerate impulses which it is the practical aim of religion to transform.

THE SECOND GREAT EDUCATIONAL VALUE: ETHICS

In the order of educational values religion ranks first because, as has been said, it is the primary revelation of God as an actual, and man as a potential, Gliedganzes. The second rank in the hierarchy of educational values must be assigned to ethics. By the word ethics we designate "the whole of the formal part of life that fits man to live in the institutions of civilization." [1] It is in and through the great institutions of the family, civil society, the state, and the church that the individual learns practically to live as a Gliedganzes. In the elementary and secondary schools the medium for the study of social institutions is history, which is really a study of the development of man's corporate selfhood. In the kindergarten the medium for a primary revelation of institutions is the dramatic game. [2]

Each one of the great institutions of society has a special function and a distinctive principle. The function of the family is nurture, and its principle is love. The function of civil society is reciprocal service, and its principle is economy. The function of the state is

[1] Rosenkranz, *Philosophy of Education*, p. 150.

[2] This report omits history in the discussion of values because in its true sense it has no place in the kindergarten. It may, however, be claimed that the kindergarten prepares in some slight degree for the study of history by inducing children to make periodical retrospects of their own typical experiences, by stories of heroes; and by celebrating the birthdays of great representative men.

to safeguard liberty, and its principle is justice. The function of the church is revelation of eternal verities, and its principle is faith. Love is the emotional equivalent of the idea of the Gliedganzes. Economy is the wise use of the members of a totality by setting to each the task to which he is by nature best adapted. Justice is recognition of the dignity and responsibility of that freedom which belongs to the individual in virtue of his character as actually member of a whole, and ideally commensurate with that whole. Faith is the spontaneous leap of the human spirit towards its own Eternal Ideal.

Not only does each human institution develop some aspect of the nature of man as Gliedganzes, but each institution also manifests a tendency towards expansion of which the realization of the Gliedganzes is the impelling motive. It has frequently been observed that the social nature of self-consciousness is adumbrated in the feeling of love. "Love," says Hegel, "is in general the consciousness of the unity of myself with another. I am not separate and isolated, but win my self-consciousness only by renouncing my independent existence and by knowing myself as unity of myself with another and another with me. The first element in love is that I will to be no longer an independent self-sufficing person, and that if I were such a person I should feel myself lacking and incomplete. The second element is that I gain myself in another person in whom I am recognized as he again is in me." [1] Love is the principle of the family, and its ideal nature as the feeling of the Gliedganzes is suggested in its

[1] Hegel's *Philosophy of Right*, S. W. Dyde, p. 165.

extension from husband and wife to children, sons and daughters-in-law, and grandchildren. Beginning as a union of two persons it becomes a union of many persons and points for its consummation to the union of all persons.

In the civic community we observe a similar expansion. The individual has wants which he can satisfy only by means of other individuals. Hence arises the economic organization with its principle of economy. The expansion of this great institution from the particular community to the nation and from the nation to the world is too patent to need illustration. The goal towards which it aspires is the devotion of each individual to the service for which he is best fitted and the dower of each individual with the fruits of universal toil and the wealth of universal experience.

The unity of men in man (or the ideal nature of man as Gliedganzes) felt in the family as love, and embodied in civil society as reciprocal dependence, is recognized in the state as law. Hegel has defined the state as "will that wills will." If we conceive will as self-determining energy, we shall have no difficulty in understanding this definition. All actions that interfere with the free exercise of self-determination attack will. All actions that abet this exercise reinforce will. The ability to curtail self-determining energy is implied in its possession, and hence the recurrent spectacle which so terrifies the weak-hearted of "freedom free to slay herself and dying while men shout her name." The great aim of providential education throughout the centuries is to teach men to do only those deeds which, being in conformity with freedom,

enhance and diffuse it. The laws of a state define the
substance of freedom so far as any given people has
learned to understand it. In the eyes of the law men
are not unique individuals, but persons participating
in a common power of self-determination. Thus conceiving man as a free agent in the world of reality,
the state metes to him the reward or punishment of
his deeds. The treaties and alliances between nations;
the growth of international law; the establishment of
an international tribunal are heralds of the great world-
union wherein each participant state shall pledge its
life, its fortune, and its honor to secure equal and exact
justice.

The object of this rapid survey of our secular institutions has been to suggest that all of them imply the
social nature of conscious intelligence and the unity of
all beings participating in this intelligence; that is, the
nature of man as Gliedganzes. In the family this unity
is felt as love; in civil society it is embodied in reciprocal dependence; in the state it is recognized by a common law. All of these institutions suggest a goal which
no one of them realizes and imply an origin which no
one of them explains. The Christian church mystically
explains the unity, proclaims the origin, and prophesies
the consummation. It declares men to be one in virtue
of their derivation from a common Father; it reveals
to them their generic ideal in a concretely presented
divine life; it proclaims their fellowship in one indwelling spirit; and it holds before them the hope of immortal citizenship in a cosmic community, where shall be
gathered together the intelligent spirits not of a single
world but of all worlds, and where at last each shall

be in, through, and for all, and all shall be in, through, and for each.

It is admitted by all students of education that the standards for educational values are the norms of the civilization into which the pupil is born, and it must now be again insisted that the supreme norm of all Western civilization is man's vision of himself as Gliedganzes, and that the more or less clearly discerned ideal which forever beckons him is that of "membership in a society of accordant free agents." "It is at the mental summons of this ideal," writes Professor Howison, "that the West as a stadium in historic progress emerges from the hoary and impassive East; and the entire history of the West as divergent from the Oriental spirit, as the scene of energetic human improvement, the scene of the victory of man over nature, and over his merely natural self, has its controlling and explanatory motive in this ideal alone. It is the very lifeblood of that more vigorous moral order which is the manifest distinction of the West from the Orient. Personal responsibility and its correlate of free reality, or real freedom, are the whole foundation on which our enlightened civilization stands; and the voice of aspiring and successful man as he lives and acts in Europe and America speaks ever more and more plainly the two magic words of enthusiasm and of stability — Duty and Rights. But these are really the signals of his citizenship in the ideal City of God. By them he proclaims: We are many, though indeed one; there is one *nature* in manifold persons; personality alone is the measure, the sufficing establishment of reality; unconditional reality alone is sufficient to the being of persons; for that alone is sufficient to a moral order, since a moral order is possible for none but beings who are mutually responsible, and no beings can be responsible who do not originate their own acts." [1]

THE THIRD GREAT EDUCATIONAL VALUE: LANGUAGE

Tested by the standard of the Gliedganzes, language must be assigned the third place in the hierarchy of educational values. Indeed, were we making a study of values in the order of their genesis, language would perforce be promoted to the first place, because without speech there could be no development of corporate life. But the order of history is not identical with the order of value, and language study, considered either in its formal aspect as training in the habits of correct speech and as equipment of the individual with the intellectual tools of reading, writing, and grammar, or in its substantial aspect as study of literature, is manifestly subordinate in value to religion, to the quickening of institutional ideals, and to the formation of habits accordant with those ideals. On the other hand, since language is the instrument which makes possible the organization of human activity and the transmission of human experience, there can be no dispute of its claim to be ranked as third in importance of the great educational values. The man who lacks sufficient mastery of speech to make other men understand what he means will have no co-workers. He who cannot understand other men's meanings will be able neither to aid nor to oppose them.

[1] *The Conception of God*, by Josiah Royce, Joseph LeConte, G. H. Howison, and Sidney Edwards Mezes, p. 93.

Not only is language the indispensable instrument of corporate life; it is also the chief means for the expansion of personality. Without speech each man would be immured forever in the prison cell of his own nature. The man who cannot read and write is able to expand his personality only to the size of those with whom he communicates through oral speech, and therefore is condemned to remain provincial and temporal. He who is able to read and write, but who fails to extend his knowledge of language beyond a colloquial vocabulary, can never enrich his personality with the larger experience of his own age, or the great experience of the historic past. He who knows only a single language must be cramped by its limitations of vocabulary and structure. He who is ignorant of the languages of the three great peoples who have contributed to the modern world its religion, its law, and its artistic and literary forms, can never fully understand his own process of becoming. In short, it is through spoken and written language that the interchange of contemporary experience is possible. It is through the written and printed forms of speech that the experience of the past is preserved and disseminated. Without language there could be no emancipation of the individual by the vicarious toil of the race, no illumination of the individual by its vicarious thought, no redemption of the individual by its vicarious suffering.

In addition to its objective values as the instrument which makes corporate life possible and as the chief means of expanding human personality, language study is important because it reveals the universal form of our mental activity, and thereby admits us to some knowledge of the nature of man as Gliedganzes. Grammar discovers that all speech has the form of a judgment. Every judgment is an expression of that essential act of the Ego wherein self-recognition is effected through the positing and annulment of self-separation. When for example, we say, "'The rose is; it is red, it is round, it is fragrant,' we separate what belongs to the rose from it, and place it outside of it, and then through the act of predication unite it again. The fundamental act of self-consciousness, which is a self-separation and self-identification united in one act of recognition, is repeated in all acts of knowing" and embodied in the judgments which express such acts.[1]

The final objective value of language is that through its adumbration of the form of subject-objectivity it points us to God, in whom alone that form is completely realized. As has been said, all human speech has the form of a judgment. Confining ourselves to judgments of determinate being, we observe that in all such judgments an individual is identified with a class; for example, the rose is red; the dog is a quadruped; John is a man. Manifestly the identity expressed in these judgments is not true. John is or may be a very defective specimen of the class man. The dog is a quadruped, but so are the cat and the cow. The rose may have redness, but it is not identical with red, and moreover possesses only one shade or tint of red. Thus in one respect it is larger, and in another smaller, than the class with which it is identified. The identity between subject and predicate which the judgment expresses breaks down in every concrete case. Therefore, we are incited

[1] *Journal of Speculative Philosophy*, vol. ɪ, pp. 118-19.

to ask, — what does this expression of identity mean, and whence does it proceed?

The answer to this question gives us new reverence for language as revealer of the form of subject-objectivity, characteristic of mind, and implied in the conception of the Gliedganzes. In the judgment mind imposes its own infinite form upon a finite experience. The form fits only eternal realities. When we identify rose and redness we seek a correspondence not to be found in the realm of sense-perception. This lack of correspondence between our general terms and the particular objects we subsume under them, has led many contemporary thinkers to deny that truth in the sense of correspondence exists at all. It has led others to a profound conviction that mind itself is truth, and that in its form of subject-objectivity as completely realized in God, we find at last that perfect correspondence between generic energy and its product, which nature and history seek, which language in the form of the judgment affirms, whose necessary implications are studied in rational psychology, and whose outcome is the conception of God as Absolute and of man as potential Gliedganzes.

Besides its objective values, language has a series of psychologic values. In acquiring the power of speech the child acquires the power of seeing each particular object as member of a class; becomes aware of differences between the particular specimens of the class; and hence perceives around each object a penumbra of shining possibilities. Seeing possibilities or unrealized ideals, mind acquires motives for action and develops will power. Finally energizing to realize these possibilities, it becomes aware of its own causative power; for to change a possibility into a reality is to cause to exist what did not exist before. Hence in learning to speak, the child unfolds will properly so-called out of blind desire and also achieves a measure of true self-consciousness.

A second psychologic value of language is suggested by the fact that since it employs signs it calls for discrimination between the sign and the thing signified, and therefore involves a double act of mental analysis. To acquire the power of speech, words must be recognized by external sense as sounds addressed to the ear, and their meaning must be recognized by internal sense or introspection. In learning to read and write, words must be recognized as forms addressed to the eye; these visible forms must be identified with the sound signs previously familiar, and finally the corresponding idea must be called up by thought. In the study of etymology, words are not only recognized as visible forms, identified with sounds and interpreted by thought, but by a deeper act of introspection identified as parts of speech. Finally, with the study of the sentence and its construction, there is advance from the recognition of signs as expressions of particular meanings to the use of signs as instruments for expressing organic unities of thought by relating meanings.

Thus far our attention has been given to language in its formal aspect as a system of signs related to meanings. We must now pass on to consider language relatively to its content, or in other words to discuss its value as embodied in literature.

It will be conceded without dispute that, aside from

other values, literature is the chief instrumentality
through which man acquires distinction of thought and
speech. The language of men and women who do not
read is prone to gyrate in a tedious round of conventional words and phrases. "Dear to me as a God,"
says Plato, "shall be he who can accurately divide and
define." Ordinary men do not make clear distinctions
in thought, and as a consequence their speech lacks
precision. Whether in spoken or written language,
style is simply the outward expression of intellect and
character. When thoughts are accurately defined,
speech is clear. When fine shades of thought and feeling
are inwardly distinguished, speech becomes delicate,
subtle, and discriminating. When each thought illuminates and is illuminated by many others, style becomes comprehensive and suggestive. When all particular ideas are organized by a master thought, style
attains unity. When this master thought is freedom,
style acquires nobility. When the ideals of freedom have
been felt as imperatives and faithfully obeyed, style
becomes commanding and coercive. When ideals are
not only obeyed, but loved, style becomes fervent and
glowing. When a man has lived long, intimately, and
lovingly with his thoughts, they will have associated
with themselves interpreting natural images and correspondences. To see clearly, define precisely, asso-
ciate largely, love fervently, believe with conviction,
act with fidelity, and live in constant communion with
one's own spirit, is the only way to create linguistic
expression which is lucid, comprehensive, glowing,
commanding, poetic, and beautiful. In short, nothing
but distinction of mind can create distinction of speech.

Literature is the expression of distinction of mind in ascending degrees. To study literature is to achieve some measure of this distinction. The pupil becomes aware of inarticulate depths in himself. The feelings which vaguely stirred his heart, the thoughts which haunted his subconsciousness are made known to him. As he learns to understand himself, he begins also to understand his fellows. If it be true that the proper study of mankind is man; if it be granted that the most practical knowledge is that which enables the individual to combine with his fellow men; then there can be no question of the high rank of literature in the hierarchy of educational values.

The attempt has been made to show that literature helps the individual to know himself and his fellow men by defining and illustrating wide ranges of thought and subtle intricacies of feeling. It has, however, an even higher mission, for it is in and through literature that the genetic evolution of human deeds is revealed. Goethe has likened the characters in a great drama or novel to watches with crystal cases. Looking through one face of the crystal case, we see the moving hands; looking through the other, we see the power that moves them. In our contact with living men and women, we become aware of what they do, and explain their deeds by an act of more or less feeble introspective analogy. In studying the men and women of literature, we are helped by the introspection of great geniuses who have discovered in themselves the emotional and intellectual antecedents of all human deeds. "It may be said in general," writes Dr. Harris in *Psychologic Foundations of Education*, " that a literary work of art, a poem, whether lyric, dramatic, or epic, or a prose work of art, such as a novel or a drama, reveals human nature by showing the growth of a feeling or sentiment first into a conviction and then into a deed: feelings, thoughts, and deeds are thus connected in such a way as to explain the complete genesis of human action." [1]

With regard to the value of this revelation the same great educator writes as follows: —

"No matter how well equipped we might be as mathematicians or scientific experts of any kind, if we lacked the power of seeing this genesis of actions out of feeling in our fellow men and in ourselves, our lives would become a chaos of misdirected endeavor. We never could adjust ourselves to our human environment, we should take offense where none was intended and make collisions with our associates; for we should first misunderstand their motives; next, seize on the wrong means of persuasion and conciliation; finally, end in misanthropy. With regard to ourselves, we should be equally powerless to control our passions and desires, not knowing whither they tended nor where they were to be repressed.

"The narrow life can be lived through without much knowledge of literature. Intuitive practice in reading the feelings of one's fellows, and in noting the effect of these feelings on their actions which follow, fits the individual for his narrow sphere. But there is as much difference between the knowledge of human nature that rests entirely on individual observation of the people of one's environment and that founded on an acquaintance with the best literature as there is be-

[1] *Psychologic Foundations of Education*, p. 327.

tween an Indian doctor's acquaintance with plants and the lore of a skilled botanist." [1]

The attempt has been made to suggest two great values of literature. It creates distinction of thought and speech. It reveals the growth of action and habit out of feelings and ideas, and thereby helps men to understand themselves and their fellows. A third and still higher value derives from the fact that literature portrays man as a member of social institutions and is therefore a revelation of the Gliedganzes, or divine human type, so far as this has been discovered, and also a revelation of the agreements or disagreements of individuals with this generic or divine humanity.

The theme of a literary work of art is usually an attack of the individual upon some one of the great human institutions, and the recoil of that institution upon his attack. It is in virtue of the fact that it portrays collisions between the individual and the social whole that literature becomes an adequate revelation of human nature. To quote Dr. Harris once more: "When at harmony with the social environment the individual does not reveal the limits of his individuality nor the all-conquering might of the institutions of society. It is only in the collisions between the individual and the social order in which he exists that the whole of human nature is revealed in both its phases as individual and as social whole." [2]

No one who has studied the great world-poets

---

[1] William T. Harris, *The Educational Value of the Tragic as compared with the Comic in Literature and Art*, p. 5.

[2] William T. Harris, *The Educational Value of the Tragic as compared with the Comic in Literature and Art*, p. 60.

Homer, Shakespeare, Dante, and Goethe can fail to be
aware how largely he owes to them knowledge of himself, understanding of his fellows, insight into the
trend of human history, and comprehension of the
value of human institutions. It is only necessary to
summon before imagination the figures of Achilles,
Agamemnon, Ajax, Odysseus, Clytemnestra, Helen,
Penelope, Macbeth, Hamlet, Lear, Desdemona, Portia,
Faust, Mephistopheles, Wilhelm Meister, Lothario,
Mignon, and Natalia to assure ourselves that without
the concrete types of character exhibited in literature,
we should know little either of ourselves or of the men
and women with whom life brings us into relations. It
is only necessary to recall the theme and structure of
each of the great world-poems to realize how wonder-
fully they interpret history and clarify the meaning of
human institutions. The *Iliad* re-creates in its readers
the impulses out of which Occidental civilization was
born and flashes a warning light upon that brittle in-
dividualism by which alone it may be wrecked. The
Odyssey portrays in a series of poetic images the conscious emergence of those domestic, social, national,
and religious ideals which the history of the West has
been one long struggle to embody. The *Divine Comedy*
paints each typical deed which man can do; describes
its emotional antecedents; traces its social consequences; tests it by the standard of human solidarity,
and points as the goal of earthly existence to divine
life realized in a cosmic community. The dramas of
Shakespeare show a series of collisions between the
individual and some ethical ideal, and portray the
recoil of the social whole upon his deeds. The last

world-poet advances unshrinking into that eternal hell where the conscious spirit is at war with its own form, and writes in words of flame the battle with and victory over agnosticism. To study with sympathy and interior comprehension Goethe's exhibition of Faust "in conflict with himself, in conflict with family, society, and state, and in conflict with art and religion," is to be redeemed by vicarious experience from the torments of intellect damned by the knowledge that it cannot know.

The attack of the individual upon social order and the reaction of that order upon the attack is the persistent theme of literature. The principle underlying both the attack and the recoil is that of human freedom. It is in virtue of the fact that man has formal freedom, or the power to act as he may choose, that the individual is able to make his attack upon the social whole. It is in virtue of the fact that the social whole has attained some degree of substantial freedom, or vision of the kinds of deeds which are consistent with freedom itself, that it is able to mete to the individual just rewards and penalties. The final revelation of literature, therefore, is the revelation of human freedom with its correlate of moral responsibility, and so great is its respect for the freedom it celebrates that it leaves its votaries free even to reject freedom. It wins by allurement, but never coerces by authority. It announces no moral imperatives, but appeals to "admiration, hope, and love;" stirs liberating and aspiring impulses and is content to warn against evil by portraying its ugliness and tracing its results. Free itself through love, it dares to trust man's love and freedom, and by this generous faith calls forth the energy through which he "erects himself above himself."

The reader who is able to recognize identity of thought under dissimilarity of statement will need no assurance of the fact that, alike in its language, its portrayal of concrete types of character, its evolution of deeds out of feelings and ideas, its projection of the impulses which have determined the march of history and its revelation of a social solidarity which guarantees free individuality as the goal of human existence, literature is one of the great revelations of man as Gliedganzes. It remains to be said that alike in poetry and prose the art of literature adumbrates through the sensuous elements of rhythm, symmetry, and harmony, that form of self-consciousness of which the Gliedganzes is the final explication. The psychology of these several elements will be considered in greater detail in connection with the educational values of architecture, sculpture, painting, and music. Literature has been treated in detachment from the other fine arts because of its higher rank in the order of educational values.

The reader who has followed understandingly the discussion of the three great norms of religion, social institutions, and language will be aware that an effort has been made to set forth both their objective or practical, and their subjective or psychological value as determined by the common standard of the Gliedganzes. In brief epitome of the thoughts suggested, it may be said that the objective value of the Christian religion is that it offers an eternal guarantee for that conception of humanity through which the single spirit "knows itself as self-active member of a manifold system of persons," and that its psychologic value lies in the fact that it stimulates the highest degree of self-activity by endowing each individual with supernatural value through its revelation of self-consciousness as the form of the divine first principle. From the practical point of view the value of the four great human institutions is, that through the family infant humanity is protected and nurtured; through the organization of civil society the individual human being is fed, clothed, sheltered, and enlarged by participation in the wider human experience; through the state justice is meted to responsible men; through the corporate life of the church altruism becomes the incarnate ideal. From the psychologic point of view the value of the family lies in its development of the feeling of love; the value of civil society, in its substitution of reciprocal service for selfish greed; the value of the state, in its power so to quicken the sense of corporate selfhood that for its sake the individual is ready to renounce his life; and the value of the church, in its appeal to those celestial impulses of faith, hope, and charity which are the emotional equivalents of a compelling insight into the nature of divine reality as absolute Gliedganzes.

Passing from the summarized values of religion and ethics to those of language, and considering language first in its formal aspect, we define its psychologic values as the gift of power to see universals, and the development of introspective activity in deepening degrees. Its objective values are that it is the instrument of human combination and of rational investigation, and that in its structure it reveals the essential nature of thought. In its æsthetic aspect as literature its objective merits are that it assists human combination through increasing man's power to understand his fellows; that it reveals the nature of human institutions and the trend of history; and that in the formal elements of rhythm, symmetry, and harmony it enshrines the structure of reason. From the psychologic point of view the merits of literature are that by its exact and subtle distinctions it makes men aware of their own inarticulate depths, and confers upon them some degree of ability to define themselves; and that by tracing the evolution of actions and habits out of feelings and ideas, it stimulates introspective and retrospective activity, and makes men aware of their own process of becoming.

The three great values considered lead all others in every stage of the educational process. The remaining values differ in their relative rank in different stages of that process. For example, the relative ranks of mathematics and the fine arts differ in the kindergarten and the elementary school, as do also the relative ranks of the sciences and industries. In the remainder of this report we limit ourselves to that ordering of educational values which, tested by the standard of the Gliedganzes, seems appropriate to the best development of children between the ages of four and six.

It has been said more than once in this report that only a self-conscious being can be a Gliedganzes, because only in self-consciousness can a generic energy duplicate itself in its product. It has also been stated that self-consciousness is the realized form of

self-activity. The justification for this statement is
that in self-consciousness alone is the self-active energy
its own environment. It follows that the ascending
stages of human development may be described as
ascending degrees of the realization of self-activity,
in self-consciousness, and it also follows that the order
of this ascent should determine the order of education.
In short, self-activity is the principle of psychology,
and therefore should be the consciously accepted
principle of education.

Granting that self-activity is the principle of psychology and education, we set ourselves the introspective task of observing what it does and soon discover in ourselves one invariable method of procedure. We act: then we become conscious of as much
of ourselves as that action reveals; finally we reflect
on the form of the activity itself and thereby ascend
to higher self-knowledge. This method of self-activity
justifies the educational procedure of the kindergarten,
which for children between the ages of four and six
assigns a higher value to the practical and fine arts
than to science and mathematics. It is through self-
expression in the several forms of industry and the
several forms of the fine arts that the native curiosity
of children is directed towards the simpler questions
which science asks and answers, and it is through
the relations of form, size, number, and proportion to
practical problems of construction that native interest
in mathematics is best developed. Hence, the fourth
place in the order of educational values as represented
in the kindergarten must be assigned to the practical
and fine arts.

THE FOURTH GREAT EDUCATIONAL VALUE: THE
INDUSTRIES AND THE FINE ARTS

Having given our reasons for assigning to the practical and fine arts a relatively high rank in the order of kindergarten education we must now consider their more general significance as two of the great human values. We begin with the value of industry, not because we rank it higher in the educational order than the value of the fine arts, but because it will be easier to show the superior value of the latter after consideration of the former.

The Value of Industry

In a pregnant passage of the *Education of Man*, Froebel attacks the conventional view that the chief end of industry is the supply of material needs. "The debasing illusion," he writes, "that man works, produces, creates only in order to preserve his body, in order to secure food, clothing, and shelter, may have to be endured, but should not be diffused and propagated. Primarily and in truth man works that his spiritual, divine essence may assume outward form, and that thus he may be enabled to recognize his own spiritual, divine nature and the universal being of God. Whatever food, clothing, and shelter he obtains thereby comes to him as an insignificant surplus."[1]

The two distinctive deeds of man throughout the centuries are the making over of himself and the making over of the world. The objective value of industry is that it is the instrument through which the transformation, or re-creation, of the world is effected, and

[1] *The Education of Man*, p. 32.

the final motive of industry is the desire of the creative divine spirit immanent in man to fulfill the purpose of the same spirit immanent in nature. "If," writes Professor Münsterberg, "we observe the economic factors, wherever commercial and industrial life find their proudest development, we must feel that egotistic greediness has been on the whole the small coin in the market, but that all great transitions and developments demanded very different impulses. To create, and to create with the whole soul for that wonderful work of the economic development is the desire and the ambition of the true worker. The gain is estimated because it indicates that the problem is solved, and that the conquest is completed; and that which is earned is used again for new progress. To take part in the work, to toil for the enterprise, is the joy of life. In pioneer days it comes to its most enthusiastic expression. Young and old, poor and rich, are joined by the one feeling that it is a gigantic work which they are to build up together. To open a land, to make the desert fertile, to dig out the treasures of the soil, and to send the works of industry over the globe, to awaken in the millions new and ever new demands, to satisfy them in a million ways — that is an inspiration and ideal which stands, in the feeling of the worker, not lower than justice and freedom and truth and morality. Where one blade grew and two are now growing, where one railroad track went through the valley and now two are built, where one chimney smoked and now a thousand testify to useful labor, there an absolutely valid progress has been secured by which the world has become more valuable. And such a noble view of economic life is detachable from the soil as well as art and philosophy; it can spread and has always spread at the periods of the golden ages of industry."[1]

The ideal described frees us from the debasing illusion that industry is merely the means by which man supplies his material needs, and defines it as a more or less conscious effort to complete the desire for development in nature by helping nature to fulfill its mission as servitor of man. "Economy," writes the author already quoted, "is always a system of natural goods serving the human community." Conceiving nature "in its purposive adjustment as the real content of economy, the way is open to estimate economy also as pure value.˙ The community which satisfies its hunger and protects itself against the climate, or which, many stages higher, gathers together the treasures of the globe by steamers and railroads to enjoy life, fulfills only personal purposes. But the nature which nourishes and protects man, and in endless transformation distributes itself everywhere in order to fulfill the human purpose, really offers an over-personal value." "Just as the conscious labor of the arts alone can complete that aim of the outer world towards inner unity which manifests itself in the beauty of nature, in the same way the desire for development in nature completes itself only in the industrial life."[2]

The thesis maintained in the passages cited is that through industry man satisfies a desire and realizes a purpose resident in nature. Reverting to the concep-

[1] Münsterberg, *Eternal Values,* pp. 308–09.
[2] Münsterberg, *Eternal Values,* pp. 310, 311, 316.

tion of the Gliedganzes and reminding ourselves of its final implication, we would complete this thesis by defining matter as a "mode of motion of spirit," and by the statement that in the light of this definition fulfillment of a desire resident in nature really means fulfillment of the will of God. It is the spirit immanent in nature which feels the desire; it is through the self-sacrifice of that spirit in taking upon itself the lowly form of matter that man is blessed with a world which he can re-create and thereby realize in himself the image of his creator.

Epitomizing this discussion of the values of industry, we may say that through the practical arts the purposive aim of nature is realized, and thereby the divine will energetic in nature is fulfilled. It is not claimed that a conscious awareness of and sympathy with this will is characteristic of the great majority of workers. The claim is, rather, that industrial life should be elevated by awakening in the minds of all laborers the ideal of which it is the expression. The industrial world has proved by the invention of special vocations that it understands one great feature of economy. The joy which comes to each worker who has found the vocation to which he is adapted by native gifts and impulses should give him some presentiment of the meaning of all vocations as instruments for realizing ideals resident in nature and wakening to consciousness in the mind of man.

If man be really a Gliedganzes, — if he can realize that ideal only as he becomes truly self-knowing, and if he can attain self-knowledge only by putting himself out of himself, and then looking at what he has done,

— then, tested by the standard we have adopted, the practical arts have an inalienable right to a place in the educational process because they are among the important instruments of self-revelation. It does not fall within the province of this report to discuss the agencies through which education in the arts should be given to older children. We limit ourselves to confession of our conviction that they have a distinct place and value in the kindergarten, and we offer as reasons for our conviction the two facts already pointed out, that exercises in the practical arts satisfy the native desire for creative activity and meet the psychologic demand that the mind shall express in order to know itself.

It is a fact, fraught with deeper meaning than many of us realize, that the practical arts tend constantly to take on the form of the fine arts. The cultivation of the soil is a practical art, but the garden, with its rhythmic arrangements, its contrasts of light and shade, its accordant colors, and its consciously studied adjustments to the surrounding landscape, is a work of fine art. Pottery and weaving are practical arts, but the vessels which man shapes into fair proportions and the rhythmic and symmetric designs with which he adorns his fabrics are works of fine art. The rude hut built for shelter against the elements is a work of industry, but the forum and temple with their harmonies of adjustment are works of fine art. This tendency of the practical arts to take on the form of the fine arts is explained by the fact that man puts himself into whatever he does, and since he is intrinsically a self-active being "the shining of self-activity" will be manifest in the work of his hands. The "shining of self-activity," as we shall attempt to show, is beauty, and wherever man creates beauty he creates a work of fine art.

Plato's definition of the beautiful as "the splendor of the true" has become so familiar that its meaning has been lost. It is only really understood when interpreted in the light of his insight into the self-moved as divine first principle of the universe. Self-movement is another name for self-activity, and the philosopher who recognizes self-activity as final truth can only mean by the "splendor of the true" the "shining of self-activity" in and through material things. "One of the good definitions of art," writes Dr. Harris, "describes it as a means of manifesting the divine in material form for the apprehension of the senses and the reason. This definition makes art one of the three highest products of the soul. The three highest activities of the soul deal with the beautiful, the good, and the true. Religion deals with the revelation of the divine as good; art deals with its manifestation as the beautiful; and philosophy deals with the definition of the divine for pure thought."[1] Defining the divine as realized self-activity, we define beauty as the manifestation of self-activity, whether in the works of nature or of art.

The first characteristic of self-activity is that it is self-originated, and therefore free. It follows that objects are beautiful in so far as they reveal freedom. We are potentially free beings and denizens of a universe which may be best described as a struggle to-

[1] *Psychologic Foundations of Education*, p. 351.

wards freedom. Any object is beautiful which suggests either the struggle for freedom, the devout aspiration towards freedom, or the physical adumbration of freedom. Beautiful is the serene moonlight and its reflection in the tossing sea; beautiful the mountain which aspires towards the sky; beautiful the free flight of the bird; beautiful the athlete who has made of each limb the willing servitor of free energy; beautiful the face which expresses the triumph of the free spirit over all chaotic and warring impulses.

Defining beauty as the shining of self-activity and art as the manifestation of the beautiful, we conclude that "material things become works of art when they are so disposed that they seem to manifest the self-determination of a living soul within them."[1] We demand of a work of art that it shall seem to be alive both as a whole and in its parts. "To a sympathetic vision," writes Professor Sturt, "the stones and beams of the cathedral are severally instinct with life. The strong straight pillars sustain the upper fabric with an air of well-girt purpose; the arches spring; the timbers knit the roof; the buttresses thrust sturdily against the pressure of the roof; the spire soars into the sky. The eye instinctively interprets these dead mechanic things in terms of living power; and those forms are grateful to it which assist its instinctive interpretation."[2] In short, the unifying principle of art is interest in a vital whole.

A self-activity must first of all act. Its action, in so far as it is self-determined, is free. Hence beauty, or the "shining of self-activity," is, as we have seen,

[1] Professor Sturt, *Personal Idealism*, p. 297. [2] *Ibid.*, p. 297.

primarily a revelation of freedom. In acting, however, an indivisible self-activity necessarily creates an organic unity, or in other words its product is a living whole wherein each part is both means and end to all other parts and to the whole. If, therefore, the end of art is beauty, and beauty is the shining of self-activity, all works of art must not only reveal freedom, but must exhibit that organic character which results whenever manifold parts or elements are made instrumental to the manifestation of a single meaning or purpose. The natural organism which manifests most completely the highest type of self-activity is the human form. Hence the greatest works of art take on this form. Hence also man tends to view as quasi-personal, "every totality which subserves meaning in a way analogous to the human body."[1]

It has been shown that since man is a self-active being he will so dispose the material things through which he expresses himself that they will manifest freedom and exhibit organic unity. There remains for consideration the significant fact that precisely as in freedom and organic unity man celebrates the substance or nature of self-activity, so through the manner in which he disposes material he exhibits in ascending degrees the structure of that self-consciousness which is the realized form of self-activity.

Analyzing self-consciousness we discover that it implies, first, identity of the self with the self; second, distinction of the self from the self; third, the active process of mediation between the self as subject and the self as object, whose outcome is the pervasion of

[1] *Personal Idealism.*, p. 298.

all the details of thought and life by a single meaning. Differently stated, in its primary and most abstract self-recognition the Ego can only say I am I; ascending to higher self-knowledge, it defines itself not only as identical, but as antithetical; attaining its highest consciousness, it knows itself as a unity pervading a manifold of distinctions.

When we study the history of the fine arts, we become aware of an order of development correspondent to the several phases of this analysis of self-consciousness. In the earliest stage of its history, the exclusive accent of each art is upon regularity or rhythmic succession, and through the tireless iteration of a single sound, or a single architectural, graphic, or plastic element, the self symbolizes that identity which is the primordial fact of conscious intelligence. In the next higher stage of development, emphasis is placed upon symmetry which expresses not abstract sameness, but identity under difference. In its highest forms, art "boldly discards both regularity and symmetry as chief ends, while retaining them in subordinate details, and concentrates its effort upon that expression of the subordination of matter to the soul to which has been given the name of harmony. The Apollo Belvedere, for example, has no symmetry of arrangement in its limbs and yet the disposition of each limb suggests a different disposition of another in order to accomplish some conscious act upon which the mind of the god is bent. All is different, yet all is united in harmony for the realization of one purpose." [1] In a word, harmony is

[1] *Psychologic Foundations of Education*, p. 356. I have taken the liberty of making some condensations and transpositions.

that particular disposition of material things through which organic unity is manifested, and as an art form it corresponds to the highest stage of self-consciousness, which knows itself as an identity pervading its own differences.

The careful reader of this report will have observed that, while in the discussion of literature attention was concentrated chiefly upon its content, the discussion of the fine arts has concentrated attention chiefly upon their form. All that has been said of the form of the fine arts in general applies to literature, which like architecture, sculpture, painting, and music reveals the distinctive quality of self-activity which is freedom; creates the organic unities which, alike in life and thought, are the integrated expressions of self-activity, and in the sensuous elements of rhythm, symmetry, and harmony adumbrates the structure of self-activity. Conversely, all that was said of the content of literature is true of the content of the other arts, which like literature portray the collisions of passion with a rational social order; the conflict of lower and higher ethical ideals and the ascending insights into Divine Reality.

Comparison between the Industries and the Fine Arts

Having considered the respective functions of the industries and fine arts, it is not difficult to show that in the order of educational values the latter take precedence of the former. In both the industries and the fine arts man transforms or re-creates the objects of nature; in both the final incentive of activity is self-revelation in the interest of self-knowledge; but the self-revelation of man in the fine arts is far more complete than in the practical arts because it unveils the structural form of reason. It is something to build a hut: more to build a Parthenon; something to shape a basin: more to model a Jove; something to stain a floor or dye a cloth: more to paint a Transfiguration. It means something to the little child to practice the industries, but it means far more to receive an initiation into the fine arts.

The mystic Plotinus says of nature that she is greedy of beholding herself. Therefore she completes the process of her self-development in man. Translating this thought into language determined by the conception of the Gliedganzes, we affirm that the divine spirit immanent in nature cannot be satisfied until it duplicates its own form in a self-conscious being. As participant in the divine form man in turn will be greedy of beholding himself; will aspire to create images of freedom and organic unity; and will impress upon his creations those ascending forms of order which are ascending revelations of the structure of self-consciousness.

THE FIFTH GREAT EDUCATIONAL VALUE: MATHEMATICS

Reverting once more to the fact that this report attempts the double task of discussing the great human values in and of themselves and of ordering them in their relation to the education of children between the ages of four and six, we remind our readers that the industries and fine arts were granted precedence over mathematics because of the psychologic order of development. To those who have comprehended that order it should be evident that through creative exercises in the several forms of the practical and fine arts there will be awakened in the minds of children a sense of mathematical relations and a demand for mathematical aid, and that with this emergence of mathematics into the field of consciousness it should be granted its own distinct place in the circle of educational activities. With this brief statement of our reason for its assignment to the fifth place in the educational order of the kindergarten, we pass on to consider its several values in the process of education as a whole.

The traditional course of study in elementary and secondary schools assigns high importance to mathematics in the several forms of arithmetic, algebra, geometry, and trigonometry. The practical value of this course in mathematics is that it confers upon students some degree of mastery of the instrument through which man theoretically and practically masters nature. Without mathematics that discovery of quantitative relations which is the greatest deed of science would be impossible. Without mathematics there could be no adequate development of the practical arts. To mathematics we owe our ability to make that estimate of the relative values of different kinds of labor upon which depends the interchange of products, and to the same great discipline we are indebted in large measure for development of the machines which are emancipating men from drudgery and compelling them to qualify themselves for higher forms of economic activity. Finally, it is by the help of mathematics that we estimate those quantitative relations

whose knowledge is so indispensable to the successful
struggle with poverty, illness, vice, and crime.

Greater than the utilitarian values of mathematics
are its psychologic values. The first of these is that,
through concentrating attention upon universal and
necessary truths, mathematics confers mental stability
and equipoise. It has been defined as "the science
which draws necessary conclusions," and again, as
"the universal art apodictic."[1] For whether mathematical concepts have been evolved from experience
or are free creations of the mind, the *relations* between
these concepts are necessary and absolute, and hence
the study of mathematics is one great instrument of
deliverance from the conception of truth as a man-
made product which changes with man in the process
of interaction between himself and his environment.

The second psychologic value of mathematics is
that it involves a transition from the thought of each
object, as related to an environment different from
itself, towards the thought of self-relation. The
mathematical studies of elementary and secondary
schools deal with the category of quantity. This category, as Dr. Harris points out, involves a double
thought. "It first thinks thing and environment
(quality) and then thinks both as the same in kind
or as repetitions of the same. A thing becomes a unit
when it is repeated so that it is within an environment
of duplicates of itself." "It is manifest that we cannot
count objects except in so far as we abstract from their

[1] Definitions by Professor Benjamin Peirce and Professor
William Benjamin Smith, cited by Professor Keyser in his monograph on *Mathematics*.

difference. We can count one, two, three oxen, but we cannot say that one ox, one sheep, and one tree are three oxen, or three sheep, or three trees ; but we can say that they are three things, or three units of any class that includes them. We must abstract from their quality, — that which distinguishes them from others, — and go back to a common class in order to count them. The same is true of all extensive magnitude. We must regard the mass as made up of similar units of extension. Take together a cubic yard of wood and the same amount of sand, and we do not have two cubic yards of sand or of wood; but we do have two cubic yards of material substance. In short, in order to have quantity there must be some common genus or species and repetitions of the same individual."[1]

Let us suppose for a moment that there existed in the world but a single specimen of each given object. We should then speak of the house, the tree, the apple, but we should not speak of one house; one tree; one apple; nor of a house, a tree, or an apple. *One* means component unit of a group of similar ones, or, in other words, it means one member of a class of objects. Membership in a class implies common origin. The members of any true class are simply a number of individual objects produced in the same way, or for the same final purpose. Broadly speaking, productive processes are of three kinds — the mechanical processes of inorganic nature, the generative processes of the vegetable and animal worlds, and the adaptive processes by which human beings convert objects of nature to their own uses. To illustrate, the first kind

[1] *Psychologic Foundations of Education*, pp. 342-43.

of process — sand is defined as small grains of stone derived from the disintegration of rocks ; snow is the vapor of the atmosphere congealed by cold and aggregated into flakes. Passing to the classes of the organic world, it may be claimed that if evolution has proved any one thing more clearly than another, it is that the word class in biology stands for a number of plants or animals having a common ancestry. Ascending from the works of nature to the works of man, the same conception of class meets us as the only satisfactory one. Tables, for example, are objects made by similar processes for common ends, and the same is true of houses, bridges, railways, and all other objects of human production. They can only be defined in terms of the purposes for which, and the processes by which, they are produced. In short, to think a class is to think a causal energy and its products.

It is not contended that mathematics directs conscious attention to classes conceived as generative energies plus their products, but merely that even in its most elementary form it involves withdrawal from the stage of sense perception which thinks object and environment, and a leap of the mind towards the thought of self-relation.

The third psychologic value of mathematics is that in its ascending forms it demands constantly increasing degrees of introspective activity. This demand becomes clear to us when we consider that all forms of mathematics deal with ratios, and that the difference between elementary and higher mathematics is that the former deals more with the terms of the ratio, the latter with the ratio itself. "In counting, the ratio between any given sum and its constituent units is merely stated in terms of the constituent unit. Addition, subtraction, multiplication, and division are devices for speed by using remembered countings." The fraction is "an expressed ratio of two numbers." A further step is taken in considering the relation of a single number to itself as power and root. Algebra "drops out the definite expression of the two orders of units between which the ratio exists and deals altogether with ratios." Higher mathematics deals with the relations of ratio. It is needless to do more than suggest that the advance from the simple to the complex relations of ratios involves deepening degrees of introspective analysis.[1]

Great as are the utilitarian and psychologic values of mathematics, they are surpassed by its higher objective value as an exploration and projection of the world of logic or pure thought. "It should be borne in mind," writes Professor Keyser, "that there are two kinds of observation: outer and inner, objective and subjective, material and immaterial, sensuous and sense-transcending; observation, that is, of physical things by the bodily senses, and observation, by the inner eye, by the subtle touch of the intellect, of the entities that dwell in the domain of logic and constitute the objects of pure thought. For, phrase it as you will, there is a world peopled with ideas, *ensembles*, propositions, relations, and implications, in endless variety and multiplicity, in structure ranging from the

[1] See *Psychologic Foundations of Education*, pp. 344-50, and the *Report of the Committee of Fifteen*, pp. 242-44. See "Development of Mathematics and their Mutual Relations," by George H. Howison, *Journal of Speculative Philosophy*, vol. v, pp. 144-79.

very simple to the endlessly intricate and complex."[1] "Now, and this is the point I wish to stress, just as the astronomer, the physicist, the geologist, or other student of objective science looks abroad in the world of sense, so, not metaphorically speaking but literally, the mind of the mathematician goes forth into the universe of logic in quest of the things that are there; exploring the heights and depths for facts — ideas, classes, relationships, and the rest."[2] Finally the mathematician not only explores the inner world, but he also projects it. Says the author already quoted: "To facilitate eyeless observation of his sense-transcending world, the mathematician invokes the aid of physical diagrams and physical symbols in endless variety and combination; the logos is thus drawn into a kind of diagrammatic and symbolical incarnation, gets itself externalized, made flesh, so to speak; and it is by attentive physical observation of this embodiment, by scrutinizing the physical frame and make-up of his diagrams, equations, and formulæ, by experimental substitutions in, and transformations of, them, by noting what emerges as essential and what as accidental, the things that vanish and those that do not, the things that vary and the things that abide unchanged, as the transformations proceed and trains of algebraic evolution unfold themselves to view — it is thus, by the laboratory method, by trial and by watching, that often the mathematician gains his best insight into the constitution of the invisible world thus depicted by visible symbols." [3]

[1] Cassius Jackson Keyser, *Mathematics*, p. 25.
[2] *Ibid.*, pp. 85–86.   [3] *Ibid.*

It has been shown that mathematics explores and projects the facts and relations of mind. It remains to be said that pure logic "is the theory of the mere form of thinking";[1] or to state the same truth in terms determined by the conception of the Gliedganzes, pure logic is an explication of the mode of behavior of that self-determining energy which achieves in self-consciousness its perfect realization. With this insight we define mathematics as an exploration and projection not only of the contents of mind, but of the structure of mind, and therefore as a discipline which breaks one more path towards the conception of a completely realized self-consciousness as absolute first principle of the universe and towards the conception of man as duplicate of the divine form.

THE SIXTH GREAT EDUCATIONAL VALUE: SCIENCE

In his *Grammar of Science*, Professor Karl Pearson asserts that "the classification of facts and the formation of absolute judgments upon the basis of this classification, — judgments independent of the idiosyncrasies of the individual mind, — essentially sum up the aim and method of modern science."[2] On a later page this statement is amplified and illustrated as follows: "The unity of all science consists in its method, not in its material. The man who classifies facts of any kind whatever, *who sees their mutual relations and describes their sequences*, is applying the scientific method and is a man of science. The facts may belong

[1] Professor Royce, *The Problem of Truth in the Light of Recent Research*. For an explanation of the "form of thinking," see Part III of this report.

[2] Karl Pearson, *Grammar of Science*, p. 6.

to the past history of mankind, to the social statistics of our great cities, to the atmosphere of the most distant stars, to the digestive organs of a worm or to the life of a scarcely visible bacillus. It is not the facts themselves which form science but the method in which they are dealt with." [1]

To all who accept this definition it must be evident that the category of science is relativity. Relativity means dependence. Since each thing is relative to every other there is reciprocal dependence. To truly apprehend any object is to apprehend the totality of its relations. Discovery of this totality of relations is the goal of science. That the goal is an endlessly receding one does not alter the fact that it determines the direction of all scientific activity.

The objective values of science can scarcely be overestimated. This great discipline is transfiguring our domestic, economic, political, and religious creeds. It is modifying social conduct. It is changing the treatment of disease and forcing a serious consideration of all the tendencies of contemporary civilization which conspire to produce a degenerate and feeble race. It has revolutionized our means of transit, indefinitely increased the agencies of intercommunion, and proved itself one of the mightiest of the many influences now coöperating towards the creation of that cosmopolitan humanity wherein the ideal of the Gliedganzes shall be approximately realized.

Passing from the objective to the psychologic values of science, we would mention, as the first of these, that science disciplines the mind to think essential relations.

[1] Karl Pearson, *Grammar of Science*, p. 12.

It is the great path of escape from that mischievous habit of arbitrary analogizing which led the pigeon in Wonderland to brand Alice as a serpent because she ate eggs. It is also the instrument of emancipation from puerile superstitions belonging to the neolithic plane of intelligence, yet still tyrannizing the minds and weakening the wills of the great majority of human beings.

A second psychologic value of science is that it forms the habit of suspending judgment and testing inferences. It seeks no short cuts to reality. It knows no "holy back stairs." It dares to call its inferences working hypotheses and subjects them to the most rigorous tests before promoting them even to the rank of accredited theories. The discipline of science tends, therefore, to develop intellects whose processes are rigorous and whose conclusions are sound.

The moral influence of science is an exalted one. The scientist is a votary of the search for truth. He is prompt to surrender his dearest hypothesis if it fail to bear the experimental test. He renounces prejudice and pride of opinion. He loves truth more than any preconceived idea of truth. He is "an endless experimenter with no constraining past at his back" and his mind is plastic to the full extent that the growth of knowledge requires.

The final psychologic value of science is that through disciplining the mind to think essential relations it confers upon its loyal votaries the power to "see by wholes." "Agassiz," writes Dr. Harris, "saw the whole fish in a single scale; Lyell could read the history of the glacial period in a pebble; Cuvier could see the entire animal skeleton in one of its bones. The spirit

of specialization aims to exhaust one by one the
provinces of investigation with a view to acquire this
power to see totalities."[1]

In the Second Part of *Faust*, Goethe has pictured the
outcome of scientific specialization under the image
of Homunculus, the little man in the bottle. He has
also pictured the aspiration of science in the longing of
Homunculus to break his bottle. He who really sees
a relative whole will desire to see the inclusive or absolute whole. Hence science continually aims to extend
the vision of totalities from mere limited provinces of
the world to the world itself.

While the ultimate aim of science cannot be realized
in any finite time, we must be forever grateful to this
great discipline for the bridge it has even now con-
structed between the conception of the cosmos as an
infinitude of particulars to the conception of the cosmos as an interrelated totality. For, as has been said,
the category of science is relativity, and, as may now
be added, universal relativity implies an independent
self-related whole. If A depends upon B and B in turn
depends upon A, then both A and B are complemental
elements of a whole which includes and transcends
them.

As the supreme practical achievement of science is
the universal intercommunion through which cosmopolitan humanity (the human Gliedganzes) shall be
created, so its supreme theoretical achievement is the
transition it makes from the category of atomism to
that category of self-relation which is an initial definition of the divine Gliedganzes.

[1] See *Psychologic Foundations of Education*, pp. 36, 234.

The survey and appraisement of educational values now completed will have fulfilled its lesser purpose if it convinces readers of this report that representatives of the Froebelian ideal have a conscious standard by which they seek to determine the subject-matter and the goal of education. It will have accomplished its greater purpose if it commends the criterion accepted to the judgment of candid students. It seems to us self-evident that the goal of education should be a true world-view and a conforming life. It seems also self-evident that if this goal be accepted, both the subject-matter and method of education should be determined by it. Finally, we are convinced that the substance of a true world-view is embodied in the conception of God as realized Gliedganzes, of man as potential Gliedganzes, and of nature as a process whose goal is a being possessing the form of self-consciousness.

In presenting the objective and psychologic values of the several great educational norms, we have tried to suggest that we conceive the supreme value of each one of them to be the emancipation of the human spirit by revelation of its ideal nature, and challenge to the exercise of its free activity. Every human value is an end to itself, not the instrument of an end external to itself. Every human activity in so far as it takes on ideal form becomes akin to play.

We conceive creation as an eternal play of the divine spirit. We recognize in the plays of childhood a primary revelation of the free self-activity of the human spirit. We conceive all great human values as higher forms of play. The true lover of any great value devotes himself to it not because of a purpose it subserves, but because of the joy with which it blesses. The free spirit seeks ever and alone its own worthy end — freedom.

It remains to be frankly confessed that we ourselves do not believe our educational ideal can be realized without regeneration of our entire social life. While life is pagan, education cannot be truly Christian. We hold that the substance of Christianity is embodied in the conception of the Gliedganzes. We hold also that in so far as Occidental civilization has a distinctive and worthy impulse it is in the incarnation of this ideal. We are convinced that the time has come when our domestic, social, economic, political, and religious life should be renewed through attempts for its more adequate embodiment. We believe that the universal unrest of men is the pledge of their confused search for a higher social order. Froebel was wont to affirm that the world needed renewal of life. Not until the old order has changed, making way for the new, can we achieve that unification of life which was his confessed aim. Meanwhile we conceive the kindergarten and the kindergarten normal school as agencies conspiring to the creation of that higher order necessary to their own adequate embodiment.

PART III

THE GENETIC-DEVELOPING METHOD

THE phrase genetic-developing method occurs for the first time in educational literature in Froebel's letter to the philosopher Krause written in 1828. The following very general formula of that method had been given in the *Education of Man*, published in 1826: "Do this and observe what follows in this particular case from thy action and to what knowledge it leads thee." [1] In the letter to Krause this formula is repeated and amplified.

"The point of departure for all manifestation, all existence, all knowledge and insight, is Doing or the Deed."

"From the deed, therefore, must true education proceed; in the deed must it germinate; out of the deed must it grow. Upon the deed must it found itself. It proceeds from the *living, creative deed; from the creative, self-observant deed; from the deed which sees into and through itself*. All true doing instructs, strengthens, creates, and is itself creative. Therefore all true doing at its culmination point reacts to protect life, to sustain life, to nurture life. Life, deed, recognition, *these are the three notes of a single chord*. Now the emphasis must be upon one note, now upon another, now upon two united. When they are uncon-

[1] *Education of Man*, p. 5.

ditionally separated, the result is what we see and feel
so constantly in life, a struggle between life and death,
a suspension between the two." [1]

Thoughtful kindergartners are sometimes perplexed
by an apparent contradiction between these descriptions of the genetic-developing method and the recurrent statement of Froebel that the point of departure for all human development is the heart. To quote
only one of these statements, we read in the *Pedagogics
of the Kindergarten* that "the center, the real foundation, the starting-point of human development and
thus of the child's development, is the heart and emotions: but the training to action and thought, the
corporeal and the spiritual goes on constantly and in-
separably by the side of it; and thought must form
itself into action and action resolve and clear itself
in thought, but both have their roots in the emotional
nature." [2]

The German word translated in this passage by the
phrase emotional nature is *Gemüth*. As used in the
writings of Froebel, this word always refers to the undifferentiated totality of the spiritual nature and implies
the submergence of thought and will in that emotional
awareness which is the aboriginal mode of consciousness. We cannot feel without feeling about something,
neither can we feel without a tendency to do something. On the other hand, feeling can only be known
as it is manifested. When a child smiles, we infer one
state of feeling, when he screams we infer another.
Running and romping indicate a tone of feeling dia-

[1] *Aus Froebel's Leben*, pp. 141, 42. Italics are mine.
[2] *Pedagogics of the Kindergarten*, p. 42.

metrically opposed to that suggested by a quiet posture, meditative eyes, and folded hands. In a word, spontaneous deeds imply and reveal emotional attitudes and it is in action as revealer of Gemüth that education finds its point of departure.

If education is to begin with the deed, it is manifestly of great importance to know the kind of deed with which it should begin. We must be generous enough to acquit Froebel of the foolish fallacy that it makes no difference what one does provided only he is doing. The aim of the kindergarten is to induce children to do the kind of deeds from which will follow educative results. When little children act spontaneously, they act from some impulse. Whether such impulses be good or bad, they are strengthened by expression. It is the duty of education to stimulate the actions which express healthy impulses, and to restrain the actions which express evil or morbid impulses. The best way of restraining the latter is by inciting the former. The little child vents his feeling of all kinds. Out of these vented feelings we are to select those whose reactions will result in forming the type of character implied in the conception of man as Gliedganzes, and by carefully considered incitements we are to get these selected deeds constantly repeated.

Thus far we have considered only that first demand of the genetic-developing method which may be summarized in the statement that children are to be educated through the incitement of selected forms of self-expression. It should, however, be evident to any student, who gives serious attention to Froebel's description of the method, that it is very imperfectly apprehended if it is limited to a demand for self-expression even in selected forms. This limitation has reacted most injuriously upon the practical conduct of kindergartens, and it is therefore important to call attention to the fact that as conceived by its originator the genetic method demands not only self-expression, but contemplation both of the product and process of self-expression. It is not satisfied with the deed, but insists upon the self-observant deed. It will tolerate no lax and careless self-observation, but calls for the self-penetrating deed; the deed which sees into and through itself. Mental activity in all its forms involves introspection, and introspection in turn often involves retrospection. To the failure of education to guide introspective activity are due many intellectual perversions and moral catastrophes. It is therefore of the highest importance that children should be helped to exercise sane introspection and wise retrospection. Let us be bold and avow our conviction that Froebel's emphasis upon the "self-penetrating deed" is no less novel and original than his emphasis upon the creative deed, and that, unless we consciously aim to influence creative, introspective, and retrospective activity, we do not fully carry out the genetic method.

It is easy to make Froebel's idea seem ridiculous by imputing to him approval of degrees of introspection and ranges of retrospection which any sane person would condemn. In a condensed statement it is difficult not to create misunderstanding. But kindergartners who know the *Mother Play* will recognize in its pictures and commentaries the delicate indirectness and wise restraint with which both introspective and retrospective activities are incited and guided. The "All-Gone" picture, for example, aims to awaken in children through varied illustrations of heedlessness a nascent sense of the nature and consequences of their own heedless acts. The "Little Window" and the "Bridge" use visible analogues to quicken awareness of emotional attitudes. The picture and commentary which interpret the "Light-Bird" make a transition from catching and holding with the hands to catching with the eyes and holding with the mind. In the commentary to the "Pigeon House," Froebel describes a mother who helps her little child to overlook the experience of a single day. The "Children on the Tower" is the retrospect of a longer period, and the "Little Artist" a bold attempt to make and project a still more comprehensive survey of experience. The kindergartner who halts before the ideal of encouraging some degree of introspective and retrospective activity must not only reject the pictures and commentaries mentioned, but admit her lack of sympathy with the spirit of the entire *Mother Play*.

It is in their relationship to moral development that introspective and retrospective activities are most important, and the chief demand of the genetic method is that a mass of subconscious experience shall not be allowed to give direction to life and character, but that from earliest childhood the free human being shall be helped to take possession of himself.

Within the past two decades Froebel's view on this subject has received indirect confirmation from an unexpected source. The source referred to is the psycho-analytic method of studying functional nervous disorders. The basis of this method is described as follows by Dr. James J. Putnam, Professor of Neurology at the Harvard Medical School: "The method rests on the view that as each person's mental life goes on, and almost from the moment of his birth, he stores up the experiences, motives, and emotions which are to largely form the basis of his character and conduct by collecting them into two groups. The first of these groups of experiences and emotions comprises those which represent the life we will to lead or which we acquiesce in — in other words, the life of morals and conventions; — the other group contains those experiences and emotions which we cannot utilize in our willed life and so strive to suppress and hide even from ourselves."

The treatment of nervous disorders based upon this view sets as its aim the unification of the self through wisely guided introspection and retrospection. The educational hint conveyed by the treatment is that schism of the self might be prevented by helping children from the beginning of life to face the experiences they instinctively hide and suppress.

No person possessing the least degree of introspection can fail to be aware of a difference between his ideal and actual self. Such awareness is, indeed, the condition of moral progress. To be aware of an ideal greater than our present achievement, but towards which we are honestly and resolutely pressing, is, however, a very different thing from the duplicity which either indulges, tolerates, or hides an actual self different from the self which we accept as ideal.

There must be difference between vision and attainment, but there need not be inner contradiction with its correlates of hypocrisy and despair.

Every disciple of Froebel knows that he conceived education as a process for the unification of life. He consciously aimed to prevent that awful schism between the better and worse self which is the hidden torment of so many human lives. He believed that little children might be so watched, guarded, and guided as to preclude the subconscious accumulation of disastrous tendencies, and he was sure that they should be helped to face all their little sins and follies, and instead of hiding them from themselves and others look into and through them and turn away from them. The word *Sammlung*, translated by the phrase inner collectedness, suggests the ideal of Froebel as it relates to moral education. From the beginning of life children shall be helped to deliver themselves from slavery to imperative appetite and inordinate desire. They shall look into and through the acts into which they have been betrayed by heedlessness, greed, and vanity, and through "the self-observant deed" master the driving impulse.

Two demands of the genetic method have been considered. It begins with the deed. The deed must see into and through itself. One more explanation must be made before the method can be understood. We are told it must move from life and that its outcome is to protect, sustain, and nurture life. To interpret this statement it is necessary to know the meanings which for Froebel are stored up in the word life. A careful scrutiny of his use of this term in many different contexts indicates that it means to him experience in its twofold aspect, as, on the one hand, a series of immediately presented persons, objects, and events, and on the other as an immediate emotional response to this presentation. The statement that education must move from life means, therefore, that we must seek our point of contact with children in immediate presentations and native reactions. The statement that the outcome of the genetic method is to nurture life means that its final issue is the regeneration of the emotional nature. Regeneration is effected through selection from among immediate presentations and native reactions, of those having ideal value, and through the creative, introspective, and retrospective activities by which these selected presentations are assimilated.

The writer of this report halted long between alternative presentations of the genetic method. Allured by the desire to present all of its implications in logical order, she rebelled against the illustrations which distract attention from a process of thought in order to clarify some one of its stages. But the rebellion of intellect was overcome by the constraint of sympathy, and in view of the fact that the primary object of this report was to help kindergartners to clearer understanding of the kindergarten, it was decided that the simpler implications of the genetic method should be illustrated before passing on to consider those which were more difficult. We therefore pause in our exposition of the method in order to apply our present knowledge of it to the development of the first and greatest educational value — the value of Religion.

In the earlier part of this report an attempt was made to discriminate between Christian theology and the Christian religion. The Christian religion embodies a mystic consciousness of God as transcendent, immanent, and incarnate. Christian theology inventories, organizes, and interprets the data of the Christian consciousness, and thereby attains the ontologic insight defined in the conception of God as completely objectified self-consciousness and therefore as completely realized Gliedganzes. The aim of Christian education should be to provide a genetic development of the normative experience through which the Christian consciousness is perpetuated. This normative experience is dependence upon and communion with a God whom we know as our Father; as incarnate in a historic person; and as a spirit energizing within our own souls and recognized by each one of us as also immanent and energetic in all other souls.

The genetic development of this normative experience implies its possession by the person who assumes the responsibility of religious education. She who aspires to give Christian education should first of all look honestly, piercingly, and persistently into herself, in order to assure herself of her participation in the Christian consciousness. A few questions may be suggested which will blaze a path for this indispensable act of introspection.

Do you know as a fact of inward experience that something speaks within you which is greater than yourself? Does this greater something sometimes appeal to you, sometimes warn you, sometimes chide you, sometimes command, sometimes commend you? Are you at peace when it approves and at war when it condemns? Do you recognize the presence of this greater something in other people as well as in yourself? Do you know its voice when it speaks in great literature? Do you detect its lineaments when embodied in great art? Do you recognize it as the unseen power that guides human history and shapes human institutions? Does it reveal itself to you in the speech of the great prophets and the love of the saints? Are you sure that in the words of One who speaks with authority you hear its clearest utterances? If you can honestly answer all these questions in the affirmative, you are a participant in the religious experience whose characteristic mark is its "immanent-transcendence" and whose final presupposition is defined in the doctrine of the Holy Spirit.

When you have discovered in yourself this great experience, ask yourself a second series of questions. Do you know that this immanent-transcendent Spirit, which you will now be ready to say is trying to get itself incarnated in you, has succeeded in incarnating itself more completely in other people than in yourself? Are the heroes who die for great ideals, the statesmen who consecrate themselves to the upbuilding of noble states, the great missionaries flaming with love for cannibals and lepers, more perfect incarnations of the immanent-transcendent Spirit than you or I? And finally, did this Spirit dwell most surely, incarnate itself most completely, in the great historic personality from whom our religion takes its name?

Whoever can answer these questions affirmatively is a participant in that religious experience whose theological presupposition is the Logos or Incarnate Word.

It may seem strange that the religious experience whose theological presupposition is the doctrine of an Eternal Father has not been given priority over the experiences defined in the doctrine of an indwelling Spirit and an Eternal Logos. Is not the order of experience from the Father to the Son and the Spirit? It is because we answer this question in the negative that we have ventured to present the inverse order. Doubtless we recognize a power which smites our eyes in the lightning's flash and our ears in the thunder's roar; which shakes our souls with terror when the storm wind rages on land and sea, and which hovers before intelligence in its most general form as the final invisible cause of all visible effects. But we do not know this great First Cause as a loving Father until we have learned to know the Spirit and the Son. It is the still small voice of the divine within us and the concrete revelation of the divine in the world which make possible apprehension of the transcendent and eternal reality as a loving Father. Without the sense of community and the historic manifestation of self-sacrifice we may know an omnipotent cause, but we cannot know a God of love, who has given us the one perfect gift — Himself, and who asks of us the one adequate return — ourselves.[1]

[1] This statement must not be construed to mean that children shall not begin to know a Heavenly Father until after they have learned to know the Spirit and the Son. The analogy of human fatherhood may suggest Divine Fatherhood. But a progressive Christian experience follows the order indicated.

If the foregoing description of Christian experience be accepted, and if we wish to apply the genetic method to the supreme educational value, we must next seek the indigenous germs in the child's soul from which may be developed the several conceptions of God immanent, God incarnate, and God transcendent. To epitomize thoughts which will be illustrated in the remainder of this section of our report, there must be an evolution of the knowledge of God as indwelling Spirit from the original sense of community; an evolution of God incarnate from concrete embodiments of the divine self that slumbers, dreams, and stirs in every human soul and from the struggle within each soul between the divine and the natural self. Finally, from the native impulse to search for causes a path may be broken towards the thought of a great first cause; and through the reaction of the sense of community and the incarnate ideal upon this thought there will develop the living conception of Divine Fatherhood.

We read in the *Education of Man* that "the feeling of community first uniting the child with mother, father, brothers, and sisters, and resting on a higher spiritual unity, to which later on is added the unmistakable discovery that father, mother, brothers, sisters, human beings in general, feel and know themselves to be in community and unity with a higher principle, with humanity, — with God, — *this feeling of community is the very first germ, the very first beginning of all true religious spirit*, of all genuine yearning for unhindered unification with the eternal, with God." This sense of community is explained as a stirring of the immanent Spirit and it is added that "the Spirit that lives and is manifest in the finite has an early though dim feeling of its divine origin, and that this vague sentiment, this exceedingly misty feeling, should be fostered, strengthened, nurtured, and later on raised into clear consciousness — into full comprehension." [1]

Let us carefully epitomize the several statements in this very suggestive paragraph.

I. The young child has a native feeling of community with others.

II. He discovers that all the people who make up his little world have communion with each other.

III. He recognizes likewise that they commune with an invisible Person.

IV. The recognized feeling of community is the beginning of a religious life.

V. The source of the feeling of community is the Divine Spirit that dwells in man.

VI. One great object of religious education is to lift the dim feeling of the divine within the soul into clear consciousness.

Since the feeling of community implies both actual relationships and an emotional reaction, it fulfills the initial demand of the genetic-developing method. Whenever this sense of community is fostered, a preliminary form of religious education is being given. The point of departure for such a religious education is to be found in the relationship between mother and child. From this initial point the sense of community is extended to other members of the family, to friends, to human beings in general, and (in virtue of the fact

[1] *Education of Man*, p. 25.

that the Divine Spirit immanent in man is also resident in nature) to animals, plants, and even so-called inorganic forces. It is superfluous to add that no amount of formal training can enable a mother or kindergartner to perform these nurturing deeds. The Froebelian ideal of education demands the intellectual, moral, and emotional rebirth of those who attempt to carry it out. The sense of community can be truly fostered only by those who with whole hearts believe that it is the primal witness of an indwelling Divine Spirit and to whom the one thing needful is conscious union with this Spirit.

There is a prophecy current in the Christian church that its history is to include three great dispensations, of which the latest shall be the dispensation of the Spirit. Many signs indicate that we are in the morning twilight of this final dispensation. Within the visible church there has burst forth a fresh flame of missionary impulse and a conscious aspiration for unity among all the various creeds in Christendom. In Asia, whose one great deed seems to be the creation of religions, there has arisen a prophet whom his disciples describe as the heart or life center of all the impulses towards brotherhood now circulating throughout the great human organism. Whatever may be the errors or insufficiencies of socialism, it is another witness to the prevailing power of a deeper sense of community between men. But most significant of all the omens of a new dispensation is the undeniable fact that out of the synthesis of many differing peoples in our own country there is developing that "cosmopolitan affection" which is the indispensable condition of a higher social morality.

These differing but convergent phenomena point towards a world-transforming process. The seemingly impossible mandate, "Thou shalt love thy neighbor as thyself," is translating itself into a native impulse, and "from the depths of anonymous life" there is emerging an "imperious kindliness" which constrains to altruistic deeds and which will not permit men to be happy while their fellowmen are miserable.[1] The Froebelian method of education which consciously begins the evolution of religion by fostering the feeling of community is therefore one expression of an impulse which in different forms is characteristic of our age and in which the devout observer detects with awe the hand of God shaping a new historic era.

It is well to begin religious education by fostering that sense of community which is the pledge of human brotherhood. He that loveth not his brother whom he hath seen, how shall he love God whom he hath not seen? But brotherhood is not religion, neither can it be maintained without religion. Communion between men implies the generic unity of mankind. The generic spirit which makes all men one is the God in man. Communion with this indwelling God is prayer. Prayer is the characteristic act of religion, and the chief aim of religious education as a whole should be to foster the prayerful spirit. The mere definition of this aim suggests a revolution in the prevalent conception of religion and in prevalent methods of religious education. There is a widespread tendency to conceive the essential act of religion as an effort to speed the coming of an ideal civilization, and there-

---

[1] Jane Addams, *Newer Ideals of Peace*, pp. 20, 21.

fore to spend much time running about trying to improve the world without any clear idea in what improvement consists. The conception of religion defended in this report holds, on the contrary, that religion is a progressive tendency towards communion with God transcendent, God immanent, and God incarnate; that such communion is based upon community of nature between man and God, and that its issue is a serene life whose outward deeds are its natural and spontaneous self-expression.

It may be because our conception of prayer has remained savage and heathen that we find it so difficult to enter sympathetically into the idea of its central position in a truly Christian experience. To limit . prayer to petition, and above all to petition for material and transient goods, is really to deny Christianity, and there can scarcely be a grosser caricature of religion than that which conceives God as a vast reservoir of power to be drawn on at our will and for our benefit. The aim of religious communion is not to prostitute divine energy to human whim, but to regenerate human intellects, consecrate human wills, and renew human hearts by making them participant in divine purposes. To fix thought on the eternal is prayer. From this highest consecration of our power of voluntary attention spring repentance for sin and gratitude for the great gift of being, ceaseless aspiration towards the source of being, trust in divine goodness, and the spontaneous leap of partial towards perfect love.

If a mother be herself religious, or in other words if her life be lived in constant dependence upon God, she will pray. The reaction of her prayer upon the mind of her child is his second forward step in the religious life. Indeed, it may be said that actual religion as distinct from its germinal cell (the sense of community) begins with the child's feeling that the one person upon whom he is dependent depends in her turn upon an invisible power. "It is, therefore," writes Froebel, "not only a touching sight for the quiet and unseen observer, but productive of eternal blessings for the child, when the mother lays the sleeping infant upon his couch with an intensely loving look to their Heavenly Father, praying Him for protection and loving care."

"It is not only touching, and greatly pleasing, but highly important and full of blessings for the whole present and later life of the child, when the mother, with a look full of joy and gratitude towards the Heavenly Father, and thanking him for rest and new vigor, lifts from his couch the awakened child, radiant with joyful smiles; nay, for the whole time of the related life between mother and child this exerts the happiest influence. Therefore, the true mother is loath to let another put the sleeping child to bed, or to take from it the awakened child."[1]

After a while the child who has seen his mother pray will wish to pray himself. One of the most remarkable songs and commentaries in the *Mother Play* shows with what tender and delicate indirectness this nascent and only semi-conscious desire should be met. Its first suggestion is that sacred acts must not be intruded upon secular moments, and therefore that we must await some signal from the child himself before we

[1] *Education of Man*, pp. 25, 26.

venture to incline his heart towards prayer. The song and picture referred to presuppose that it is evening, and that the little one who all day long has been busy with many things will soon be laid to sleep. His quiet posture, clasped hands, and introspective eyes assure us of the meditative moment, and apprize us that from fragmentary thoughts, feelings, and deeds he has withdrawn into the wholeness of his central selfhood. Gently and carefully the mother seeks to quicken a vague awareness of what is passing within him. She tells him a story of little children and all they did in one happy day. She shows him a picture of these happy children, tired and sinking into sleep. She clasps her own hands to represent the sleeping children and sings the prayer they said before they slept. The little child's own intertwined fingers begin to mean something to him. They are children who played as he has played, who were tired as he is tired, who are sleeping as he would sleep, and who before sleeping prayed as now he feels he would like to pray.

The sympathetic reader is doubtless already aware that with the experience just described we have advanced to that phase of the genetic method which demands introspection and retrospection. The child has been helped to look into himself. He has been helped to take a backward glance over a single day. Finally, he has been helped to discover a desire stirring faintly below the threshold of consciousness.

We have considered the three primary stages in the evolution of Christian experience and have sought to show that their root is the native sense of community; their blossom a nascent longing to pray, made aware of itself; and their final presupposition the God immanent in, and yet transcendent of every human soul. We must now consider that second path of approach towards the Christian consciousness which begins with recognition of our own double selfhood and whose climax is the vision of God incarnate.

This report presupposes in its readers awareness of an ideal self which is different from the actual self; of a universal self which is different from the particular self; of a permanent self different from and transcendent of the series of selves created and outgrown. Only those who know their own double selfhood can understand that its discovery creates the most dramatic moment in the life of a child. It is a moment fraught with fate, and there is no crisis of experience demanding clearer insight in order to meet it with a redeeming response. The child has discriminated between his actual self and an ideal self. The self he recognizes as ideal is the one he has learned to define through the reaction of those about him upon his deeds. What they praise he has begun to call good, what they blame he has begun to regard as evil. Three great dangers threaten him. Through desire for social approval he may try to seem what he is not and so fall into duplicity. Duplicity in himself will make him suspect duplicity in others and betray him into debasing views of human nature. Finally, he will hide from himself as well as others the acts and feelings which contradict the accepted ideal self and thereby will distribute all his experiences into two mutually repellent groups. In short, while vision of an ideal self is the condition of moral development, it brings with it the possibility of a disastrous schism in the soul.

Spiritually naked and unashamed the young child has wandered hitherto in the Eden of his home. Now, to him as to his great forbear, there is revealed what he should and should not do. Betrayed chiefly by heedlessness, temper, and lust into actions which contradict the revealed ideal, he begins that terrible game of hide-and-seek which often continues throughout life. He hides through fear; he hides through shame; he hides through vanity; he hides from mother and father, from brothers and sisters, from the world, from God, and from himself. He sews for himself concealing garments of hypocrisy; he skulks in caves of hidden motive; he parries attack with keen-edged blades of sophistry; he retreats into solitary fastnesses of pride. He will not be known and he will not know himself. Worst of all, he hides under masks of conscience, blind to the fact that his imperious ought is nothing but an enthroned passion or a crowned ambition. Hiding and hidden, he steals through life haunted forever by premonitions of the great unmasking which awaits every soul made in the image of God.

It argues something very wrong in our education of children that transition from the unmoral to the moral life should so often make them worse instead of better, and perhaps the most important question which a mother or kindergartner can ask herself is: How shall I help the child to see an ideal and guide himself by conscious choices of the will, without betraying him into hypocrisy and falsehood and creating in him a contradiction so great that he will never be able to resolve it? As has been said, progress in the moral life demands vision of an ideal beyond present attainment. An unattained ideal must not only beckon but condemn. The question to be solved is: How shall we conduct the young soul safely through the dangers inevitably associated with self-condemnation and thus prevent a necessary schism from deepening into an insoluble contradiction?

We know the answer made by religion to this question when it was asked by man in the childhood of the human race. In that mystical account of man's first discovery of his double selfhood which reaches into the profoundest depths of the soul, we read that contemporary with the revelation of sin was the promise of a redeemer. A child born of woman should bruise the serpent's head.

With the deepening of moral consciousness came the conviction that the redeemer from sin must be born not only of woman but of God, or, translating this mystic intuition into terms of conscious intelligence, it was felt that there could be no deliverance of man from the curse of sin, no attainment by man of the ideal self, no reconciliation of man with the cosmic order, unless generic humanity was divine humanity, and it were possible that God immanent should become God incarnate.

The redemptive power of this insight derives from the fact that the ideal revealed is one of perfect love. The God who cares so much for men that He cannot be satisfied until He has given them all He has and all He is, is not a God before whom any soul need shrink in cowardly terror even when smitten by the sense of sin. He is not a God from whom man needs to hide. Rather is He a God towards whom every sinning soul may run for succor. Emerson proved his interior vision of Christianity when he wrote —

> "Fear not, then, thou child infirm,
> There's no god dare wrong a worm";

and Browning showed the boldness born of faith that "sees into and through itself" when he dared affirm that

> "A loving worm within its clod,
> Were diviner than a loveless God."

In the light of this revelation of religion we discern an answer to the question how a young soul may be safely conducted through the dangers incident to the dawning vision of an ideal. This answer is that when we reveal the true ideal, which is love, the dangers vanish. The revelation is first made through the attitude of the mother. The child who trusts his mother's love will not hide his naughtiness, but run to her to be delivered from it. Her response to his appeal must reveal love as both pitiful and imperious. No mother does redeeming work unless she makes her child feel that the demands of love are as inexorable as its forgiveness is assured. Love implies either actual or potential worth in its object. It challenges to perfection because it believes perfection possible. It can forgive so long as forgiveness is needed, because it knows that this possibility, however delayed, can never be lost. Love is, therefore, the ever renewed confession of faith in divine immanence, the ever renewed hope of divine incarnation.

The attempt has been made to describe that crisis

of experience marked by the birth of conscience. It has been shown to involve four phases. The child has recognized his own double selfhood. He has recognized the double selfhood of those around him. He has discerned a coercive ideal hovering over himself and others. He has violated that ideal and is smitten with the sense of sin. The mother has responded to his troubled conscience with a love which suffers while it delivers. Is it only a mother who can thus meet and overcome evil, or may it be that her redeeming love is but a reflection of the redeeming love of God?

The moment has come for the revelation of a deliverer, but this revelation must be very gentle and indirect. For a revelation which outruns need will create skepticism, and as every premature disclosure of good is the ancestor of evil, so every premature disclosure of truth is the ancestor of a doubt or a denial.

The world literature of the childhood of the race abounds with stories which meet the needs of the child in this most momentous crisis of his history. Wide-eyed he will listen to tales of the beautiful princess held captive by a wicked giant, and of the hero who journeys far, suffers long, and combats mightily for her deliverance. Sometimes he will identify himself with the wretched captive, sometimes with the conquering hero, because in very deed he is both, and in his own soul as battle-ground must meet and slay himself as foe, and free himself as captive held in chains. Later he will be stirred with strange surmises as he hears the great myth of Herakles or listens to the story of Achilles renouncing wrath and freely accepting death for the sake of his cause. But the question

which these and kindred tales may help to quicken in
his soul will be fully answered only by the legends and
history of the race elected to answer it for all mankind. The myth of Eden interprets the first act in the
history of his soul. By the free decision of Moses to
forsake a palace and throw in his lot with slaves, new
ardors are inspired and new horizons won. At last the
revelation of the Cross sets the seal of eternity upon
time and the seal of the cosmic order upon the noblest
impulse of man. Then is the final ardor quickened and
the infinite horizon spread.

When we attempt to state Christian experience in its
simplest terms, we say it is assurance of the fact that
looking into the face of Jesus we behold the face of
God. Christianity is worship of a God whose character
is like the character of Jesus. Jesus so loved men that
he gladly embraced death in order to save them. If
God be like him his eternal life is an eternal cross and
passion. It is this conception which defines Christian
faith. It is the command, Take up thy cross and follow
me, which defines Christian duty. The trouble with
our moral conventions is that they have not recognized
the centrality of loving-kindness. It is only as every
duty is conceived as derivative from and related to this
supreme obligation that it can be enjoined without
creating that deplorable schism which makes so many
men not one person, but two or even many persons.

A genetic development of ideal human character is
possible because some degree of love is present in all
men in the form of immediate impulse. Moral education should be centered in the effort to abet the native
struggle of this divine impulse against all the impulses

which contradict it. Religious education should be centered in the effort to reveal God as love. The concrete revelation of love is made in the Cross. Without the sacrifice of Calvary, Jesus might have been the world's greatest teacher and prophet. With it, he becomes the world's Redeemer, a figure unique in history and resplendent with the glory of eternity. In the temporal world, Love hangs forever on the Cross; in the Eternal world, it is enthroned upon the seat of judgment and summons all men to its dread assize. In the order of time there is no last judgment for any human soul, but in the permanent order of the spiritual universe self-sacrificing love is the ultimate criterion of character, and men are in hell or heaven as it repels or attracts them.

There is a widespread and uneasy sense that something is wrong with our moral conventions. Such uneasiness indicates that the collective mind is in travail and a nobler social conscience about to be born. Conventions are agreements which embody the results of collective experience. It is because through that experience for nearly two thousand years has been working the leaven of the Christian ideal that our domestic, economic, national, and religious conventions are now being challenged, and that the hearts of men everywhere are crying for renewal of life. The Cross is the sacred symbol of an infinite and eternal Reality. Eternal Reality is what in human life we call the unrealized ideal. It is not wonderful that two thousand years should be insufficient for the realization of an ideal that is infinite. The miracle is rather that in the paltry period of two thousand years it should be ac-

cepted by so many souls as a moral imperative and
that the conscience of the Occidental world should be
convincing itself of sin and panting for deliverance
from the baser instincts inherited from brute and
savage ancestors.

We have traced two aspects of that genetic-developing experience through which an approach is made
towards the Christian conception of God. There remains for consideration the conception of God transcendent, and its approach through ascent from effects
to causes and from all secondary causes to a primal
cause.

It is characteristic of the human intellect that it
begins at once to be dissatisfied with the immediate
aspect of experience and to explain all that is perceptible by the senses as effects of outlying causes. This
search for causes is itself explained by the fact that
being a causative being man knows himself as producer
of objects and acts, and therefore divines an analogous
origin of all things and events. Furthermore, he knows
himself as the single cause of a related multiplicity of
acts, and projects this self-knowledge as an intuition
of one great primal cause.

The characteristic attribute of a great first cause is
sovereignty. As God immanent is the pledge of cosmic
fellowship and God incarnate the revelation of cosmic
love, so God conceived as transcendent or as primal
cause gives assurance of cosmic power. It has been
well said that failure to hold to the sovereignty of God
is a lapse into the impiety of the intellect. God is love:
but if love be not omnipotent, then love is not God.
Recognition of its sovereignty is our apprisal that it will

never abate its challenge to perfection, never withhold the pangs which failure to respond to that challenge must forever provoke.

A genetic development of the idea of divine sovereignty is made by abetting the conscious search for causal explanation and by fostering the presentiment of one great first cause through a series of illuminating analogies. When we incite children to trace the history of a piece of bread, through baker, miller, farmer, to the wheat field, and to discover the dependence of the growing grain upon earth, sun, air, dew, and rain; or, again, when we call attention to the relationships between the needs of nestlings and the localities in which birds build their nests and the season in which they hatch their eggs, we are stimulating causal interest and forming a habit of mind which will issue in that search for ever completer chains of causality which must culminate in intellectual vision of a primal cause. But we cannot be content to postpone the sense of divine sovereignty until it is discovered as a logical necessity by conscious intellect. We crave the benign and stimulating influence of this conception upon the child's unfolding intelligence and will. Therefore, recognizing the saltatory power of mind and aware that the prescient imagination must outrun understanding, we foster the power of mystic divination by means of those natural analogies which so powerfully affected the evolution of religion in the childhood of the race, and through the lightning flash, the invisible but mighty wind, the overarching sky, and the all-revealing light, quicken the solemn sense of divine transcendence and omnipotence. For now, as in the days of yore, Jove hurls his thunderbolts from Olympus; Ahura-Mazda triumphs over the fiend of darkness; Jehovah rides upon the wings of the wind, and forever above and beyond this world gleams the Eternal City which hath no need of the sun, neither of the moon to shine in it, for the Lord God doth lighten it and the Lamb is the light thereof.

It has seemed best to illustrate what we have thus far learned of the genetic method through the evolution of the supreme educational value. It is hoped that the following points have been made clear: —

I. The point of departure for the genetic method is life conceived as interaction between the individual and his social and natural environment.

II. The environment presents itself as a fellowship to be shared, an ideal to be obeyed, and a world to be investigated and re-created. The individual responds with a feeling of community, a consciousness of double selfhood, a tendency to search for causes, and a desire to exert causal activity.

III. The presupposition of the threefold incitement and response is the completely realized Gliedganzes, or Triune God, and the Christian religion may be defined as an ever growing awareness of this presupposition and an ever increasing volitional and emotional response to that ideal of perfect love which it embodies and defines.[1]

[1] It has been no part of our purpose to consider the agencies by which religious education should be given. In order, however, to avoid all possible misconception, we desire to affirm our entire sym-

FURTHER IMPLICATIONS OF THE GENETIC-DEVELOPING METHOD

It has been already said in this report that the principle alike of psychology and education is self-activity. *It is characteristic of this principle that it is also a method.* For self-activity must have some way of acting, and this general mode of action will be its method. Self-activity achieves its ideal form in self-consciousness. Self-consciousness involves awareness both of the results of self-activity and of its process. We first act: then look at what we have done: and finally at the way we did it. It is through this introspective and retrospective gaze that mind ascends from undifferentiated feeling to sensation, perception, conception, and all higher forms of mental activity. The ascent from sensation to perception is made by an act of introspection which looks both at the result and the process of sensation; the ascent from perception to conception is made by a deeper introspective act which scans the product and process of perception. In short, every ascent of mental activity is accomplished through an introspective survey of the next inferior mode of action, and the so-called "faculties" of the mind must therefore be conceived as vortical ascents of a single indivisible energy.

The genetic-developing method is nothing more nor pathy with that national ideal which prohibits the teaching of any particular creed in our public schools.

The aim of our discussion has been twofold — first, to suggest an insight which as it seems to us may be assimilated by different religions and become the basis of one universal world-view; and second, to indicate the incitements by means of which the emotional equivalents of this insight may be generated in the hearts of little children.

less than the conscious attempt to apply the native method of self-activity in education. We spy upon mind and discover how it acts; then make its spontaneous mode of procedure our criterion of educational method.

It has been customary to describe three principles as fundamental to Froebel's educational theory, — the principle of organic unity, the principle of development, and the principle to which is sometimes given the name of self-activity and sometimes the name of interaction. We are urgent in our insistence that Froebel's educational theory has but one fundamental principle — the principle of self-activity; and we hope that as this report proceeds our reason for this insistence will become clear. For the moment, we limit ourselves to a statement of our reasons for preferring the older word self-activity to the newer word interaction, and to an attempt to show that development and organic unity must be conceived as descriptions of the process and result of self-activity.

The substitution of the word interaction for the word self-activity is defended on the ground that "in an organic unity there cannot be any arbitrary or external action of one part upon another, it is rather an interaction of the parts of an organic unity."[1] We hail this thought as a notable advance over the idea of a fixed environment, to which the individual must adjust himself and the idea of a predetermined self, that is, a self in which faculties exist prior to their exercise. We cannot, however, accept organic unity as our highest principle. Such acceptance seems to us the out-

[1] "Kindergarten Problems," *Teachers College Record*, November, 1909, p. 355.

come of one of the most dangerous of those biologic analogies to which are due so many of the confusions of contemporary thought. The members of an organism are complemental elements in a whole which forever transcends them. They differ from each other and from the whole to which as members they belong. Furthermore, no organism is ever at any one moment the whole of itself, nor does any particular organism ever duplicate the species to which it belongs.

The final principle accepted by the signers of this report is not organic unity, but the Gliedganzes conceived as completely realized self-activity. In the light of this completely realized self-activity we interpret all lesser forms and degrees of self-activity.

We freely grant that the self-activity of little children, and, indeed, of human beings throughout life, is of inferior type. A perfect self-activity would have to be self-environing. Only a creative subject which has duplicated itself in its object can be wholly self-related and therefore perfectly self-active. The term interaction appropriately describes one aspect of that inferior mode of self-activity manifested by the members of an organism. It may also be generously interpreted as referring to the fellowship or communion of individuals in a social whole. But even under the most liberal interpretation it fails to suggest the fact that, whether perfect or imperfect, self-activity has a constraining form or inner law, and that in human beings this inner law affects both creative and apperceptive deeds. Hence the acceptance of organic unity as the comprehensive principle of education, and the degradation of self-activity into a mere phase of this principle, create in the kindergarten a practical procedure foreign to and subversive of that genetic-developing method which is Froebel's· most original contribution to the art of education.

It should not be difficult for any one who has insight into the principle of self-activity to understand that development is its process of unfolding and that education may abet this process by stimulating related deeds. We have all been made familiar with the idea that we cannot have a single sensation which is unaffected by our previous sensations. It is no less true that deeds subsequent are affected by deeds antecedent. It is, however, to some extent inevitable that the feelings and deeds from which development proceeds will not always agree, and hence that there will be clashes and contradictions in the developing process. The aim of education should be so far as possible to avoid these contradictions by inciting concordant deeds and emotions.

Students of abnormal psychology are at present having much to say of obsessions or extra voluntary ideas, feelings, or emotions, presenting themselves automatically in consciousness either alone or in combination. These obsessions arise when particular mental states get dissociated from the main stream of the self-conscious personality and then connect themselves with other contents to form a kind of isolated complex. Any analogous experience will then call up this disliked and intrusive complex, and the resisting personality becomes temporarily or permanently the victim of a fixed idea. In normal persons a similar contradiction exists in inferior degree. One value of recent studies of the abnormal is that they have given a genetic explanation of a fact of common experience and thereby have cast light on the problem of how this regrettable and painful experience may be minimized. Manifestly, one of the efforts of early education should be to prevent the formation of these dissociated complexes. Hence the unifying of consciousness through stimulating concordant deeds and through introspective scrutiny and rejection of clashing deeds is one of the most important means of preserving mental health. It is towards this unification of consciousness that Froebel aims in his effort to abet continuity of development.

The bearings of the ideal of continuity upon the development of intellect are no less important than its bearings upon the development of will and feeling. In this final relation it calls for a genetic evolution of the several great human values which it conceives as revelations of that aboriginal self-determining energy whose realized form is self-consciousness. An effort has been made in this report to illustrate the earlier stages in the evolution of a single value. The Froebelian method will be adequately understood only after it is applied to the evolution of all values and to all stages in the evolution of each value.

It is inevitable that large ideas should shrink when they enter small minds, and it must be frankly confessed that in this way the ideal of continuity in development has too often shrunken into a method of arrest. Not discerning its wider implications as related to the evolution of human values, and not understanding that, in evolving from within the child the norms of his generic selfhood, she was developing him, the narrow-minded kindergartner has fondly fancied that all she had to do was to make every possible combination of vertical and horizontal lines before venturing to use a slanting line, or every possible combination of the numbers one and two before daring profanely to dream of applying the number three. Through this shrinkage of the idea of continuity into what was called the logical evolution of the gifts and occupations, the developing method was changed into a method of stultification which deserved all the scornful criticism it received. It is doubtless true that even to-day some representatives of the kindergarten do this arresting work. But the time is past when any intelligent person can suppose that Froebel would have countenanced such a caricature of his idea. Furthermore, among the kindergartners who follow Froebel no practical tendency is at present stronger than the tendency to oppose the imposition of fixed series, to curtail so far as possible the given elements out of which series unfold, and to recognize that saltatory power by which in proportion to their natural vigor of intelligence children leap from differences of degree to differences of kind.

Conceiving the child as self-active, believing that education might abet the process of self-activity and save it from falling into glaring self-contradiction by genetic evolution of the values which are its own approximate self definitions, and by incitement of the deeds and feelings which are the volitional and emotional equivalents of these values, Froebel held finally that upon every plane of development there might be that integration of experience which he sometimes described as a spherical totality and sometimes as an organic unity. When he used the phrase spherical totality to express this idea, there hovered before him the thought of a force which since it projected equal radii in all directions could be conceived as terminating in successive spheres of increasing size; when he used the phrase organic unity his mind was influenced by the famous Kantian definition of an organism as a living whole wherein each member was both means and end to all the other members and to the whole. In both cases he was trying to think as clearly as possible a self-determining energy which through a variety and succession of interrelated acts, feelings, and ideas integrates itself into a structural unity.

The aim of the foregoing analysis has been to show that Froebel has but one fundamental principle — the principle of self-activity — which approximately realizes itself in processes and integrates itself in their results. The so-called principles of development and organic unity are in reality interrelated aspects of self-activity.

Thus far in our discussion of the genetic method we have suggested only its more obvious implications. It has been shown that its presupposition is life; its point of departure the deed; its first demand, the incitement of deeds pointing towards the values of life and restraint of deeds which antagonize those values; its second demand, the introspective and retrospective scrutiny through which deeds become self-penetrating, or in other words through which self-determining energy becomes aware of itself. It has been further shown that the genetic method is simply the conscious attempt of education to reinforce the native principle of self-activity in its spontaneous effort to objectify itself in processes of development and integrate its results in a vitally related totality or organic unity.

Froebel's own statements of the deeper implications of the genetic method are contained in his references to and discussions of what in kindergarten terminology is known as the law of Mediation of Opposites. Our next task, therefore, must be to explain as briefly as possible what we understand to be the meaning of the Froebelian law.

The first requirement necessary to the correct understanding of the Mediation of Opposites is a precise definition of the word law. Many persons seem to think of a law as external to the energy it guides and restrains and to assume that were it not for this external coercion the energy itself would behave in quite other ways. Understood in this sense any law imposed upon mind would be an attack upon its freedom. The question emerges whether this is a correct conception of law. The physicist speaks of the law of gravitation and affirms that in virtue of this law all objects attract each other in direct proportion to their mass and in inverse proportion to the square of their distance. Manifestly, the law of gravitation merely summarizes our experience of the way in which this force behaves. Should we ever find, as some physicists are beginning to claim, that facts contradict the formula, we should conclude we had been mistaken in our law.

Understanding that a law is not an external edict binding a reluctant energy, but a fixed form in which an energy acts in virtue of its own constitution, we may briefly define the Froebelian law as the universal mode of action of the energy we know as mind. Because mind is what it is, it behaves spontaneously and yet unvaryingly in a certain way. This spontaneous and yet unvarying mode of behaviour may be called its law.

"I wish," said Alice to the Cheshire Cat she met in Wonderland, "I wish you would n't keep appearing and vanishing so suddenly. You make me quite giddy."

"All right," said the Cat, and this time it vanished quite slowly, beginning with the end of the tail and ending with the grin, which remained some time after the rest of it had gone.

"Well! I've often seen a cat without a grin," thought Alice; "but a grin without a cat, — it's the most curious thing I ever saw."

Anybody may see anywhere a cat without a grin. It is only in Wonderland that one may see a grin without a cat. The kindergartner who aspires towards a real understanding of the Froebelian law must be prepared to go through with an experience which for a time will make her no less giddy than Alice. The form or law of mind will appear and vanish, and just when she is most sure she has seen it, it will disappear most completely from her sight. Let her, however, be patient and resolute, for after a while the vanishings will cease, and when the vision abides there abides with it a joy which transfigures life.

If it be understood that the phrase "form of mind" means simply an unvarying way in which mind be-

635030

haves, we may next look into ourselves to discover if
in reality there be any one mode to which our mental
activity always conforms. We shall perhaps recognize
this mode of action most readily in our moral life and
as summarized in such formulas as "It is only with
renunciation that life, properly speaking, can be said
to begin"; "Surrender happiness and win blessedness";
"Create selfhood by crucifying self"; or, in most
vigorous epitome, "Die to live." No one who has
made an honest and persistent moral struggle can fail
to know himself as an incarnate paradox. As was said
in an earlier portion of this report, each human being
is a slave, an enslaver, and a deliverer, and is engaged
in a war wherein he is both of the contending parties,
the ground of conflict and the fruit of victory. The
paradox thus illustrated in the moral conflict holds
in all spheres of human experience and may be pictori-
ally suggested by all forms of achievement. Each man
is an architect, who is also the quarry whence comes
his marble and the temple he rears; a sculptor who is
his own clay and the statue he molds; a musician who
is the symphony he creates and the instrument upon
which it is played; a poet who is at once his own legen-
dary material and his song; in short, a self-active
energy which is its own creator, its own stuff, and its
own product, and which in order to achieve its product must overcome the persistent obstacle variously
suggested by the malleable yet resisting clay, the
recalcitrant marble, the imperfect musical instrument,
and the obscure legend.

These crude and external pictures of an unpicturable
reality are only intended to assist unaccustomed minds

to approach a difficult thought. That thought itself is most briefly stated as negative self-relation. The kindergartner who wishes to understand the Mediation of Opposites must discipline herself in thinking until she can see with her own intellectual eyes that any pure self-activity must be a self-related negative, and until she is able to deduce from this insight its more obvious consequences.

This difficult thought may be gradually approached. We are to think a pure self-activity, that is, an activity which acts upon itself. For if it acted upon anything other than itself it would be related to this other instead of being self-related, and relationship to another always implies some degree of determinism, and therefore contradicts the idea of pure self-activity.

When we see that a pure self-activity must act upon itself, we are ready to approach the more difficult insight that in so doing it dirempts itself at once into determiner and determined, or into energy and product. In acting upon itself, therefore, a pure self-activity produces within itself a realm of passivity and particularity. It makes itself, and necessarily makes itself that which it is not. Hence its act is negative to itself.

It is easy to illustrate the essential negativity of a pure self-activity by the analogy of all imperfect self-activities. Every generic energy in the vegetable and animal world is an imperfect self-activity, and every such energy is at any given moment contradicted by its product. Neither the acorn, the sapling, nor the full-grown tree duplicates the generic energy, oak; nor is this energy duplicated even in the total process of life which includes these several products. For the generic energy we name oak includes many species, and the particular oak is only a single specimen of a single species. A generic energy which is always trying unsuccessfully to duplicate itself is a negative which can negate itself but not negate its negating act, and which therefore is unable to overcome the tragedy of its inherent form.

The relation of a negative activity to itself may be illustrated on a higher plane through our own processes of thinking and willing. The particular thought is only one of myriads which we might think, the particular deed only one of myriads which we might do. Hence every thought is in a very real sense an arrest of thinking, and every particular deed, as Goethe tells us, "impedes the onward march of life."

We implicitly recognize this contradiction between thinking and doing on the one hand, and thought and deed on the other, by our condemnation of the intellectual narrowness and rigidity due to mechanical reiteration of accustomed thought, and by our disapproval of action which has so long limited itself to fixed ruts as to be incapable of pioneer effort.

The contradiction with self into which the act of determining must plunge a pure self-activity supplies the incitement to renewed act. For reflect: A pure self-activity must be an energy having the mark of universality. It is the potentiality of all possible deeds. It acts, and by this act determines itself as particular. Being universal, it is repelled by this particularity and acts again to annul it. In its first aspect, this act of annulment is a restoration of universality; in its second aspect, it is a new determination which again plunges self-activity into contradiction with itself and incites new effort to cancel the contradiction. Hence through its own inherent constitution a self-related negative becomes its own perpetual self-incitement and maintains itself as an eternal process, which, in the words of the philosopher who has seen most deeply into the miracle of self-activity, "pulsates within itself without moving itself and vibrates within itself without ruffling its repose."

The characteristic feature of a negatively self-related activity is that its inhibition is its renewal. It is this negative self-relation which we mean when we speak of the form or law of mind, and it is because we see that this form cannot be denied without affirming it that we claim for it the quality of absolute truth. Having made our own statement, we give ourselves the pleasure of citing the more adequate statement of Professor Royce. "What," he asks, "is thinking?" And replies: "Thinking is simply our activity of willing precisely in so far as we are clearly conscious of what we do and why we do it. And thinking is found by us to possess an absolute form precisely in so far as we find that there are certain aspects of our activity which sustain themselves even in and through the very effort to inhibit them. One who says: 'I do not admit that for me there is any difference between saying yes and saying no' — says 'No,' and distinguishes negation from affirmation even in the very act of denying this distinction. Well, affirmation and negation are such self-sustaining forms of our will-activity and of our thought activity. *And such self-sustaining forms of activity determine absolute truths.*" [1]

The question may be raised whether, even granting that mind is a self-related negative, its constitution has any bearing upon the method of education. It remains, therefore, to be suggested that this inherent constitution of mind acts both as an apperceptive agency and as a determiner of the form of all creative activity. It was because of this form that the selective interest of primitive men fastened upon those natural phenomena wherein it was adumbrated. It is in virtue of this form that the sensuous elements of every art are regularity, symmetry, and harmony. It is because of the coercion of this inner law that every great human value breaks its own path towards that conception of the Gliedganzes wherein is clearly revealed the constitution of the positive out of the negative. Finally, it is because of the fact that this mode of behavior is the most essential feature of mental life in all stages of development, and that from earliest childhood its constraining influence far surpasses that of any special impulse or tendency, that it may not be ignored in education.

When we wish to learn most clearly of the way mind loves best to act we turn to the poets. No student of great literature can fail to be aware how all great poets delight in mere sport with the "form or law of mind," and also how, when they turn from sport to the keener joy of self-revelation, the same great law determines the theme and structure of their poems. Readers of

[1] Josiah Royce, *The Problem of Truth in the Light of Recent Research*, p. 86.

the Odyssey will remember the punning device by which the crafty hero outwitted the Cyclops. Giving his name as Noman, he made it impossible for the blinded giant to declare who had blinded him without affirming that no one had blinded him. Professor Snider has said that the pun of Odysseus is the deepest ever made or that it will ever be possible to make, because it rests on the duplicity inherent in the negative. To the same inherent duplicity we owe the grotesque pictures of Dante and Virgil escaping from hell by climbing up the legs of the reversed Devil into the sunlit world. The last world poet had his own little free play with the negative when he dispatched Faust to seek his all in the nothing of Mephistopheles. Eckermann tells us that when asked to explain the mysterious scene Goethe raised his brows, opened his eyes, and assumed a mysterious air. He was enjoying a fun which only those who knew his open secret could share.

Great poets are not satisfied to sport with the negative, but more or less consciously determine the theme and structure of their song by this constraining form. The Iliad is a concrete portrayal of the moral paradox, "Die to live." The Odyssey transfigures all tales of geographic wandering into the search of the soul for itself. The poet of the church shows the negative will negating its own negativity and becoming holy; the poet of the individual traces the process of the intellect through the same self-refuting, self-reaffirming cycle; and the great poet of society never tires of showing how the social whole by its negative reaction upon negative deeds makes them the instruments of their own undoing. Literature would not be a revelation of life did it not reveal the inner law which controls life. Turn where we may, we shall find that life, whether lived or pictured, is a great dialectic process which is perpetually illustrating the creation of the positive by the negation of the negative.

It is to this universal process that Froebel gives the name Mediation of Opposites, and it is because we recognize it as the absolute form of all mental activity that we cannot agree with those kindergartners who either reject or ignore the so-called Froebelian law. Recognition of the inner law, however, is perfectly distinct from acceptance of the particular devices of instrument or method which Froebel created under the inspiration of this insight. It is possible to accept the Mediation of Opposites and reject all Froebel's applications of this principle. It is possible to accept some of his applications and reject others. Each particular application should be intelligently tested and accepted or rejected upon its own merits. But the inner law itself is a definition of the structural form of self-activity and any educational method which rejects or ignores it imperils itself by denying an agency prepotent in its influence both upon creative and apperceptive activities.

The universal law or form of mind is the true key to the genetic-developing method. In Froebel's recurrent statements of this law we are always apprized that "every individual being, if it would attain its destiny, must manifest itself in and as unity, in and as individuality, and in and as manifoldness in ever increasing diversity." His statements have too often been misunderstood because the word unity has been explained in a static sense. Froebel's own phrase is energetic unity, and his reference is to the universal or self-determining phase in the process of self-activity. The phrase "ever increasing diversity" points to the results of that constant annulment of particularity through which new particulars are posited, and the word individuality defines that concrete union of uni-versality and particularity which is both the eternal antecedent and the ever renewed consequent of the self-determining process.

In its practical relation to educational method the significance of the Froebelian law is that it makes a further explication of the native developing-process of self-activity. We have already seen that this pro-cess involves the ideas of continuity and integration. We should now see that it involves the ideas of a con-tinuity incited by and maintained through the posit-ing and annulment of antitheses, and hence that it explains the final origin of those clashing deeds whose result is the formation of dissociated complexes. In the light of this revelation of the final source of moral evil and intellectual error, we discern that most im-portant exaction of the genetic-developing method, that upon every plane of experience there shall be a resolute facing of the intellectual aberrations and moral perversions into which children have been ac-tually betrayed and a conscious attempt to help them assimilate and thereby transcend negative deeds and wayward fancies. To this requisition of restraint is added a requisition of incitement, and from insight into the Froebelian law emerges the demand that both creative and apperceptive activity shall be heightened by concrete presentation of those terminal contrasts of action, sentiment, and idea which are so much more readily apprehended than nearer and finer distinctions.

"The key to every man," writes Emerson, "is his thought. Sturdy and defying though he look, he has a helm which he obeys, which is the idea after which all his facts are classified." [1] To the reader who has understood this report it should be evident that the helm which Froebel's mind obeys is the Mediation of Opposites. The conception of the Gliedganzes is attained by developing the theoretic implications of this master-thought. The kindergarten translates this same master-thought into deed through its attempt to mediate the apparently excluding antitheses of play and work. In view of the fact that the writer of this report has devoted a whole book to the elucidation of this attempt, its further exposition seems superfluous, and the signers of this report restrict themselves to reaffirmation of the following statements from the report presented to the Committee of Nineteen by the conservative members of that body.

We hold that the highest form in which the native activity of childhood expresses itself is play. We accept the Froebelian definition of play "as self-active representation of the inner life from inner necessity and impulse." We believe that mind grows into self-consciousness through self-revelation. We conceive the characteristic mark of the kindergarten to be emphasis upon the activity of self-expression as prior to the activity of assimilation. We are earnest in our

[1] "Circles," *Essays*, First Series.

conviction that kindergarten exercises must preserve the form of play. We recognize as a distinctive merit of the kindergarten that from the native plays of childhood it makes a selection determined by their relation to the values of human life. Through his studies of childhood, Froebel became aware of the fact that some plays point toward the practical arts, some toward the fine arts, some toward science and literature, and some toward the ethical life of man as embodied in social institutions. In these creations of the human spirit he found his standards of value. In various forms of play he recognized the tendencies of which these values are the higher expression. Through recognition of this relationship between native manifestations and human values he was enabled to graft upon selected forms of play the higher realization of their own ideal. The value of thus transforming play is that it develops the child through his own free impulsion. It augments the energy of ideals instead of paralyzing them. The values of life must not be conceived as artificial flowers fastened by some external hand upon a plant which could never have produced them, but as the perfect blossom in which the plant completes its life and provides for its own renewal.

We further hold that by accenting plays pointing toward the values of life the kindergarten creates a selective interest which leads children to single out from the complex of experience its valid and necessary as opposed to its contingent elements, and thereby, as Froebel expresses it, "breaks a pathway through the tangles of human life." It is becoming increasingly recognized that the "likenesses and differences we

observe in facts are not merely thrust upon us without
our consent and connivance. They are the objects of
our attentive interest and they obviously vary with
this interest." [1] It is also admitted that selective interest precedes voluntary attention. Finally, it is granted
that the native selective interest of young children
often fastens upon non-essential and sometimes upon
harmful presentations. It is necessary, therefore, to
create a selective interest which will single out in
rational proportion the valid elements of experience.
The means by which this higher selective interest is
aroused is the exercise of selected forms of activity.
In succinct summary what a child does has a reaction
upon his selective interest, and therefore indirectly
determines which among the many influences stream-
ing toward him shall be welcomed by his mind and
become the material out of which he builds himself and
his world.

KINDERGARTEN SYMBOLISM

Whoever accepts the idea that kindergarten exercises shall preserve the form of play accepts symbolism
in its more inclusive sense. The Standard Dictionary
defines a symbol "as something (not a portrait) that
stands for something else and serves either to represent
it or to bring to mind one or more of its qualities." It
adds: "A symbol is chosen either arbitrarily or on account of some supposed resemblance between it and
the object it symbolizes." In kindergarten terminology
the word symbol is restricted to *resembling* objects and
acts, and the word sign is used to denote any object
which stands for another, not in virtue of some resem-

[1] Royce. *The World and the Individual*, vol. II, p. 48.

blance, but in virtue of our social agreement. As illustrations of such conventional signs may be mentioned the letters of the alphabet, diacritical marks, mathematical figures, schematic drawings, telegraphic dots, and all words whose metaphorical meaning has been submerged in their agreed-upon sense.

This distinction between the symbol and the sign is not a mere distinction of convenience. It rests upon a psychologic discrimination between two marked stages of mental development — the stage wherein the individual does his thinking almost exclusively with pictures and the stage wherein to a large extent he thinks with definitions. Only in so far as he thinks by definition can he use conventional signs. For conventional signs imply social agreement, and social agreement implies common definition of classes of objects and acts.

Defining symbolism as the representation of one object or act by another which in some way resembles it, we become aware that in this wider sense all make-believe play is symbolic. The little girl who makes-believe she is her own mother, the boy who makes-believe that his stick is a horse, are both illustrating symbolism in its broader meaning. The kindergarten, therefore, does not impose upon make-believe play an alien law, but merely recognizes its own most salient characteristic when it encourages the little child to make-believe that his ball is a bird when it hops or a pendulum when it swings, or that he himself is a horse when he trots or a soldier when he marches.

The distinctive feature of symbolism as shown in childish play is its identification of different objects through some single striking mark. The same symbolic activity is manifested in childish speech. It is characteristic of infantile intelligence to seize its object under some one striking aspect and to identify with it other objects sharing this selected mark. For example, a ceiling is grasped as something high, and straightway the word ceiling is applied to the sky, or the word "coo-coo," spoken when the mother hides her face behind a handkerchief is understood to mean disappearance and is promptly extended to the sun vanishing below the horizon.

The reaction of childish symbolism upon mental evolution is a very important one. It leads, on the one hand, towards conscious grasp of the activity or attribute through which different objects have been identified, in detachment from all objects, and on the other, first, to an uneasy suspicion, and later to a clear recognition of excluding distinctions between the identified objects. Thus symbolic activity is the characteristic feature of that cycle of self-activity through which ascent is made towards the concrete definition of particular objects and towards the clear discrimination between image and idea.

A careful study of the speech and play of any particular child consciously directed towards discovery of the ties through which he identifies different objects would perhaps throw more light than any other investigation upon that native form of reaction through which each human being builds up his own individuality. Between the boy who plays he is a horse by prancing, kicking, bucking, and running away, and the boy who trots steadily in cheerful response to voice

and bridle, there is a difference which cannot be wholly
explained by the influence of environment; and between two sisters, one of whom plays mother by perpetually spanking her baby while the other as make-
believe mother goes through the most varied forms
of tender service, there is a contrast which wise education may not ignore.

Since it is through his peculiar reactions against the
influence of environment that each child builds up his
individuality, all children should have plenty of time
and opportunity for free play and in free play should
be interfered with as little as possible. The process of
building individuality may, however, be abetted in
several ways. The first of these is improvement of
the environment against which the child reacts. "It is
inevitable," writes Professor Baldwin, "that the child
make up his personality under limitations of heredity
by imitation out of the copy set in the actions, temper,
emotions, of the persons who build around him the
social enclosure of childhood." The prime duties of
parents and kindergartners are to protect the child
from bad models and supply him with good ones.
They should also observe with care what special persons, objects, and actions are most frequently imitated,
for in such imitations the child reveals the native bias
of his temperament, indicates the line of his possibilities, and suggests the dangers to which he is prone.
They should divert attention from persons or things
which monopolize imagination and threaten to derange
balance of character by subjecting it to the tyranny of
too few ideas. They should procure for the child that
variety in the persons and objects of environment

which is "the soul of originality and the fountain of the ethical life." Finally, by gentle and indirect suggestion they may help children to substitute higher for lower reactions. For example, it may be suggested to the child-mother who is over-fond of spanking her crying baby that perhaps it cries because it is uncomfortable, and that, if she would hold its cold feet to the fire or find the pin which may be pricking it, its screams and kicks would cease.

While free play is indispensable to the development of individuality and while it may be influenced by good copy, by variety of copy, by diversion of attention from monopolizing ideas, and by indirect suggestion, it is manifest that, if play is to be made the instrument of any form of corporate education, there must be developed games whose accent is not upon the individuality through which one human being is distinguished from another, but upon that rational human type or generic spirit in which all individuals participate, and whose historic achievement has been the evolution of the great human values. The traditional games of the nursery and the playground point towards these values, and it is in these traditional games and not in the free play of particular children that we must seek for the prototypes of kindergarten activities. The relationship of Froebel to the traditional games of childhood is analogous to the relationship between the poet who interprets and transforms an obscure myth and the collective spirit in whose depths the myth originated.

The thoughts which have been suggested are intended as a bridge from the conception of symbolism, in its more inclusive sense as the representation of one object or act by another which in some way resembles it, to the more specific conception of symbolism, defined in kindergarten terminology as play with typical objects and representation of typical facts, characters, relations, and processes. All symbolic play unites the represented with the representing object, action, or person through some selected tie. Symbolic play becomes typical when the tie selected points towards logical as distinguished from psychologic concepts.

Most adults have learned to think many simple ideas by definition, and are therefore able to use a large number of conventional signs. Many adults, however, are unable to think such ideas as are embodied in the institutions of church and state except in symbolic form. The difference between the adult and the child is simply that, while the average adult does much though not all of his thinking through definition, the child does most though not all of his thinking with pictures. Children need to have all ethical ideals presented in the form of concrete examples, and all general thoughts presented under some image of sense. The kindergarten attempts to bridge the chasm between the mental image and the general idea through play with typical objects, and through representation of typical acts, facts, characters, relations, and processes.

The statement that children think mainly with pictures must not be understood to imply that they have no general ideas. Professor Preyer proved conclusively that his child had attained one general idea in his eleventh month, and in learning to use language all children acquire the power of seeing objects as individuals belonging to classes. In early childhood, however, such general ideas as are expressed by abstract nouns are entirely beyond the range of intelligent apprehension. Speak to a child of heroism, social interdependence, or patriotism, and you might as well speak to a deaf person. But tell him the story of David, let him play such games as the farmer, miller, baker, carpenter, and wheelwright, encourage him to march like a soldier, and to wave high in air our national flag, and you not only stir the emotional equivalents of these ideals, but prepare the way for their definition to intellect. Most of the symbolism of the kindergarten takes the form of typical representation. The greater number of kindergarten games; the rhymes and stories throwing into relief selected types of character; the careful selection of typical facts as approaches to the different sciences; the use of archetypal forms as playthings; the use of organically related gifts; the many concrete illustrations of essential relations and evolutionary processes; the development of forms of beauty and knowledge by the mediation of antitheses, are one and all illustrations of that form of symbolism defined as representation of typical acts, objects, characters, relations, and processes. As has been said, this form of symbolism differs from spontaneous play only in the ties selected to bind together the represented and representing act, object, or person. The insight which creates this whole series of symbolic activities is that through play the child determines in large measure the direction of his attention and the trend of his character.[1]

---

[1] For a more complete discussion of this form of symbolism see *Educational Issues in the Kindergarten*, pp. 37-75.

While the concrete presentation of types is the predominant form of kindergarten symbolism, it is not the exclusive form. It has already been suggested that the symbolic activity of free play is a potent factor in the building of individuality. All kindergartens offer opportunity for such free play. They also encourage a minor form of free play in connection with the typical game. For example, after mother and father have been pictured by all the children under their typical aspects, each child is encouraged to show something mother or father does; or, again, while all the children play in the same way their visit to a toy-shop, each child selects for himself the toy he prefers and invents his own way of representing it. Finally, through the constant free selection by the children of preferred typical games, native tendencies are both revealed and developed.

In addition to free play and typical representation the Froebelian kindergartner frankly accepts that form of symbolism described as correspondence. Reverting to the definition of a symbol, we read in the Standard Dictionary that it is "something (not a portrait) that stands for something else and serves either to represent it or to bring to mind one or more of its qualities; *especially* something so used to represent or suggest that which is not capable of portraiture, as an idea, a quality, state, or action. Thus the oak is a symbol of strength, the sword of slaughter, the trident of Neptune, white of purity."

It is only necessary to reflect for a single moment upon these several illustrations of a symbol to become aware of differences in the ties by which they are related to the objects, persons, or qualities which they are said to symbolize. The oak symbolizes strength and the sword slaughter because the former is very strong and the latter was for many ages the matchless death-dealing weapon; the trident symbolizes Neptune because it was the instrument conferred upon him by mythology as an expression of his dominion over the sea; white symbolizes purity because both imply the idea of stainlessness. Two of these symbols — the oak and the sword — are what we have called typical objects;[1] one — the trident — is connected with its object by the tie of an exclusive association; one — whiteness — is a physical quality connected with a spiritual quality through the analogical tie of stainlessness.

With the single exception of the flag, which is rather a sign than a symbol, the kindergarten avoids the tie of conventional association between representing and represented objects. Its types are concrete illustrations of human values, and its activities, therefore, contribute to the development of those valid objective concepts in which all individuals may participate. To these typical activities it adds representations wherein the tie between the representing and represented objects is like that between whiteness and purity, and which fall under the more restricted definition of a symbol as a natural object, action, or event which is analogically related to some spiritual fact or process.

The significance of that form of symbolism which

---

[1] In such expressions as "heart of oak" the symbolism is of the type to be defined as correspondence.

deals with concrete types is that through it mind makes
the transition from the mental image to the concept.
The significance of that form of symbolism defined as
correspondence is that through it mind makes the
transition from concepts of material objects, actions,
and processes to their spiritual counterparts.

The researches of comparative philologists prove
that all words expressive of immaterial conceptions
were originally derived by metaphor from words
expressive of sensuous ideas and it is recognized by
all students of language that without the analogizing
activity of mind speech could never have progressed
beyond the merest rudiments. To the same analogizing activity written language owes the hieroglyph.
Metaphor and hieroglyph which interpret spirit in
terms of nature have their counterpart in animism
which interprets nature in terms of spirit. Out of the
union of metaphor and animism arose the great myths
which embody man's first discovery of his own essential nature. Intuition of the correspondences between
nature and the soul still creates the poet and enables
him to "call the particular fact to its universal consecration."

Since analogizing activity has played such a prominent part in the mental development of the race, it
would be passing strange if it played no part in the
mental evolution of the individual. If, perchance, it
be an important ally in the process of mental development, it would seem that its influence should not be
ignored in education. Recent studies of dreams go far
to show that the tie of analogy between mental and
physical facts has a preponderating effect in determin-

ing the character of men's nightly visions.[1] They also suggest that in this as in all forms of symbolism the particular ties selected throw light on individual character and history, and they would seem to indicate that a favorable bias might be given to character by an early direction of attention to those simple and noble analogies between nature and the mind which most powerfully affected imagination during the long childhood of the human race.

Let us approach this most difficult phase of kindergarten symbolism by considering some of its wider implications. Few persons will deny that children respond by alterations of mood to alterations of weather and season. Thunder, lightning, and the darkness so strange to day, call forth a mood very different from that which springs responsive to sunshine and blue sky. The emotional undertone of the springtime is different from that of winter. Something buds in the hearts of children in response to the budding life around them, and nature calls them to the park and field as she calls young lambs to the meadow. To take a narrower but scarcely less important illustration, we all know that children react to order with serenity and are ruffled by disorder, and perhaps most of us know both from happy and humiliating experience how immediately children are affected by the spiritual atmosphere created by our own mental states. Complementary to these responses of childhood to environmental influence is the tendency com-

[1] Prof. Dr. Sigm. Freud, *Die Traumdeutung;* Dr. Karl Abraham, *Traum und Mythe;* Otto Rank, *Die Mythen von der Geburt des Helden.*

mon to all children to impute to objects around them
a life akin to their own. It is only drawing from these
familiar facts their further conclusions when Froebel
urges that, through light, shadow, star, moon, and
wind plays, we may deepen the influence of these great
phenomena, and by directing sympathetic attention
to their significant aspects revive in the children of
each new generation the great mythic experience of
the race. It is only trusting analogizing activity a
little further when he claims that the apparently free
flight of the bird may stir obscurely the feeling of freedom. It is only believing a little more consistently in
the influence of an orderly environment when he insists that by the use of an organically related material
children develop in their own minds a sense of essential
relations. It is only an attempt to meet that craving of the spirit for self-revelation and self-discovery
which created the animistic interpretation of nature
when he offers a series of playthings which are an objective counterpart to the process of mental development.

Several reasons have conspired to prevent the general acceptance of this particular form of kindergarten
symbolism. Perhaps the reason which has consciously
exercised the widest deterrent influence is that the suggestion of analogies has been construed to mean the
interpretation of analogies. The truth is that the
analogy itself is an initial phase in the process of
definition. When one savage says of another that he is
foxy, he has connected the animal and the man by the
characteristic which is later defined as cunning. When
primitive man calls his own breath, wind, he has caught
his first far-off glimpse of spirit.

The kindergartner who believes in the use of natural analogies as helps in the evolution of spiritual ideas simply recapitulates this historic process. Her method is, first, to seek a point of contact with experience, then to play a game which throws into relief the salient feature of such experience, and finally to suggest its implicit analogy. For example, on some auspicious morning the children come to the kindergarten tingling with excitement over their battle with the wind, and eager to tell how it blew off their hats, made their hair fly, and almost threw them to the ground. This experience gives the wise kindergartner her point of departure for games like the Weather-Vane, the wind-blown trees, and the flying of kites. Following the representation of wind-blown objects a picture is shown which suggests many more things the wind does. A story is told of an invisible giant and his mighty deeds. The minds of the children are stirred to wonder and they question what the wind is and whence it comes. Their question is answered by the suggestion of an analogy whose aim is simply to quicken the feeling of faith in invisible power. "*You cannot understand* now what the wind is nor where it comes from, but you see what it does. Look — your own little hands move, but you cannot see what moves them."

As an actual encounter with the wind gives the point of departure for the Weather-Vane and its allied games, so a day of brilliant winter sunlight after days of depressing cloud gives the point of departure for the play of the Light-Bird. No kindergartner who has watched little children play this game can doubt the eagerness with which they try to catch the flickering reflection or question their faith that it may be caught. When after vain experiment they give up the impossible attempt, they are gladdened by the suggestion that though they cannot catch it with their hands they may catch it with their eyes, and so, too, they may catch the rainbow, the sunset, the beautiful colors of flowers, the blue sky, the dear faces and smiles of father and mother.

One more illustration must suffice to suggest the way in which the Froebelian kindergartner uses analogies. In the early fall the children learn the games of the baker, miller, and farmer, in each one of which is represented a series of activities. During this same period they learn to make different kinds of chains. On some morning when they are patiently adding link to link comes the suggestion, Let us make another kind of chain, and the effort to stimulate relating activity by leading to a more conscious representation of the links in that chain of service at one end of which is the breakfast roll and at the other the farmer sowing grain. To dramatic representation follows the drawing of chain pictures. The unmistakable result is the direction of selective interest to relations and processes.

The signers of this report are convinced by long experience that acts of analogizing like those described are among the most important of all forms of kindergarten symbolism.

A second reason which has deterred some kindergartners from the use of analogies is that recognition of the value of correspondences has been erroneously

supposed to carry with it acceptance of the Sweden-
borgian doctrine of correspondence, according to
which each particular object of nature is exclusively
related to a particular phenomenon of mind. It seems,
therefore, well to state that the Froebelian use of
correspondences implies no such exclusive tie, but
holds, on the contrary, that the same mental phenomenon may be adumbrated by different natural images,
and that the same physical image seized under different aspects corresponds to different phenomena of
mind. The Froebelian procedure implies nothing
beyond what is implied in metaphor, trope, simile,
personification, myth, fable, allegory, and all poetry.

The final source of prejudice against that form of
symbolism defined as correspondence is undoubtedly
antagonism to the particular correspondences suggested by Froebel in the kindergarten gifts. The attitude of any kindergartner towards these disputed
counterparts will be largely determined by her acceptance or rejection of the insight to which Froebel gave
the name Mediation of Opposites and which has been
explained in this report as identical with the insight
defined in Hegelian terminology as the self-relation
of the negative. Since we are anxious to evade no
question whose divergent solutions tend to produce
contrasting types of kindergartens, our next task shall
be to explain the relation of this insight to the organization of the Froebelian gifts. Before attempting this
explanation, however, we desire to avow our conviction that insight into the form of mind is of far more
urgent necessity than acceptance of any specific application of this insight, and to confess our belief that

among the applications made by Froebel the most
notable are the mediation of the individual and the
social whole in the embryonic community of the kindergarten; the mediation of substantial and formal
freedom achieved by freighting play with the great
human values; the mediation of image and idea
through typical facts; and the mediation of material
and spiritual concepts through carefully selected
analogies.

THE KINDERGARTEN GIFTS

It is difficult to describe in detail one value of the
kindergarten gifts without seeming to imply an emphasis which we should deplore. We therefore preface our
discussion of the organizing principle of the gifts by a
statement of the several values which we accept in
common with other kindergartners.

The kindergarten gifts are first of all playthings.
They offer material for building, for plane, linear, and
point representation; for various forms of constructive
activity and for plastic production of different kinds.
Among their values, that which is both primary and
greatest is that they incite and develop creative activity.

The kindergarten gifts are playthings through which
approaches are made towards the several industries
and fine arts. Of especial value are the approaches
towards sewing, embroidery, weaving, basket-making,
and pottery among the industries, and towards architecture, sculpture, drawing, and painting among the
arts.

The several values above mentioned are accepted

by all kindergartners who do not discard the Froebelian instrumentalities either in whole or in part. The signers of this report hold further that these instrumentalities open the best path of approach thus far broken towards the great value of mathematics. It will be necessary to consider this approach in and for itself before we can describe intelligibly the symbolism of the kindergarten gifts.

The creative idea of the kindergarten is that what the child does will determine both what he observes and what he becomes. If, therefore, in his play he recurrently produces geometric forms and recurrently changes one form into another, he will become interested in these forms and their relations and will be quick to recognize similar forms and relations in his environment.

As planned by Froebel the kindergarten gifts offered a fairly complete introduction to geometric forms and their interrelations. Through playing with these forms, furthermore, children were constantly incited to notice their plane and linear boundaries, the intersection of lines, and the several kinds of angles. Attention was also necessarily directed to numerical facts and relations, and finally the very important concept of ratio was illustrated through perceptions of proportionate sizes.

The mathematical basis of the Froebelian gifts needs no justification or defense, for all productive activity demands this basis and so does every effort to increase the power of rapid and exact sense-perception. The world presents itself to sense as a complex of diverse forms. Differences in these forms can be grasped sharply and spontaneously only by a mind furnished with discriminating concepts. "All that the greatest minds of all the ages have done toward the apperception of form through concepts we find gathered into a single great science — mathematics." [1]

The kindergarten gifts suggest an idea which they do not completely exemplify. The history of the kindergarten movement in the United States has been characterized by two streams of tendency; one towards the entire elimination of this informing idea and the other towards its more adequate embodiment. Kindergartners who have been swept into the former stream prove the trend of their thought, first, by eliminating forms of knowledge and, second, by eliminating a number of the Froebelian gifts. Kindergartners who represent the second tendency make recurrent efforts to develop further implications of the one informing idea by additions to the Froebelian instrumentalities and by a systematic evolution of peas-work, clay and cardboard modeling. [2]

In 1906, Miss M. M. Glidden published a monograph which has greatly helped to clarify the idea embodied in the kindergarten gifts. The author had found in Froebel's personal diary a note dated July, 1836, describing a series of cuts by means of which the cube was divided into six tetrahedra. The cuts

---

[1] Herbart's *A B C of Sense-Perception* (William J. Eckoff), p. 143.

[2] It is impossible to accomplish in the kindergarten all that Froebel desired to accomplish through the use of his gifts and occupations. The signers of this report believe that there should be an extension of Froebelian ideals and instrumentalities into the elementary school.

are described by Miss Glidden as follows: "Placing the knife upon the diagonal of the square surface of the cube and cutting part way down, so that a line is made connecting diagonally opposite corners of the cube, and treating each surface of the cube in the same way, the cube will be divided into three equal irregular square pyramids. The base of each of these is the square face of the cube. Two faces are right isosceles triangles, two others are obtuse scalene triangles. If each of these parts be split down the center, the cube will be divided into sixths" (tetrahedra).[1]

Convinced by her studies of Froebel that this note suggests the division of the cube which he intended to carry out in his Seventh Gift, Miss Glidden makes the following comment upon her discovery: "At first glance, the Seventh Gift appears uninteresting and of little value. The odd, wedge-shaped pieces suggest little, but when one sees that the solid angles shown in the interior of the Seventh Gift are the same as the exterior angles of such a form as the pentagonal dodecahedron, one begins to think possibly there is more in it. When one finds that whatever the exterior angles of a mathematical form may be, it may always be found in the interior of a rectilinear form by applying the Seventh Gift cut, one feels that he has discovered a principle. And again, when one finds that the ultimate unit of the Seventh Gift, an irregular tetrahedron, is the form into a certain number of which all mathematical solids can be resolved, one could shout with Froebel, 'Eureka! I have it!' It is a universal mathe-

[1] M. M. Glidden, *A Mathematical Study, Froebel's Building Gifts, Seventh and Eighth*, pp. 14, 15.

matical element; this is the key which unlocks all mathematical form." [1]

The value of the Seventh Gift lies in the method of cutting which it suggests. It is by applying this cut to other rectilinear solids that the variously proportioned tetrahedra are found, into certain numbers of which all mathematical solids may be analyzed. These tetrahedra are, therefore, a medium of exchange and comparison between different solids. To quote Miss Glidden once more: —

"The inner diagonal lines shown by the cut of the Seventh Gift become the outer angles of any regular mathematical solid which has axes of approximately equal length. The slant of the outer angle depends upon the proportions of the rectilinear solid to which the Seventh Gift cut is applied. This makes it possible to easily build up complex mathematical forms or with equal ease to analyze them, and secures to the one who makes this study an unusual knowledge of mathematical form, size, relative proportion, and the mental development that goes with it."

"If a complex solid like a pentagonal dodecahedron can be made easily to take the form of a rectilinear plinth, its cubic contents can be ascertained at a glance; and if this rectilinear prism (analyzed in a similar but not identical manner) can be rebuilt in other forms, — for example, an octahedron or isosahedron, — then a bridge between these forms has been found and their relation to each other may easily be seen."

"Every mathematical solid can be resolved into

[1] M. M. Glidden, *A Mathematical Study, Seventh and Eighth Gifts*, pp. 6–7.

tetrahedra, similar to those of the Seventh Gift, when it is divided into sixths. The proportions of the sides of the tetrahedra may vary in different forms, but the fundamental shape is the same. These tetrahedra may, therefore, be considered as universal units, elements, the simplest units into which mathematical forms can be analyzed." [1]

The Seventh Gift cut does not explain the organization of the kindergarten gifts, but it tells us that Froebel is trying to find some clew to the genesis and evolution of form and to the relations between different forms. When we have analyzed a number of solids into these little tetrahedra, built up a number of solids from them and used them as a medium of exchange and comparison between different solids, we can never again see these solids either as fixed or as isolated. Each one of them has revealed itself as one phase of a formative process and as an integral member of a related series of forms.

The series of forms whose genesis, evolution, and interrelation are suggested by the application of the Seventh Gift cut are all bounded by planes. There are, however, a number of geometric solids bounded by curves, and there are others bounded partly by curved and partly by plane faces. Are these solids, therefore, to be considered as belonging to three distinct series or is it possible that all geometric forms are members of a single system? We notice that as we increase the number of sides on a plane figure it approximates in shape to a circle, and that as we increase the number of

[1] M. M. Glidden, *A Mathematical Study, Seventh and Eighth Gifts*, p. 26.

faces on a polyhedron it approximates in shape to a
sphere. Defining a circle as a polygon having an infinite number of sides, and a sphere as a polyhedron
having an infinite number of faces, we get our first clew
to the organization of the kindergarten gifts, which
is that they illustrate, in the evolution of geometric
forms, the general law of advance from an undifferentiated unit to those highly complex wholes wherein
the most perfect unity is achieved through infinite differentiation and integration. For this reason the kindergarten gifts move from the sphere conceived as
excluding to the sphere conceived as including all possible faces, corners, and edges, and to this movement
of solid from sphere to sphere corresponds the evolution of geometric planes wherein the circle is both the
terminus *ab quo* and the terminus *ad quem* of a generative process, and the movement of lines from the curve
with return thereto through the intersection of straight
lines of different inclinations. Each solid, plane, and
line is, therefore, apprehended not in detached and
solitary independence, but as an integral member of
a related series. The exact place of each solid in the
series is determined by its greater or lesser approximation to the sphere, the exact place of each plane by
its greater or lesser approximation to the circle.

The second clue to the organization of the kindergarten gifts is suggested by the order of their presentation. For while, as has been explained, the organization of geometric forms into a system is made possible
by the conception of the sphere as both their procreant
ideal and their final goal, the order in which the different forms are made known is determined by the insight

to which Froebel gave the name Mediation of Opposites, and which, as applied in the kindergarten, demands the presentation of contrasting extremes of form and the gradual elimination of the antitheses through an intermediate series. Thus the solid gifts posit and annul the antitheses of sphere and cube; the planes posit and annul the antitheses of circle and square; and the linear gifts first accentuate and then cancel the seemingly excluding extremes of curved and straight lines.

In Froebel's conception all forms are products of indwelling force. If unimpeded in its activity, this force would diffuse itself equally in all directions, and its most perfect material expression, therefore, is the sphere. In nature's geometry, as written in crystal forms, we behold the progressive attempt of indwelling force to realize its spherical ideal. Since, however, this indwelling force is correlated with other forces which hold it in tensions of varying degree, it must manifest its spherical tendency by giving rise to a series of forms which exhibit an advance from particular-sidedness toward all-sidedness, and hence, departing from rectilinear, strive incessantly to approach curved outlines. The significant feature of this process is that in its effort to make a sphere, force begins by making its opposite, and only by a progressive annulment of rectilinear limitation does it finally achieve its ideal incarnation. This natural evolution of sphericity through the positing and annulment of limitation ·is precisely repeated in the kindergarten, and since each illustration of a truth is one step toward its adequate apprehension and definition, the gifts undoubtedly build a bridge over which, within the limits of their own petty experience, children may pass from the conception of mutually excluding extremes to the conception of a single ascending order.

Acceptance of the organizing idea of the kindergarten gifts does not necessarily carry with it acceptance of Froebel's guess with regard to the genesis of crystal forms. That guess was not a scientific hypothesis, but an act of poetic analogizing. It is interesting, however, to remind ourselves that from contemporary crystallography we hear of "sterile liquids containing substances in solution that require the presence of a crystalline 'germ' to bring about the birth of crystals." It is also worthy of mention that the new science of plasmology would seem to be rapidly establishing the fact that form and structure are due to the interplay of different forces.

The mathematical values of the Froebelian gifts are that they throw into relief the self-relations of detached forms and the interrelations between different forms; that they express all these relations in terms of number; and that they direct attention to formative and transforming activities. If science means seeking essential relations and discovering totalities, then Froebel's procedure is truly scientific and the wise use of his instrumentalities will tend to develop the scientific habit of mind. In connection with the use of the gifts changes of form in natural objects should be noticed, for example, the rounding of pebbles by the action of water, the manifold alterations of form in bubbles caused by reciprocal pressure, the "flattening of chestnuts in their cases, of peas in their pods, and of sheaves of

straw in piles; the difference between the round cell of
the solitary bee and the cells in a hive where pressure
on space has straightened out the sides of the cells
until the limiting form — the hexagon — is reached."[1]
Finally, mathematical imagination should be stimulated by directing attention to "the fluidity and inter-
changeableness of natural curves," such as the reflection curves "made by the sunlight falling on moving
liquids or the light-curves at the bottom of a clear
stream caused by the ripples on the top." [2]

When we understand the organizing idea of the
kindergarten gifts, it is very easy to interpret their
symbolism. Since they furnish a concrete example
of that evolutionary process which exhibits a change
from an "indefinite, incoherent homogeneity to a
definite, coherent heterogeneity," they belong among
the symbols defined in kindergarten terminology as
typical acts, facts, characters, relations, and processes.
Since the process exemplified recapitulates that mode
of behavior which is the form of mind, and since the
child participates in this form, the organized totality
of the gifts is also symbolic in the sense that it offers
a series of correspondences to his own self-developing
activity. It is not asserted that the child is aware of
these correspondences. The claim is simply that he
enjoys and readily apprehends what agrees with his
own inherent form. In the kindergarten gifts as in a
mirror he beholds himself, and like the primal self-
activity rejoices in his own image.

It has been claimed as one of the great discoveries

[1] M. S. Boole, *Preparation of the Child for Science*, p. 126.
[2] *Ibid.*, p. 113.

of our age that "Mathematics is Symbolic Logic and Symbolic Logic is Mathematics."[1] If this twain be, indeed, one, and if recognition of their identity be among the most remarkable of contemporary mental feats, then why did not Froebel make a valuable contribution to education when he made it possible for little children to illustrate, in the evolution of archetypal forms, the relations, processes, and structure of thought?

The structure of mind is the most potent of all agencies in determining creative activity. It is also the most potent of all apperceiving agencies. Until these insights have become wide awake in our own minds, we do not know how to abet the self-developing activity of childhood. We thwart the strongest of all native tendencies, and by forcing self-expression into artificial paths arrest development.

The contentions of the Froebelian kindergartner are that play with organized material organizes the mind and that the most efficient principle of organization is the form or law of mind itself.

Several reasons have conspired to bring the kindergarten gifts into disrepute and to create antagonism to their mathematical basis, their organizing principle, and their traditional method of use. The first of these reasons is that, while the mathematical basis of the gifts is recognized, it is not clearly conceived; the second, that, while the plan of Froebel for the true use of his gifts demands at least four years for its realization, the kindergarten rarely holds its children for more than a year; the third, that the organizing principle of the gifts has been so narrowly conceived as to lose

[1] Cassius Jackson Keyser, *Mathematics.*

all its significance; and the fourth and final reason, confusion between the idea of projecting in images the natural logic of mind and the very different idea of making children logical by a forced and unnatural method.

With this discussion of the Mediation of Opposites, as illustrated in the organization of the kindergarten gifts, we complete our survey of the genetic-developing method. It has been shown that the presupposition of the method is life, conceived as immediate presentation and immediate response to this presentation, and that its goal is life renewed, transfigured, and unified. It has been stated that its point of departure is the deed and that it demands those introspective and retrospective activities through which the deed learns to see into and through itself. It has been claimed that during the period of early childhood the highest form of the deed is play and the kindergarten has been defined as that mode of education which freights the form of play with the values of human life. It has been further shown that the native make-believe play of childhood is symbolic in its form, and therefore that in the use of symbolism the kindergarten does not impose upon play something foreign to its spirit, but borrows its own characteristic mode of expression. Finally, the attempt has been made to suggest that the genetic-developing method is simply a conscious effort to abet the native movement of self-activity, which, proceeding from the deed, advances to awareness of its results and its process.

If the kindergarten is ever to realize its own ideal,

its representatives must have a clear conception of the Gliedganzes; must appraise educational values by this criterion; and must comprehend that genetic-developing method whose aim is to evolve values instead of imposing them. Practice must shape itself differently as values, their criterion, and their method of development are differently conceived. The need of the present, therefore, is the discussion of these several questions. Any external uniformity of practice not based upon a common vision would only impede the historic development of the kindergarten.

It is because we crave to share a vision which has brought inspiration and joy to us that we have given so much space to discussion of the several forms of symbolism in their relation to the genetic-developing method. It is for the same reason that we refrain from any attempt to justify the particular symbols preferred by Froebel. Our present effort is to win so far as may be recognition of principles which seem to us fundamental. When these principles are recognized, we shall heartily coöperate with all persons who may be striving to create conforming practice.

The aim of the first section of this report was to describe the ideal of the Gliedganzes and to present it as the realized form of self-activity. The aim of the second section was to suggest that each great human value is an approximate definition of this universal form. The aim of the present section has been to call attention to the fact that self-activity is not only its own goal and its own standard, but also its own method. The aim of the final section will be to describe the kindergarten practice which seems to us most nearly in conformity with its one great principle. While, however, we are sure of our principle, we are equally sure that in reducing it to practice we must have done many things we should not do and left undone many things we should do. We are ourselves in process of development, and the blindness which darkens our minds and the obduracy which clings to our wills must react upon our practical achievement. Truth is final and we can abate no jot or tittle of the claim we make for the principle of self-activity. Life, on the contrary, is a dialectic process wherein the one thing permanent should be self-outgrowing. Not in the program we shall present, nor in the program towards which we struggle from afar, will our ideal be realized. Yet that ideal will forever inspire fresh effort, and each more approximate realization will bring clearer vision to the kindergartner and purer and more joyous life to the little child.

PART IV

THE KINDERGARTEN PROGRAM

THE larger sanction of the kindergarten is to be sought in its contribution to the building of character. During the period of early childhood mental and moral habits are being formed and emotional attitudes are establishing themselves. If, in these early years, children are not trained to be careful, they will be forming habits of carelessness; if they are not learning to govern temper, they are forming a habit of being governed by temper. If they are not learning to be industrious, punctual, orderly, clean, kind, and courteous, then they are confirming disastrous tendencies towards idleness, procrastination, disorder, uncleanliness, selfishness, and rudeness. In these early years, moreover, they are forming intellectual as well as moral habits. If they are not being taught to "stop and think," they will be arrested in the habit of heedlessness. If they are not cultivating a healthy selective interest, they are becoming victims of whim and random suggestion. If they are not filling imagination with concrete pictures of purity, beauty, and nobility, then they are sullying it with base or belittling it with petty images. If they are not learning to see essential relations, they are forming the habit of arbitrary classification. If they are not learning to think consecutively, to test inferences, and to suspend judgment, then they are drifting into mental habits of superficiality, precipitancy, and reckless analogizing, and preparing themselves for all the misery attendant upon vibration between the extremes of intellectual slavishness and intellectual anarchy. Last but not least, all little children are either developing an emotional undertone correspondent to ethical ideals or sinking into slavery to the unregenerate impulses which antagonize those ideals.

The aim of the kindergarten program is development of the mental and moral habits, the emotional undertone, and the imaginative vision which are implied in the conception of man as Gliedganzes. The object of all education is to help the pupil to find himself as a whole and also as a single member of the great living whole — God, nature, and humanity. As an integral phase of the general educational process the kindergarten accepts this common aim and moves towards its realization in ways determined by the psychologic order of development.

The ideal of the Gliedganzes must be clearly distinguished from the ideal of social efficiency. The words social efficiency imply a giver but not a receiver — a man equipped for leadership but not himself in need of help. The kindergarten ideal may be more nearly stated as social reciprocity. But all statements which fail to throw into clear relief relationship to God and to nature, as well as relationship to man, fall short of the ideal of education as determined by the conception of the Gliedganzes.

In the first section of this report an effort was made to show that all great educational values are approximate revelations of the Gliedganzes. Three attitudes may be taken towards these values. They may be denied or ignored; they may be imposed; or, finally, their native process of self-unfolding may be abetted. The kindergarten chooses the third attitude. It helps children to do better what they themselves are blindly trying to do. Therefore, it quickens within them both a faint awareness of their own inner life and trust in those who are responding to this craving.[1]

As the aim of the kindergarten is determined by the conception of the Gliedganzes, so its practical attempts to carry out this aim are determined by the genetic-developing method. The first emphasis of this method

[1] "First of all," writes Froebel, "and before any other reflection from without comes to the child, the following observation as the sun of his whole future life must shine upon him and warm him — the reflection that the fostering care, the development and formation, the realization of my inmost *life as a whole in itself, and as a member of a great living whole*, is the object of all which is done for me from without; of all which is done for me by older people, and especially of all which is done for me by my parents. If now the lively appreciation of what has been done to cultivate his inner world by parents and other people fill the soul of the child *so that he may feel and find himself at the same time as a whole and also a single* member of a higher life unity, then will true love and gratitude toward his parents, respect and veneration for age, germinate in the mind of the child. Then will the vivifying anticipation of the lovingly pervading unity and fount of all life blossom in his soul, and bear imperishable fruits in his character, and be an abiding quality of his action.

"To assist parents and children to obtain these highest gifts and blessings of life is the single and innermost aim of these plays and means of employment." (*Pedagogics of the Kindergarten*, pp. 114, 115.)

The most important statement in this passage is that the child is to be so treated that he will feel that what is being done for him corresponds with his own inmost nature and needs. This demand and the effort to meet it constitutes one of the most distinctive peculiarities of the Froebelian method.

is upon self-expression in the form of typical deeds. Its second emphasis is upon those introspective and retrospective activities through which children gain their first awareness of the results and process of self-expression. It cannot be too often repeated that, conceived in its entirety as "the deed which sees into and through itself," the Froebelian method is the most effective yet discovered for preventing that accumulation of blind, tempestuous, and colliding impulses which so constantly wrecks life and disintegrates personality.

Defining the aim of the kindergarten as the germinal development of those mental and moral habits and that emotional undertone which are implied in the conception of man as Gliedganzes, and defining its method as the incitement of typical deeds through which children shall be helped to see into and through themselves, let us next remind ourselves that the presupposition of our method is life conceived, on the one hand, as immediate presentation, and on the other, as immediate response to this presentation. In other words, the actual experience of children is to supply our point of departure for the development of the Gliedganzes by the incitement of typical deeds and the stimulation of that gentle and indirect introspection and retrospection through which the deed gets eyes to see into and through itself.

For many years there was divergence of opinion among the representatives of the kindergarten as to whether it were either possible or desirable to find a basis of common experience and whether it were either possible or desirable to incite typical deeds. Happily this divergence of opinion is now so far overcome as to be practically negligible and this report assumes that the common experience and the typieal deed need no further defense.

Accepting the idea that the program shall find its point of departure in the common experiences of children, we next set ourselves the task of inventorying the elements of this experience. So soon as we consciously begin this task we become aware that the first great common experience of the children is life in the kindergarten itself. Let us try to realize what this experience means by entering into the mind of a new pupil admitted to an already organized kindergarten. Up to this time the little boy, now four years old, has spent his life with the members of his own family. Most of them are his elders and make allowances for him. In the kindergarten the very first things he learns are what he must do and what he must not do in order to become an acceptable member of the little community to which he now belongs. He must not knock over his neighbor's blocks or scatter his sticks or snatch the mat he is weaving. He must open his box at the right moment in order not to keep the children who are prompt from beginning their building. He must have his weaving or folding in his portfolio at the end of an exercise in order not to detain his comrades who are eager to march to the circle. He must not jerk, push, slap, or pinch his companions. Again, these little companions are clean and will not like him unless he is clean. He notices that they listen to what the kindergartner says and obey her words. They water the plants, put away the gifts, set the chairs in order.

Insensibly he conforms to the general spirit, and through the contagion of a prompt, industrious, orderly, cheerful, obedient, and kindly community he begins to form the habits necessary to all corporate life. After a while the kindergartner begins indirectly to present these habits as ideals. There are stories of children who were active, useful, polite, and kind. There are fairy stories whose heroes won fair princesses and became great kings through the exercise of these elementary virtues. There are games wherein the children represent typical forms of the service of men and animals, of plants, and even of the elements. The picture of a life in which each serves all and is served by all begins to hover in dimmest outline before his imagination and reacts to make the little boy more ready to do his own small part. In short, fundamental habits are being formed, fundamental sympathies cherished, and fundamental ideals defined, first, through actual life in an embryonic community, and second, by a representation in play and story of the services of the larger community and the natural world.

We have tried to suggest briefly the reaction of an organized kindergarten upon an individual child. Let us now attempt to follow the self-organizing and self-defining activity of the kindergarten itself. We will assume that it is the first week of the school year and that a new kindergarten is being opened. The kindergartner who understands and appreciates the influence of environment will have spared no pains to make the first impression of the kindergarten room both pleasant and suggestive. It is, therefore, bright with sunshine and flowers. A single picture — the Madonna and

Child — hangs on the wall. Suspended from the ceiling are several groups of balls of different colors, and boxes containing similar balls stand on an accessible shelf. A sand table invites to immediate delights, and perhaps upon the tables at which the children are to sit are temptingly displayed boxes of bright-colored beads, and large needles conveniently threaded.

To this new environment in early September come forty or fifty little children four and five years old, no one of whom has ever attended a kindergarten. For the nonce let us eliminate the kindergartner; suppose the children alone and ask ourselves what they will do. We may be sure that they will make more or less shy advances towards acquaintanceship, will soon learn each others' names, will measure themselves against each other in running games, and after a while will unite in playing some simple traditional ring game. They will spy the sand table and will soon be sifting sand through their open fingers, burying their hands in the sand, poking holes, hollowing wells, and piling hills. The bright-colored beads and threaded needles will tempt them to string necklaces. The balls will suggest rolling, tossing, whirling, and hiding games. The hiding of balls will be followed by the hiding of children. Finally, the flowers will assuredly be noticed, and the picture of Mother and Child will attract sympathetic attention.

Let us now restore the eliminated kindergartner and ask ourselves what she should do. The answer is a very simple one. She should watch the children and from their spontaneous deeds open paths of approach towards the several great human values. She may lead from the mere covering of hands in the sand to the making of huts. She may bring twigs which the children will be delighted to plant around these huts in holes of their own poking. She may suggest that each child draw a boundary line around his own cave. She may lead the children to make paths from cave to cave and thus create a rude village. She may turn away from constructive activity to rhythmic arrangement, and suggest that the holes poked in the sand be poked at equal distances. After a while she may substitute shells for holes and incite the children to original creation of rhythmic and symmetric designs.

Like the sand table the bead-stringing offers a point of departure for the development of creative activity and for approach to constructive values, art values, and mathematical values. The children may string necklaces, bracelets, wreaths, and decorations for the kindergarten room. It is fair to assume that left to themselves they will string in somewhat disorderly fashion. The kindergartner intervenes with the suggestion that they alternate one white and one red bead, thereby introducing a practical exercise in number and color. Later the most varied and beautiful arrangements of beads may be made by more complicated alternations of number and color and by the addition of alternative forms and sizes.[1]

Turning our attention from sand and beads to balls, we are almost bewildered by the number and variety of educational exercises for which they supply the point of departure. Rolling balls is a fine arm exercise.

[1] It is to be understood that these arrangements are to be discovered by the children.

Rolling first to some particular child and later to hit a box or cube is an excellent eye exercise. Attention to the path taken by a ball impelled with force begins the acquaintanceship with the straight line. Attention to the several movements described by whirling balls begins the acquaintanceship with circular, spiral, and vortical lines. The sinking and rising balls introduce the children to the vertical line. The fruit and bird games call attention to color and number. The spinning games (especially when the spinning sphere is contrasted with the spinning cube) suggest the unchangeableness of the sphere under all varieties of position and all accelerations of movement. The search for objects like the sphere begins the classification of objects under geometric archetypes. The method followed in developing all these exercises is to give the children opportunity for free experiment; to observe what they do and towards what human values this deed points; to suggest new exercises developing the implications of their free deed, and to incite the children not only to do something, but to notice what they have done.

We have dwelt at some length upon the first gift and occupation exercises because the application of the genetic method to gifts and occupations seems to be far less generally understood than its application to games. It has long been recognized that the first thing which must be done in a new kindergarten is to overcome the feelings of shyness and strangeness, and help the children to feel at home in their unaccustomed environment. These little strangers must get acquainted with the kindergartner, her assistants, and each other. They must also get acquainted with the kindergarten room. This primary demand of acquaintanceship determines the games played during the first few weeks, and all kindergartners know the goodly series of naming games, greeting games, wandering games, hiding games, recognition games, and visiting games which have been evolved to meet it. It is worthy of mention that these games call only for the simplest physical activities and that they involve none of the quick transitions of movement characteristic of games played towards the end of the year.[1]

It has been already said that the first great common experience of kindergarten children is life in the kindergarten itself. The program may perhaps be most briefly defined as an attempt to reinforce, influence, and interpret this self-evolving life. Let us, therefore, ask ourselves what lines of development have been started by the experiences already described.

The children are now acquainted with the kindergartner and with each other. They have enjoyed many things in common. They have dug wells, piled hills, and hollowed caves in the sand. Long chains of beads of their own stringing, and paper chains which they have interlinked hang in gay festoons before their eyes. The balls have rolled and wandered from child to child. Other rolling games have developed in which the ball has been aimed at some chosen object and the stead-

---

[1] The first demand of the genetic method in its application to games is emphasis in the early part of the year upon pure movement games, such as walking, running, skipping, hopping, swinging of arms and legs, sinking and rising. Its second demand is advance to simple imitative games involving these movements, for example, hopping birds, running horses, swinging pendulums.

fast cube has proved itself a satisfactory target. The
flowers have been given fresh water every day, and as
they faded, new and different flowers have taken their
places. The kindergartner has suggested how pleasant
it would be to go some day all together to a park or
field where many beautiful flowers might be seen and
gathered. The single wandering game has developed
into the flying bird; the collective wandering game into
the streamlet; and the words of both have rehearsed
the wonders of the great out-of-doors. A story has been
told of little Thumbelina who wandered far and wide
and the marvels of her experience. Finally, the game
of "Little Travelers" has been played and imagination
stimulated in each little child who tells of the land from
which he came. Are not the children ready for a new
experience, and shall not our next attempt to abet the
self-unfolding life of our little community be made by
taking them on an excursion?

Only those kindergartners who have for years made
excursions with their children can realize how greatly
they enrich the self-unfolding life of the little community and how many points of departure they yield for
approach towards the several great educational values.
Some slight sense of their importance will, however,
be suggested by considering even the four excursions
now often made during the weeks intervening between
the opening of the kindergarten in September and
the first climax of the program in the Thanksgiving
festival. The first excursion is made during the fourth
week after the opening of the kindergarten and is usually to some park or field. On this excursion the children see horses, dogs, squirrels, pigeons and pigeon

houses, different kinds of birds and butterflies. Often they find snails and cocoons. Generally they see ant-hills. Sometimes they come across different strange insects. They dig tiny pebbles out of the ground. They gather many kinds of wild flowers. They blow the feathery tufts of the dandelion and snap the capsules of the jewel weed. Burdocks cling to their clothes, and sometimes they are pricked by thorns and stung by nettles. In a second excursion several weeks later, they see birds flying southward, trees shaking their leaves, and squirrels gathering nuts; they find nests which have fallen to the ground, gather fall leaves of different colors, pick up nuts, and discover many kinds of seeds. Their third excursion is to a bakery, and the fourth, and last before Thanksgiving, is to a market where they see sheaves of wheat, stalks of corn, and a wonderful variety of fruits and vegetables.

We have been trying to analyze the common experience of children during the first few weeks of life in the kindergarten. Not yet, however, is our analysis complete. For every day all these children have been coming from and returning to homes. Their total experience is an alternation of life between two communities and a gradually self-establishing connection between them. Is it not inevitable that as the children domesticate themselves in their new environment and begin to feel in sympathy with the kindergartner and with each other that they should wish to tell about the homes in which hitherto their lives have been lived. There is a baby brother in one home, a baby sister in another, and in a third a grandmother who tells wonderful stories. Willy's mother took him on Saturday to a circus. Gretchen has had a birthday party and a cake with candles. Peter's father goes with the whole family to the park every Sunday. Connections with the home are establishing themselves in other ways. Dora's mother brings her to the kindergarten every day and often lingers through the opening exercises. Harry's sister comes with him, and tiny Margaret has as daily escort her proud young father. Joe's brother brings a message that he is ill and the kindergartner hastens to cheer him with a visit. It is needless to go into more detail. The chain which binds the kindergarten to the home is forging itself.

At the meeting of the International Kindergarten Union, in St. Louis, Mrs. Anna Garlin Spencer, so well known through her wise philanthropic work, said that of all the agencies now working towards the solution of that most imperative problem, — the assimilation of our immigrant population, — the one which in her judgment was working in the sanest way was the kindergarten. Other agencies, she explained, were dismissing the adult immigrant from consideration; solacing themselves with the assurance that these foreign-born men and women would soon be dead, and concentrating efforts upon the single task of making American citizens of their children. The result was a severance of the family tie, and development in children of a contemptuous attitude towards fathers and mothers.

The least reflection should assure any intelligent person that attack upon primal relationships is attack upon the roots of virtue. It is by filial faith, love, and

obedience; by fraternal kindness; by consideration and
tenderness for grandparents, and by the stimulation
of nurturing impulses through small services to helpless infancy that each new generation nourishes in its
heart those primal affections from which are precipi-
tated our moral ideals. Teaching a child to scorn his
parents and to despise his home is not educating him
for citizenship, but for contempt of law and order. We
must educate for a national, nay, rather for a cosmopolitan, manhood, but the child five years old cannot
be a citizen of the world.

> "Man is made of social earth,
> Child and brother from his birth.
> Near to his heart the household band,
> Father, mother, sister stand:
>
> . . . . . .
>
> Virtue to love, to hate them vice."

One incidental feature of the interaction between the
two communities — the occasional visit of a baby
brother or sister to the kindergarten — has proved itself
singularly prolific of educational results. Its influence
may, perhaps, be most briefly described as a point of
departure for the development of the nurturing spirit.
Nearly all children love babies and are pleased to hold
them, if only for a minute, to look at their tiny fists
and pink toes, to see them wave bye-bye, and to win
from them a coo or a smile. After such a visit they
are ready for doll plays, eager to wash, dress, and feed
baby, trundle it gently in its carriage, warm its cold
feet, put it to sleep, speak and move gently while it is
sleeping, play with it when it wakes. Having themselves played these acts of nurture, they look with
awakened interest at the pictures in the *Mother Play.*

On one page they see baby striking out vigorously with his little legs and mother playing some game like "Shoe the Horse." On another, they see mother giving baby his supper. In a third picture, she has taken him out of doors and is teaching him to beckon the pigeons. In a fourth, she is teaching him to play "Pat-a-cake"; in a fifth, to gather flowers; in a sixth, she is showing him the moon. Enough — the concrete picture of all mother does for the baby — all she once did for him begins to shape itself in the child's imagination, and interpreted by the doll plays stirs his heart with faith and love. He has begun to know himself as a nurtured being. He has begun to develop in himself nurturing impulse. "Answer me," says Froebel, addressing the mother, "answer me but one question. What is the supreme gift you would bestow on the children who are the life of your life, the soul of your soul? Would you not above all other things render them capable of giving nurture? Would you not endow them with the courage and constancy which the ability to give nurture implies? Mother, father, has not our common effort been directed towards just this end? Have we not been trying to break a path towards this blessed life?"

It will be remembered that the presupposition of the genetic method was life conceived as immediate presentation and reaction and its goal life transfigured and illuminated. We have been trying to show one small cycle of this process, the sweep from simple pleasure in seeing and holding baby to a dim awareness of self as a nurtured being and a faint stirring within the heart of nurturing impulse. The total sweep of the kindergarten program should be a vortical ascent towards clearer consciousness of the self as nurtured, more vigorous stirrings within the self of nurturing impulses, and higher attainment by the self of the courage, constancy, patience, watchfulness, and fidelity necessary to nurturing activity. Doll plays must therefore be followed by actual care for animals and plants, and the kindergarten cannot realize its own ideal until these phases of its life are more generally embodied. There are many indications which suggest that their importance is being increasingly recognized. In practically all kindergartens there are plants which the children care for, in a very large number there are gold fish, in a smaller number aquariums with several kinds of water animals, and in a few kindergartens the experiment has been made of providing a very large cage which is occupied successively by visiting animals — that is, pigeons, squirrels, guinea pigs, families of rabbits, mother hens with their broods of little chickens. No one who has attentively considered the reaction of this direct and sympathetic contact with animal life both upon intellect and character will be willing to lose its influence.

In what has thus far been written an effort has been made to describe the common experiences which give direction to the self-evolving life of a new kindergarten community during the first few weeks of its existence. Two features of that life remain to be considered; the daily luncheon of bread and milk and the little prayer and hymn with which each morning the kindergarten opens.[1]

[1] It is not claimed that these features are universal. It is believed they should be.

Considered as an educational influence the values
of the luncheon are that it affords occasion for developing cleanliness, neatness, and courtesy, that it supplies
a point of departure for representation and assimilation of the series of activities through which bread and
milk are provided, and that through the simple grace
by which it is preceded it reinforces the influence of the
opening prayer and hymn. The common purpose of
grace, hymn, and prayer is the cultivation of a devout
spirit. ·

One of the more valuable contributions of contemporary pyschology to education is its insistence upon
the reaction of motor-expression upon feeling and
thought. Froebel calls attention to this reaction in the
Mother Play and bases upon it his argument for the
development of the religious spirit through the cultivation of reverent attitudes and gestures. Faithful,
however, to his own genetic method, he likewise insists
that the devout attitude shall not be formally imposed, but evoked as the natural expression of a dawning feeling. The ways and means of meeting this
double requirement were considered in detail in the
third section of this report. It suffices, therefore, in the
present connection to repeat that only a devout kindergartner can really quicken the reverential spirit and
that nothing could be more antithetic to the Froebelian
ideal than a parrot-like repetition of devout words and
a monkey-like simulation of the prayerful attitude.

The connection between mental states and bodily
attitudes is not an arbitrary one. Between the Oriental who prostrates himself before a heavenly and earthly
potentate and the Puritan who, erect and open-eyed,

faces God and his fellow man, there is a contrast which
suggests the greatest line of scission in human history.
Between the Puritan himself and his descendant, who
with wandering mind sits in indolent relaxation in his
cushioned pew, there is another contrast it were well
to consider. It may, nay, rather, it must be granted
that reverent attitudes should be the outer and visible
sign of reverent minds, but it must also be insisted
that reverent minds are created by reverent deeds and
that unless in childhood the dawning feeling of reverence is strengthened and confirmed by habitual expression it cannot maintain itself against the besieging
temptations which tend to make life superficial, arro-
gant, and empty.

The primary purpose of the foregoing pages has
been to describe the self-evolving life of a new kindergarten community. During their first weeks in the
kindergarten the children have had the several great
experiences of estrangement from a familiar life; membership in a new community; and a series of self-establishing connections between the two. They have repeated the typical aspects of this threefold experience
in play and by this reproduction have begun its assimilation. The reader who has grasped this relation between life and play will already have divined the fact
that throughout the kindergarten year the children will
be expanding experience and projecting this expanded
experience in their games. Running like squirrels, galloping and trotting like horses, flying like birds, swimming like fishes, flowing like streams, tending babies
like mother, sowing and reaping like the farmer, ham-
mering like the blacksmith, marching like the soldier, in

short, becoming themselves different persons, animals, and objects, children create within themselves a microscopic copy of life, and therefore begin to know life. Do we ever know anything save as we make it a part of ourselves, and how shall the little child make external objects, persons, and events parts of himself unless, by doing as they do, he makes himself their copy. The essential thing is that his copy or portrait of life shall not caricature life, but shall sympathetically reproduce its defining features and its ideal expression. George Eliot has remarked that even Milton, looking for his portrait in a spoon, must submit to have the facial angle of a bumpkin. Like portraits of individuals, portraits of life may diminish and distort the original portrayed.

The play world which the child creates constitutes the spiritual environment, in which he lives and moves and has his being. Having created it, he comprehends it, and it becomes the key through which he interprets the larger world in which he finds himself. The world mind knows is always primarily a world it has made. The creator is not the mere predecessor of the knower. He is the knower's ancestor.

Hitherto, exercising his own unaided might, the child has created a play world which caricatures the greater world into which he is born. Hence his interpretation of the latter is a false and distorted one. The primary aim of the kindergarten is to help him create a miniature world which shall be a faithful portrait of the greater world in its ideal aspects.[1]

[1] For a definition of what is meant by the ideal, see *Educational Issues in the Kindergarten*, pp. 63, 64.

The question may arise, How can games having a fixed form be considered creations of children? The answer to this question is that the game assumes fixed form as the result of a process of social creation. In the *Pedagogics of the Kindergarten*, Froebel has illustrated in great detail the application of the genetic-developing method to the evolution of games, and one of the most cheering evidences of growth in the kindergarten is the increasing ability of kindergartners to follow his procedure. It should be added that excursions have proved themselves of great help in the original development of games. The children who have actually seen carpenters and blacksmiths at work, who have gone to a toy-shop, who have visited a barn-yard, who have seen men making, planting, hoeing, and raking gardens, are full of ideas with regard to the ways in which these activities may be represented in play.[1]

The reproduction of experience in the circle game is reinforced by its reproduction in and interpretation through the gifts and occupations. The increasing tendency in all good kindergartens is to make every gift and occupation exercise creative, and the spontaneous reproduction of common and typical experiences by the children is another witness to the fact that the kindergarten is really coming to understand itself.

In describing the plays of the kindergarten as reproductions of experience we have expressed one of those half-truths which become the worst kind of falsehoods when they are taken for the whole truth. We must, therefore, urgently call attention to the fact that play

[1] These illustrations do not imply that an actual experience must precede every single game. See *Symbolic Education*, note to p. 171.

is not merely a copy of life, but during the period of childhood is life itself at its highest potency. Hence play is a large contributor to experience, and in its original contributions we find our points of departure for many great human values. In our judgment it is because the contribution of play to experience is not appreciated that gift exercises are often limited to copy of life and that in occupation exercises undue stress is placed upon applied design.

To the conception of the kindergarten as a place where children reproduce experience, accompanied by blindness to the fact that it is a place where children are having experience, we owe many of the worst perversions of kindergarten practice. Children are having experience when they play circle games, when they build, model, sew, draw, or paint; when they look at a picture; when they listen to a story. Any one of these or of many other experiences may become the point of departure for a process of development.

Casting a backward glance upon the thoughts thus far considered, we may repeat once more that the presupposition of the genetic method is life conceived as immediate presentation and response, and that its goal is life clarified, interpreted, and renewing itself on a higher plane. This sublimation of life is begun in and through play, which is itself an initial expression of that loftier activity and more transparent consciousness in which it should issue.

Looking at his immediate life in a mirror of play which he has created, the child exercises that delicate, indirect, and semi-conscious introspective activity upon which Froebel insists in his description of the genetic method. The word introspection carries to many minds the exclusive meaning of a conscious analysis of mental states. No one who limits introspection to conscious self-scrutiny can understand Froebel or the genetic method. Froebel is simply thinking the double thought that through imitation the child fans to clearer flame the tiny spark of consciousness, and that this flame of consciousness by a kind of return dialectic illuminates the objects of the external world.

The introspective activity aroused by representation in play of different objects, persons, events, and processes is heightened by looking at pictures having a similar content. It is primarily because the pictures in the *Mother Play* book correspond most nearly to the series of typical representations made by children in play that Froebelian kindergartners consider their use so important. Their function is to give additional concreteness to the portrait of life sketched in the kindergarten games and to contribute to its ideal interpretation. For example, children who have played the "Family Game" are stirred to deeper intuitions of its meaning by the picture of a home interior showing father, mother, brother, sister, and baby, and surrounded by marginal pictures of family life in nature. Again, in the illustrations of the *Mother Play* book the children see not only the objects, persons, and acts they have represented, but a picture of themselves representing them, or, in other words, the inner relationship of their play to life is suggested to them and thereby a new degree of introspective activity is quickened. Their play mirrored actual experience; the pictures mirror not only experience, but the mirroring of experience. That this naïve process of double reflection is in accord with the method by which genius has always attempted to stimulate the prescient imagination, no student of literature will need to be reminded.

It should be added that while we find in the illustrations of the *Mother Play* our most valuable pictorial aids in the interpretation of experience, we do not exclude other pictures. Large collections of pictures have been made in different cities which combine artistic merit with the illustration of those ranges of experience accessible to childish imagination. Their influence upon the development of an appreciative feeling for art has been as marked as their power to quicken a sympathetic intuition of primal relationships and elementary ideals.

The interpretation of experience begun in play and continued by picture is clarified through the use of natural analogues. In the first weeks of their life in the kindergarten the children, who are beginning to feel themselves members of a little community, are helped to precipitate their feeling into an idea by looking at such floral communities as sunflowers and daisies and hearing a little about their coöperative life. When they have played putting baby to sleep and taking him up when he waked, they are interested in the sleeping four-o'clock and love to hear how different flowers wake and greet the rising sun. As the premonition of mother-love dawns in their minds, they delight in playing the "Bird's Nest"; as they begin to be dimly aware of the interrelations of industrial life, they grow interested in insect communities; and with awareness

of the vibration of their own lives between outgoing and
homecoming, they seem never to tire of the image of
themselves in the forth-flying and home-returning
pigeons. The fact that the *Mother Play* pictures include
so many of the analogues which are helpful in interpreting experience is another reason why no other pictures can wholly take their place.

The sublimation of experience begun in play and
continued through pictures and natural analogues is
completed in stories. Of these stories there are two
distinct kinds, — the realistic story whose details
correspond with the actual experience of children, and
the wonder tale which incites mind to reaches beyond
its immediate grasp. For children of kindergarten age
the best stories of realistic type are to be found in the
Mother Play. This book is indeed the biography of
childhood, and therefore the best interpretation of the
everyday life of all children. In many kindergartens
one period of twenty minutes each week is given to a
story in the *Mother Play* and to looking at the picture
which illustrates it. In addition to this mirror of actual
life other stories of realistic type are told, and occasion-
ally simple poems are learned which are rehearsals of
actual experience.

Even more important than the stories which are
a mirror of everyday life are those whose distinctive
merit is that, instead of reproducing the details of
an actual experience, they illuminate its principle. To
illustrate: During the first ten weeks of the kindergarten year many kindergartners tell the stories of "Thumbelina," "The Lion and the Mouse," "Baby Ray,"
"The Three Bears," "In the Mountain," "Susie's

Dream," "Hans and the Four Giants," "The Shoe-maker and the Elves," and "Billy Bobtail." Three of these stories ("Thumbelina," "The Three Bears," and "In the Mountain") are tales of children who wandered far from home, had wonderful adventures and joyous returns. "The Lion and the Mouse" con-cretely pictures the service which the least may render to the greatest. The two stories of "Baby Ray" re-late how all things served a helpless child. "Susie's Dream" is a story of mother love. "Hans and the Four Giants" and "The Shoemaker and the Elves" project the ideal of social service, and "Billy Bobtail" is a story of the domestication and service of ani-mals. It should be superfluous to say that these particular tales are mentioned only as illustrations of the content which in our judgment should deter-mine the selection of stories during the early part of the kindergarten year. The general thoughts govern-ing the selection are that stories of this type should differ from experience in their detail, correspond with experience in their principle, and by extending the range of this common principle expand the bounda-ries of the child's life. In short, we aspire to have our stories for children do something of what world litera-ture does for us, and we recognize as its greatest boon that it helps us to scale heights, descend into depths, and explore breadths of life which without it we had never known, and which nevertheless are connected with our own infinitesimal experience by the inter-preting tie of a common principle.

In concluding our survey of the kindergarten as an embryonic community which is evolving and assimilating a common life, it is only needful to add that this life is framed in music and set to song. It is through this musical setting that one of the strongest influences is exerted upon the "emotional undertone" of the common life.[1]

It will be remembered that when our little children first entered the kindergarten they were welcomed by a room flooded with sunshine and gay with flowers; were invited to activity by plastic sand, dangling balls, and brightly colored beads, and that the tender ideal of the kindergarten itself was suggested through the single picture of the Madonna and Child. As the year progresses the kindergarten room becomes a kind of history of the life of the happy community. As each new experience is assimilated and interpreted, pictures embodying its typical aspects are hung on the walls, and to these are added other pictures different in detail but correspondent in idea. On the blackboard are drawn chain pictures of the series of acts involved in different industrial processes. The cabinet preserves treasures collected on excursions or brought by different members of the community. In another cabinet are treasured creations of the children themselves. The plants so carefully tended are growing and blossoming. The visiting animals are a never-failing source of in-

[1] The phrase "emotional undertone" is borrowed from Professor Royce, who defines it as "the permanent common quality at the basis of any man's normal emotions" and considers it as the accompaniment of a permanent physical organization. In extending the phrase to cover the common life of the kindergarten we eliminate its physical connotation and use it to suggest how education may help to make life habitually brave and glad. See Royce, *Outlines of Psychology*, pp. 341, 342.

terest and delightful reminiscence. A walk around the kindergarten room is a retrospect of experience, and no one who has observed the reaction of this silent environmental influence can doubt its value.

The theme of this section of our report up to the present point has been the self-evolving circle of experience in a kindergarten community; its projection in play; its interpretation through play, picture, natural analogue, and story; its framework of music and its record in the kindergarten room. Summarizing the thoughts presented, we become aware that we have been considering the subject-matter of a kindergarten program, the genetic-developing method by which it is assimilated, and its immediate goal in the child's dawning feeling of himself as an individual member of a social whole. Were it possible to consider in similar detail the life of the kindergarten throughout the year, it would be easy to show that, by steps as short, easy, and natural as those already taken, the kindergarten becomes a primary revelation of the ethical ideals embodied in the institutions of family, civil society, state and church. Should there seem anything forced and unnatural in the brief description we shall now attempt to give of this revealing process, it is hoped that our readers will generously recognize that the reason may lie, not in the procedure of the kindergarten, but in the defect necessarily attaching to condensed statement.

With this appeal for a sympathetic judgment we venture to present a cinematographic picture of kindergarten experience after the three weeks which have already been considered. During the twelfth week of the kindergarten year the first climax of the program is reached in the Thanksgiving festival, and with this climax present in her own mind from the beginning, the kindergartner selects from the offerings of life those which will develop in children some faint presentiment of the beauty of universal service, some responsive feeling of gratitude, and some desire to share the work which all are doing. The point of departure for this vision of service is baby's visit and pictures of what mother does for baby. Responsive feeling is expressed in and developed through doll plays. There follow sympathetic representations, pictures, and stories of the home and the family with their interpretation through the natural analogues of the Bird's Nest and the Pigeon-House. From the home and the family there is a simple and natural expansion to industrial service. The child's glass of milk is traced backward, through milkman and farmer, to the cow; his bread, through baker and miller, to the farmer. The dependence of the farmer upon sunshine and shower is suggested. The children themselves plant wheat and corn. They also pound wheat, make bread, churn butter. They make an excursion to the bakery and another to the market, where there is unrolled before them a panorama of service. Vegetables and fruits of different kinds are brought to the kindergarten, named, examined, modeled, cut, drawn, painted, and used as elements in rhythmic design. Animal service of various kinds is suggested, represented in play, and described in story. The accent of life is placed upon harvesting as the climax of the autumn season. Finally, as Thanksgiving approaches there are stories about going to grandmother's and cheery conversations about seeing uncles, aunts, and little cousins.

The last day of the kindergarten before the children disperse for the holiday season arrives. When they enter the kindergarten there bursts upon them a picture they will never forget. The room has become a bower decorated with flowers, fruits, vegetables, masses of wheat sheaves and corn stalks and great bunches of hay. The object of this decoration of the kindergarten room is to make a pictorial summary of the children's experience and to embody in a visual image the beauty of universal service. There follows the representation of this service in the games which now evolve into a simple drama with its dances and choruses. In the center of the circle sit grandfather and grandmother waiting for their grown-up children and their little grandchildren. A family consisting of father, mother, and children enter the circle. The family song is sung. Glad greetings are interchanged, after which a tiny circle is formed around grandfather and grandmother, and the family enjoys a gay dance. Enter, a second family, and greetings are interchanged not only with grandparents but with uncles, aunts, and cousins. A larger circle is formed, and music and dance repeated. After this second dance the circle of the two families stands still while the concentric circle, including all the rest of the kindergarten children, begins the representation of industrial service. Pat-a-cake is played; the family circle sings a chorus of thanks to the circle of bakers. Then to the accompaniment of gay music the inner circle dances to the right — the outer to the left. Millers and farmers follow the bakers with intervening thanks and dances. To the pictured service of man succeeds the liveliest portion of the little drama as animal helpers of different kinds announce their presence by galloping, trotting, flying, creeping, mooing, barking, baa-ing, clucking, quacking, and shouting cock-a-doodle-doo. Last of all, the pattering rain softens the ground, there is a simple song of the sunshine, and with hearts attuned to thanks the happy little members of the kindergarten community close their drama of life with a quiet hymn.

When the children return to the kindergarten after Thanksgiving, they always have much to tell about what they did on that great day, and the kindergartner should assure to each little child the opportunity of narrating his happy experience. To the recall and interchange of individual experience succeeds the recall of collective experience through rehearsal of all the games thus far developed and through looking at pictures illustrating their themes. A final review and survey of experience is made by an excursion to a toy-shop, where the children see dolls and doll houses, tiny furniture for bedrooms, dining-rooms, parlors, laundries, and kitchens, toy animals of all kinds, vehicles of every description; ships, locomotives and cars, mills, bakeries, and farmyards. A visit to a toy-shop does for a child what a visit to a great World's Fair does for the adult. It is a reproduction on a Lilliputian scale of the world as he is beginning to know it, and therefore a final concrete summary of his experience. After this visit the game of the Toyman is evolved, each child so far as possible contributing his selected item to the dramatized retrospect of a delightful experience.

We have now arrived at the middle of December, and it should therefore be evident that the toy-shop will offer not only a retrospect but also an anticipation of experience. It will point forwards to Christmas as well as backwards to Thanksgiving, and upon the canvas of childish imagination will be painted pictures of Santa Claus, Christmas trees, Christmas stockings, and Christmas presents.

To the little child Christmas is first of all a time when from mysterious sources shall come to him treasures secretly desired. The knife he has wanted so long may hide in the toe of his Christmas stocking. A paint-box like that he saw in the toy-shop may hang from some branch of the Christmas tree. Father may give him a box of tools which will make him a carpenter indeed. The familiar poem "A Visit from St. Nicholas" projects the secret hopes and far surmises stirring in every little mind, and as the children listen to it again and again during the two weeks preceding the Christmas celebration it clarifies the experience through which they are living.

The kindergartner must share the secret hopes and anticipated surprises of her children and lead from them to the thought of surprising father, mother, sister, brother, and baby with something they want. She should interest the children in attempts to find out what these wants may be, and finally concentrate the life of the entire little community in making Christmas presents and beginning to know in a small way how much more blessed it is to give than to receive.

But why should all this giving and receiving of presents come every year on Christmas day? Why, indeed, unless on that day we celebrate our own reception of the great gifts through which we have learned to know the heart of the Divine Giver? History tells us that into the Christmas festival humanity has poured the ever accumulating riches of its spiritual experience. In it are reverberations of yule-tide and sacred trees; of the worship of the ever victorious, ever beneficent sun; of that ancient feast, the Vigil of the Mothers, palpitating with a nascent feeling of the continuity of mankind; of that great struggle within the Christian Church whose outcome was the assurance that the divine and the human are not mutually excluding, but mutually interpenetrating. We celebrate Christmas most truly when we gather into it all these strands of spiritual experience. We rejoice as did our forefathers in that mysterious life enshrined within the sacred tree. Our hearts are glad within us because once again the earth shall receive from the sun richer stores of light and heat. We express our sense of human continuity by giving our little presents to the children who are so soon to fill the places we must leave vacant. We stir in the souls of the children some presentiment of a divine humanity by telling them the story of the one divine human life.[1]

The tiniest child in a kindergarten knows the meaning of a birthday. We tell him Christmas is the birthday of the little child whose picture hangs on the wall of the kindergarten; that this little child was given

[1] The writer of this report desires to acknowledge her obligation to a Christmas sermon of the Rev. Percy Stickney Grant.

to the world by the Heavenly Father, and that when he grew to be a man he was so strong and brave, so wise, so gentle, and so loving that every one who knew him felt as if he had seen God. Then we repeat as nearly as possible in the matchless Bible words the story of the Nativity and show pictures of the Christ-Child in the manger; the mother watching over him; the wondering cattle, the shepherds listening to the angels' song, and the wise men following the Star.

As the first climax of the program was the Thanksgiving festival, so the second is the Christmas celebration. The contrast between the two climaxes is as suggestive as their connection. The Thanksgiving festival concentrates attention on all that the children have received from nature, man, and God, and strives to kindle the spark of gratitude. The Christmas celebration concentrates interest on the higher joy of giving. Marching together into the kindergarten, the children behold the Christmas tree resplendent with light and color and laden with the gifts they have worked so hard to finish. Fathers and mothers greet them with loving eyes and smiles. Little hearts flutter in anticipation of joyful surprises they have prepared for others. Christmas carols are sung, parents and friends welcomed, presents joyfully distributed and thoughts of self banished by the expulsive power of thoughts for others. "All giving," says Froebel, "is linked with receiving, or rather let me say all giving blossoms out of receiving." In the kindergarten Christmas is the blossom of Thanksgiving. The little recipient of universal gifts becomes himself a giver. In its deepest aspect Christmas is a perpetual revelation of the

self-imparting life of God — a perpetual appeal to
God's children to share the blessedness of their Heavenly Father.

Four months of the kindergarten year have elapsed.
Out of the feeling of community have been developing
the habits of industry, order, punctuality, cleanliness,
courtesy, and kindness. Through doll plays and care
for animals and plants there has been a quickening
of nurturing impulses. A dramatic, literary, and pictorial representation has been made of two of the
great human institutions — the family and civil society. Excursions have led out into the life of nature,
and natural analogies have clarified the pictures of
life beginning to form themselves in the children's
minds. The frame of the picture of life was the autumn
season. The high lights of the picture were upon the
two great festivals — Thanksgiving and Christmas.
Finally, a beginning was made in the religious interpretation of life by the revelation of God as a loving
Giver and by stirring the desire of responsive giving.

During the four months now past one thing was
done which as yet has not been mentioned. There
were constant glances forward from what was, toward
what was to be. Falling leaves, abandoned nests,
south-flying birds, squirrels storing nuts, children don-
ning warmer coats, animals covering themselves with
thicker fur were all noticed as heralds of the approaching winter. The spirit which was in the air during the
fall elections reverberated in the kindergarten children
and was seized upon as a point of departure for experiences which are to reach their climax in Washington's

Birthday. If soldiers have marched by the kindergarten, exercises have been stopped that the children might see them. If there has been a parade of soldiers anywhere within walking distance our embryo patriots have been among its delighted witnesses.

What now are the new experiences which shall determine the order of life in our little community when children return to the kindergarten after Christmas holidays? The question need only be asked to answer itself. They will wish to tell their holiday experiences and to show each other their Christmas presents. They will have heard of the New Year and perhaps of making good resolutions. Snow is falling and snow crystals may be caught. Snow is on the ground and it is time for the delights of sleighing and coasting. There is ice for skating and sliding. There are wonderful frost pictures on the windows. Other pictures no less wonderful may be seen in the glowing embers of winter fires. Best of all, around these fires in the gathering twilight children in happy homes sit listening to wonder tales. Days are short; the dark descends before children are tucked away to sleep, and night after night they may see the moon sailing high in the sky and gaze with wonder at the twinkling stars. The brilliant sunlight brings greatest rejoicing because of its contrast with ashen skies. And — climax of all the winter as Thanksgiving is climax of the autumn — there is our national festival of Washington's Birthday which in the kindergarten is seized upon as its greatest opportunity for fanning the spark of patriotism.

Having summoned before us the typical experiences which await our little community, let us now attempt to indicate as briefly as possible the reaction of the kindergarten upon them. It will be remembered that, in our retrospect of the four months during which this little community has already shared a common life, attention was called to the habits which had been gradually establishing themselves. It is now time that these habits should begin to define themselves as conscious ideals, and one aim of the kindergarten during the remainder of the year will be to abet this self-defining process.[1] The limits of a report forbid more than a single illustration of the method of definition, but it is hoped our readers will understand that the process now to be shown in the concrete example of evolving the ideal of punctuality is repeated in the evolution of all elementary ideals of conduct.

The point of departure for the evolution of a conscious ideal of punctuality is the game of the clock which is created by the children. Making themselves into clocks by imitating the rhythmic swing of the pendulum, showing the movement of the hand and reiterating the monotonous *tick-tack-tick*, they develop in themselves a kind of clock consciousness. Having been clocks they are more ready to listen to what the clock says. They look at the *Mother Play* picture illustrating the clock game, and find out what the mother is doing, what the baby is doing, what the older children are doing, and what connection there is between these several deeds and the hours struck by the clock. Having played the clock game and scrutinized the clock picture, they are ready to listen with some divining sense

[1] The reader will observe that this self-definition of habits illustrates the second demand of the genetic method.

of its meaning to a wonder story like the *Enchanted Watch*. At last the conscious question forms itself in their minds, What does the clock say to us? — and with the joy of discoverers they answer to themselves: Time to get up; time for breakfast; time to go to kindergarten; time to sing; work; play games; listen to stories; time to go home; time for dinner; time to play out of doors; time for supper; time to go to bed. Their next discovery, incited by guileful suggestions from the alert kindergartner, adds to their sense of the clock's importance. It tells grown people as well as children what to do and when. It tells father when to go to his business. It tells the teacher when to go to school. It tells the cook when breakfast, dinner, supper must be ready. It tells the milkman when to bring milk, the butcher when to send meat, the baker when to deliver bread. Within little minds stirs faint suspicion of what would be the chaos of life without the order which measure of time makes possible, and from responsive wills comes the conscious resolution to listen to the clock and obey its mandates.

It has seemed important to describe in detail the uplifting of a single forming habit into a conscious ideal through whose reaction the habit itself is fortified, because with this development of conscious ideals we enter upon a new phase in the self-evolving life of the kindergarten.[1] It will not be necessary to describe in similar detail all the new activities developed in response to seasonal incitement, as the general method of the program has been sufficiently illustrated. So

---

[1] It is to be understood that other forming habits are similarly uplifted into ideals — notably the habit of attention.

we pass over snowflake and snowball games, sleighing, coasting, sliding, and skating games, in order to devote more time to consideration of the most far-reaching influences exerted upon kindergarten children during the winter months, which are undoubtedly those beginning with the direction of attention to the moon and stars and ending with the celebration of Washington's Birthday. The connection between the terminus *ab quo* and the terminus *ad quem* of this process of development is far from obvious yet very real. We must approach its consideration by a somewhat circuitous path.

Max Müller has said that "the fact, which if fully appreciated will be felt to be pregnant with the most startling and instructive lessons of antiquity, is that *Zeus*, the most sacred name in Greek mythology, is the same word as *Dyaus* in Sanskrit, *Jovis*, or *Ju* in Jupiter, in Latin, *Tiw* in Anglo-Saxon, preserved in *Tiwsdaeg*, Tuesday, the day of the Eddic god Tyr; *Zio* in Old High-German." This venerable word, he adds, "was framed once and once only; it reveals the earliest religious thought of our Aryan race and it means — Sky." [1]

The clew to this most startling lesson of antiquity is suggested by a thoughtful writer who says that "one of the first elements in education is the sense of space, of which sense the star-dwelt heaven is probably the first awakener." [2] The meaning of this suggestion dawns upon us as we dwell upon the thought of how different it would be with all of us were we prisoners in a world

[1] *Science of Language*, vol. II, pp. 337, 576.
[2] George Macdonald, *What's Mine's Mine*, p. 176.

whose low-hanging skies were only a few miles above our heads. In such a world there could be no sense of majesty, no longing for liberty, no feeling of heights above and depths beneath, no divination by the prescient spirit of an infinitely transcendent God. For "Space is the body to the idea of liberty," [1] and liberty alone is majesty and transcendence. It is outer space which awakens the spacious soul. It is the visible symbol of infinitude which stirs and summons the infinitude of the spirit.

The infinitude of space is suggested by its sphericity. If when we lifted our gaze skyward the apparent form which met our eyes was a cube, we should know that space extended farther in some directions than in others and should quickly suspect that in all directions it was limited. The spherical form of space is "a foreshortening of infinitude that it may enter our sight; there is no imagining of a limit to it; it is a sphere only in this that in no one direction can we come nearer to its circumference than in another. This infinite sphere or spheric infinitude is the only figure, image, emblem, symbol fit to begin to make us know God. Over and around us we have the one perfect shape. It is not put there for the purpose of representing God. It is there of necessity because of its nature and its nature is its relation to God. It is God's thinking, — and that half-sphere above men's heads with influence endlessly beyond the reach of their consciousness is the beginning of all revelation of Him to men." [2]

[1] George Macdonald, *What's Mine's Mine*, p. 296.
[2] George Macdonald, *What's Mine's Mine*, pp. 296, 299. I have taken the liberty of making some omissions and transpositions.

The first suggestion of the sky is infinitude. Its second and no less pregnant suggestion is that of a spheric totality peopled with spheres. Within infinite or self-limited space revolve the heavenly spheres, and through this including yet relating environment each world receives the guarantee of individuality. The star-sown sky is a visible analogue of the inclusion of all spirits in God and a symbolic adumbration of the emancipating truth that through this very inclusion is assured "the eternal form which shall still divide the eternal soul from all beside."

The discernible suggestion of the overarching sky, coupled with the historic response to this suggestion, impels us to strange surmises when we consider that the most startling discovery of contemporary psychology is the immeasurable power of suggestion. Reverent minds are seeking to fathom its mystery. Numberless experiments are being made to test its effects. May it be that the mysterious power man is just learning to wield consciously is the power through which from the beginning God has touched to fairer issues the souls of his human children? Is it folly to suspect that the incitements of nature are suggestions from God; that her particular objects are images of divine thoughts; that her relations adumbrate connections between divine thoughts; that her laws reveal processes of divine thinking and that her frame of infinite space is the blank form of the Divine Mind?

It was from no accident, but by the constraint of divine suggestion, that in the overarching sky men began to know a sky-father. It is no chance connection which binds the dome of our National Capitol

to the dome of heaven. Without that heavenly dome
the limit-transcending power to which we give the
holy name of freedom might never have wakened in the
human soul, and without the awakening consciousness
of freedom men would never have known the correla-
tive idea of justice. The foreshortening of infinitude
in the spherical form of space is God's primal suggestion of his own infinite being. The star-sown sky is his
primal revelation of that cosmic community wherein is
realized the ideal of the Gliedganzes.

Science is the answer of man to the suggestions of
nature. The two great deeds of science have been the
expansion of the universe and its integration. Astronomy has extended the universe in space; geology in
time; and biology has made us spectators of that long
and painful travail of nature through which humanity
was born. While extending the universe, science has
also unified it, and her consummate revelation is that of
a great interrelated whole wherein "each clod vibrates
with pulsations from the farthest star," and wherein
all that *is* is inextricably linked with all that has been.

It is necessary to know our distant educational goal
in order to take even the first short steps on the path
which winds slowly upward towards that goal. In this
seventy-second year since the kindergarten was born,
it should be superfluous to say that we do not hold
that any of the thoughts we have been suggesting
should be suggested to babies. It is far from superfluous to add that only as we ourselves have intimately
pondered them shall we be able to respond with wisdom
to the astonishment of children in presence of sky,
moon, and stars.

It is a grave error to suppose that because animism is native to childhood we should meet it on a prehistoric level. The fact that children often say the moon has a nose and eyes does not justify us in telling them of a man in the moon. It may be native animism when children describe thunder as God rolling barrels, but if we acquiesce in such a description we arrest intelligence. Still worse is it when, deserting animism, we tell children that the moon is made of green cheese or that stars are holes in the sky.

In one of the most illuminating commentaries of the *Mother Play*, Froebel tells us that, "by loyal attention and response to the hints thrown out by childhood and by an education consonant with the needs of childhood, we may revive the mythic period of human history, with its dross cleansed, its darkness illumined, its aims and ideals purified." What hints thrown out by children will teach us to respond wisely to their astonishment in presence of the moon and stars? What myths of primitive men help us to interpret these hints?

The common saying that we must not be like children who try to grasp the moon apprizes us of the most universal hint childhood has given with regard to its response to the moon's incitement. The story of Babel and the many myths of sky-climbing heroes[1] apprise us that, though men learned after a while that heaven was not near, they were long in suspecting its infinite recession. Other primitive myths recount the disasters which befell men or giants who tried to seize for themselves the lights of heaven. All little children re-live these primitive experiences. The baby cries for the

[1] See John Fiske, *Myths and Myth Makers*, pp. 23, 151, 162, 168.

moon and reaches forth his hand to seize it. The little
lad has learned that it is not within reach of his arm,
but believes that by the help of a high ladder he might
attain it.

If the hints of childhood convey any educational
suggestion; if this suggestion is reinforced by primitive myths; if science has truly interpreted the intimations of nature; and if, above all, an ever-greatening
universe means an ever-greatening God and an ever-
greatening manhood, — then should not the very first
thing we do for little children, when they begin to
wonder about the sun, moon, and stars, be to call forth
in imagination some prescience of their distance and
their size? If as the cosmos has expanded in men's
minds it has been integrated by their thought, should
not our next effort be to stir some faint premonition of
the ties between the earth and the heavenly spheres
and especially to help children to realize that without
the sun there could be no water, no fire, no grass, trees,
flowers, animals, men; ocean and rivers would be ice
and the whole earth cold, dark, barren, and dead? If
"throughout the world of sense, even as an object is
sublime or fair," it is given not to one, but to all, should
we not help children to learn from this parable of
nature that all best gifts are sharable gifts, and that
"so much the more as one says *our*, so much the more
each one possesseth"? Finally, if there be a spiritual
as well as a physical astronomy and if the higher value
of the latter be to suggest the former, should we not do
well to heed the words of Froebel, who in the *Mother
Play* writes as follows: —

"Confronted by objects which he does not under-

stand, the child accepts with simple faith the explanation of his elders. Whether such explanations be true
or false, he accepts them with equal ease. Hence by
false explanations the child may be led to conceive
the moon as a man and the stars as gold pins or burn-
ing lamps. On the other hand, by means of true though
necessarily partial explanations, he may recognize in
the former a beautiful shining, swimming ball, and in
the latter great blazing suns which only look so tiny
because they are so far off.

"The one way of looking at moon and stars despite
its apparent life is barren and lifeless. The other bears
within it a seed of thought which may later develop
into rational insight. Why should we withhold from
children a living and life-giving explanation and weigh
them down with a dead one?"

In a recent novel, which is a remarkable study of the
influence of both social and physical environment,
there is an illuminating description of the reaction of
the homes of the Middle Ages upon the little children
who were born in them. "The mental and moral gloom
of these homes," we read, "hung destructively, ap-
pallingly over children. The very architecture taught
them their first bad lessons. Lifted in their nurses' or
mothers' arms, they peered from parapet down upon
drawbridge and moat — at danger. At the entrance
they saw massive doors built to shut out death, perhaps battle-hacked, blood-stained. From these they
learned violence and the habit of killing. Trap-doors
taught them treachery. Sliding panels in walls taught
them cunning, flight, cowardice, and eavesdropping.
Underground dungeons taught them revenge, cruelty,

persecution to the death. They might look down into one and see lying there some victim of slow starvation or slow torture. Nearly every leading vicious trait born in them seized upon the house itself for development and began to clamber up its way as naturally as castle-ivy." [1]

If we really believe in the influence of environment, we must often be troubled in spirit as we ponder the suggestions to sloth, gluttony, and covetousness made by too many of our contemporary homes of wealth, and must be filled with heavy forebodings of danger to our national ideal as we consider the suggestion of slums and tenement houses, of narrow streets crowded with wares easy to snatch and hide, of the commercial advertisements which everywhere attack the eye, of the countless sights, sounds, odors, and motions whose incitement must belittle and debase imagination. We hope for a time when these debasing influences shall have disappeared and when a noble humanity shall have created an environment appealing to all that is noble in the spirit of childhood. But we know that even in that distant day flowers shall discover to the heart its own tender meanings; the nurturing bird shall quicken the nurturing impulse and the soaring bird rejoice the soaring spirit; mountain peaks shall call forth spiritual climbers; the storm-tossed sea shall interpret the storm-tossed soul; and the human mind adapted to infinitude shall receive its highest incitements from moon and stars, sun and sky. For language and myth, poetry and religion assure us that these are the perpetual suggestions through

[1] James Lane Allen, *The Doctor's Christmas Eve.*

which the Divine Mind stimulates impulses akin to divinity.

In interpreting to children the rich influences which stream towards them from the sky, we have found invaluable aid in Froebel's great book, the *Mother Play*, and particularly in the songs and pictures of the Child and Moon, the Boy and Moon, the Little Maiden and the Stars, the Light-Bird, and the Window Songs. Our little children in the kindergarten love these songs better than all others, and never tire of searching out the details of the pictures. When they have taken these songs and pictures into their hearts, they are ready to listen to wonder tales of baffled attempts to scale the sky, of disasters following selfish attempts to seize the moon, of ruin which followed the desire to own or be the sun. Two great ideas wake up in their minds, — the idea of how far, far away are the heavenly spheres and the thought how wrong it is to want for themselves alone blessings which belong to all. To hear kindergarten children in whom these ideas are dreaming, stirring, waking, sing "Good Morning, Merry Sunshine," or to watch them play the game of the Light-Bird is to receive a revelation of what wise education may do in expanding and ennobling imagination.

Casting a retrospective glance over the life of our little community during the first weeks of the New Year, we become aware that what has been going on has been an approach towards liberty by two different paths. The children have been freeing themselves from merely reflex action by beginning to define and obey ideals of attention, industry, order, punctuality, cleanliness, courtesy, and kindness, and their minds have

been liberated and expanded through the absorption
of imagination in those suggestions of nature which
waken the ideas of immensity and unity. The struggle
for liberty of life through formation of the mental and
moral habits which liberty implies, and the liberation
of imagination through presentiments of the immensity of space and the universality of light are next to
be followed naturally and beautifully by a hint of the
meaning of freedom as incarnated in the state and
typified in the hero and the national flag. For now
Washington's Birthday is approaching; schools will
give holidays; soldiers will march; flags will wave;
newspapers will celebrate the father of our country;
and for a few brief days the social atmosphere will be
electric with patriotic emotion.

There is no romance of fiction equal to the romance
of our American ideal of government. With sublime
faith in humanity, we have dared to claim that every
man is capable of freedom; therefore it is not sufficient
for him to be well governed; he must himself participate in the governing power. This emancipating conception of self-government demands self-governing
men and women. Hence, if we really believe it, or even
if we accept it as a working hypothesis, it forces us to
assume the great duty of nurture. We have dared to
declare all men free. So doing, we have created the
necessity and responsibility of educating them for
freedom.

The state is the institution through which freedom
is defined, protected, and developed. It asks the question how shall men act that they may not destroy but
increase liberty, and it answers this question by enu-

meration of the deeds which the experience of the
world has shown to be productive of freedom. It makes
laws in which the deeds of freedom are enjoined; it de-
vises penalties for their infringement; it discovers that
the criterion for determining free action is the principle of social solidarity and that actions make for freedom in so far as they help each single will to coöperate
with all other wills.

It is not sufficient that the great principles of liberty
should be written in Magna Chartas, or national con-
stitutions. They can only be perpetuated as they become the inspiration of individual lives. "Millions of
individuals make the people; in millions of souls the
life of the people is pulsating; but the conscious and
unconscious working together of the millions produces
a spiritual content in which the soul of the whole people
appears as a living, self-creating unity." This living,
self-creative unity is the state or nation. It is greater
than any or all of the individuals it includes, yet it is
identical with what is deepest in each individual. It is
man's generic self,— enfolding, protecting, developing,
emancipating, his private and particular self. It is
a clarion call away from the prison cell of individual
limitation to the infinite space of rational selfhood.
It is the spiritual sky of freedom, and as the dome of the
physical heaven is studded with stars which are blazing
suns, so the spiritual firmament is studded with souls
aflame with the ideals of liberty. Such souls of flame
were the creators of our republic. Such above all
others was the father of our country.

The kindergartner whose heart thrills with our national impulse; who feels the sublimity of our national

ideal that the nation shall be not only *over* but *in* each
individual, so that America shall live in each American;
who knows that "a nation is a living, striving, passion-
ate soul with many members but with one life," —
such a kindergartner will crave to waken that sleeping
soul in the little child, or, if she may not waken it, to
stir in it the beautiful dreams which prophesy its
awakening. A little child cannot understand the nature
of the family, but he can honor his father, love his
mother, be kindly affectioned to brothers and sisters.
He cannot understand that complex organization of
industry through which each serves all and is served
by all, but he can comprehend his dependence upon
baker and miller, farmer and carpenter, blacksmith and
miner, and can realize that one day he, too, must be'
able to do some useful work. He cannot understand
the great truths of religion, but his heart is touched by
devout gesture and devout music, by the sight of wor-
shiping congregations; by the religion wrought into
architecture, sculpture, and painting, by the joy of
Christmas, the triumph of Palm Sunday, the mystery
of Good Friday, the elation of Easter. He can have no
suspicion that the nation "merges millions of individuals into one august personality," but he feels the contagion of patriotic emotion; he may be stirred by national anniversaries; he may strengthen the power of
discipline and kindle the spark of devotion by playing
soldier games; his imagination may be captured by our
national flag, and he may begin to gaze with reverence
and wonder at the great souls shining like stars in the
heaven of freedom. Let us never fall into the fatal
error of supposing that, because only little things can

be done with the little child, these little things are un-important. The great insights which are embodied in human institutions will never be the beacon lights of mature intelligence unless the impulses which are the emotional equivalents of these insights are quickened in childhood. Filial impiety is the ancestor of marital infidelity, parental indifference, and egoistic attack upon the institution of the family. Selfish disregard of the property rights of playmates breeds the spirit of monopoly and prevents comprehension of the imma-nent ideal of the industrial organization. If the heart of childhood be not fertilized with Christian ideals, we must expect a pagan manhood; and if we allow the period of childhood to pass without kindling love for our national flag, elation of spirit through national songs, reverence for national heroes, pride and joy in national anniversaries, then we have conspired to bring forth the man without a country; the dead soul which never to itself has said, "This is my own my native land"; perhaps even the anarchist with his blind and bigoted faith in government destruction and his fatuous attempt to "save humanity by blood and steel, poison and dynamite."

It will be remembered that the kindergarten has had Washington's Birthday in mind from the beginning of the year, and in anticipation of this climacteric experi-ence has missed no parade of soldiers, no suggestion of elections, no happening of the passing days which pointed towards the patriotic ideal. Marching exer-cises have been developed, and by early February the children move in rhythmic accord and are prompt to obey the word of command. The soldier game is now

developed and the ideal of the soldier suggested in the
words, "I go where my duty, my country is calling." [1]
The kindergarten room adds to its incitements a large
flag, a picture of our National Capitol, and a portrait
of Washington. The children receive smaller flags
which they bear proudly aloft when they play soldier
games. There is daily singing of national songs, and
daily cheering of the red, white, and blue. There are
stories of heroes; there are simple talks which stir some
faint sense of how our country protects each one of us.
Pictures are drawn of soldiers on the march. Tents are
made and soldiers encamped on the sand table. Chains
of red, white, and blue are linked to decorate the room,
and red, white, and blue rosettes are fashioned for and
by the children. A picture of the great national monu-
ment to Washington is shown, and the children are told
it was reared to him because he was the father of our
country. They themselves build monuments to him
with their blocks. A fathers' and mothers' meeting is,
or should be, held, and the influence of the home
solicited in reinforcement of the effort of the kindergarten. As the twenty-second of February approaches,
the best pictures portraying crises in Washington's life
are shown. They are allowed to speak for themselves,
and there is no attempt to make children understand
suggestions which are only intended to incite the ac-

[1] In order to play soldier games aright, we must take into our
hearts "the newer and more aggressive" ideals of peace. For the
soldier will not die when war dies, or rather, war itself will not die
when men cease to slay men. There is a knightly warfare to be
waged against ignorance, disease, vice, and crime. Armies of soldiers
ready to be armies of martyrs are needed for these nobler and more
generous battles.

tivity of imagination. Looking at these pictures and helped by a few tactful words which illuminate their details, the children begin to know a hero who dared, suffered, endured, prevailed. At last they are shown a picture of Washington as President. They feel the majesty of his presence and the benignity of his face, and once again he takes his rightful place, "first in peace, first in war, and first in the hearts of a new generation of his countrymen." Must we add that when his birthday finally dawns, the kindergarten community celebrates the third great climax of its experience?

It is by staying our minds on selected ideas that we invest them with power to form apperceptive masses and thereby determine the trend of character. Little children can hold their attention to any idea for only a very brief period. If we would endow any idea with prevailing influence, we must recur to it frequently and suggest it through many different concrete illustrations. Therefore, during the weeks which immediately follow Washington's Birthday the interest of the kindergarten is centered in heroes of different kinds. The game of the Knights is developed. Pictures like the beautiful English print of St. George and the Dragon are shown; the stories of David, of St. George, and of King Arthur are told; heroes of lowly service are celebrated and the children taught to "honor each toil-worn craftsman, however humble his calling, who braves danger in doing labor which furthers the general welfare." Finally, through true stories like the "Little Hero of Harlem," or "Dora and the Light-House," and imaginative stories, like "Dorilla," and "The Line of

Golden Light," are suggested the possibilities of a heroic childhood. There is no moralizing and no generalizing. Children are not admonished to be brave like David or conjured to imitate the example of Dora. The word heroism is probably never used. But the great ideal of heroism presented in a series of inspiring and appealing pictures captivates imagination and inspires emulative impulses. For it is literally true that

> "We live by admiration, hope, and love,
> And even as these are well and wisely placed
> In dignity of being we ascend."

While the ideals of heroism and freedom have been slowly dawning in the minds of our little children, the weeks have been hastening towards the great festival wherein the Christian church celebrates every year its faith in that immortal life which freedom implies, and the time is approaching when this beautiful faith must be presented in a form appealing to childish imagination. Nature is showing us what we should do and how we should do it. For seeds are opening; through the earth, tiny plants are pushing upward towards the light; bulbs are bursting into glorious blossom; trees are covering themselves with fresh leaves; and from apparently lifeless cocoons are emerging the joyous butterflies. The seeds and the bulbs say, there was life in us that was asleep, but now it is waking up. The trees say, we too went to sleep last fall, but we are waking up now more beautiful than ever. The butterflies say, we went to sleep creeping things and are waking up flying things. All things are saying, life sleeps and wakes from sleep; and when it wakes from sleep, it is more beautiful than when it went to sleep. And the kindergartner tells her children that, though life sometimes sleeps, it always wakes up again and wakes up more beautiful than before, and that soon Easter Sunday will be here, and they will go to church to thank the Heavenly Father for a life that goes on forever, and forever becomes more beautiful.

It is hoped that our readers will not need to be assured that the thoughts compacted into the foregoing brief sentences are very slowly and gradually suggested to our little children. Preparation of the mind to receive their suggestion was begun in the early fall when, during excursions into nature, the children collected cocoons, and if possible caterpillars spinning cocoons, and were helped to feel how life was going to sleep. During the fall they also put away in a safe place the bulbs which they were told would burst and blossom in the spring. From time to time during the winter they have looked at the cocoons, held them, felt their stillness, and wondered if butterflies would ever wake up in them. It often happens that one or more butterflies do come out precisely during Easter week. During this same week the bulbs burst into life; seeds planted by the children begin to germinate; and pussy willows bring a message that spring has really begun, not only in the kindergarten, but in the great out-of-doors. Finally, on the last school day before Easter Sunday the kindergarten should be gay with crocuses and daffodils, hyacinths and tulips.

Thus far we have considered chiefly the suggestions of the springtime. The secret of the kindergarten, however, is its method of inciting response to selected suggestions, and as our readers should now know, this open secret is, Let the child himself become the object to whose suggestion you wish him to respond. If therefore seeds and flowers, chrysalids and butterflies are to speak to the hearts of our children, then children must themselves be seed planted in the ground, plants springing into life, and butterflies joyously emerging from the chrysalis state.

The following extract from Pierre Loti's *Story of a Child* is a perfect description of the most thrilling experience of kindergarten children during the weeks immediately preceding Easter.

"I will now describe a game that gave Antoinette and me the greatest pleasure during those two delicious summers.

"We pretended to be two caterpillars, and we would creep along the ground upon our stomachs and our knees and hunt for leaves to eat. After having done that for some time, we played that we were very, very sleepy, and we would lie down in a corner under the trees and cover our heads with our white aprons — we had become cocoons. We remained in this condition for some time, and so thoroughly did we enter into the rôle of insects in a state of metamorphosis, that anyone listening would have heard pass between us, in a tone of the utmost seriousness, conversations of this nature:

"'Do you think that you will soon be able to fly?'

"'Oh, yes! I'll be flying very soon. I feel them growing in my shoulders now . . . they'll soon unfold.' (*They* naturally referred to wings.)

"Finally we would wake up, stretch ourselves, and

without saying anything, we conveyed by our manner our astonishment at the great transformation in our condition.

"Then suddenly we began to run lightly and very nimbly in our tiny shoes; in our hands we held the corners of our pinafores which we waved as if they were wings; we ran and ran, and chased each other, and flew about making sharp and fantastic curves as we went. We hastened from flower to flower and smelled all of them." [1]

"Butterflies, the poor butterflies that are old-fashioned nowadays played a grand rôle in my childhood." So comments the genial Frenchman as he reviews the romance of his infant days. We wish he might have seen thousands of little children in American kindergartens yearly re-creating the game he loved so well and re-creating in their own hearts the premonition out of which springs its imperishable joy.

When through making themselves into seeds and plants, chrysalids and butterflies, children have begun to be stirred by the mystery and joy of life, their dawning feeling is clarified by song and story. They sing of the sleeping caterpillars and of the wondrous change that comes to them; they sing of the butterflies lightly flitting from flower to flower; they sing of the little plant that

"... rose to see
What the wonderful! wonderful
Outside world must be."

They listen to the stories of Rhœcus, Picciola, and the beautiful parable of the "Caterpillar and Butter-

[1] *The Story of a Child*, translated from the French of Pierre Loti, by Caroline F. Smith, pp. 62–63.

fly." Last of all, through simple and intimate talks and with the help of poems like the "Mountain and the Squirrel," and "Great, round, wonderful, beautiful World," there begins to quiver in prescient hearts a feeling that the least living thing is greater than the greatest lifeless object.[1] Then we show the *Mother Play* picture of the Church. The children see the people crowding towards the church door; other people already within the church; the minister in the pulpit; the organ and the choir. We tell them that when the minister talks to the people he tells them about the life that goes on forever; that then the organ plays and all the people sing praises to God for giving them this wonderful life, and that when they have finished singing they pray for help to make life braver, better, and more beautiful.[2]

The importance of early wakening in children reverence for the great institution that reveals an altruistic God and an immortal humanity can scarcely be overestimated. The religion of any people is the final determiner of its national life. If America has a free government; an industrial organization which is increasingly seeking to endow each individual with the results of collective endeavor; a type of family life which respects the rights of all its members; and a

[1] It has been impossible to make a brief presentation without somewhat confusing the order of poems and stories. So I desire to explain that some of the stories mentioned are told not before but after Easter.

[2] Parents' meetings should be held at this time; the thoughts we have been considering should be talked over and fathers and mothers urged not to permit their children to miss the rich experience of Easter Sunday.

system of education which, from its beginning in the kindergarten to its climax in the university, aims to capacitate free souls for freedom, — it is because still in her deepest heart America cherishes faith in a liberty-loving God. This is the truth that makes us free, and without that perpetual reaffirmation by which the church keeps it alive in our souls, those specific forms of national, industrial, and domestic life which are its approximate secular embodiments would soon vanish from the earth.[1]

From the convictions which inspire our Easter program, let us now return to the self-evolving life of our little kindergarten community. Experience has shown that on their return to the kindergarten, children who have been prepared for sympathetic appreciation of the great religious festival have much to tell of beautiful churches, beautiful flowers, beautiful music, and solemn prayers. They have not understood all the words of these prayers, but they have realized that a great common feeling was throbbing in many hearts and a great common thought stirring in many minds. We give up the first week after Easter to a retrospect of this inspiring experience and we deepen and clarify its influence by singing Easter hymns; looking again

[1] The careful reader will have observed that there has been no attempt to connect the Easter service with the Christian belief in the resurrection of Jesus. Indeed, there has been no mention of death, but rather an attempt to quicken the joy of immortal life. We find it hard to believe that anyone would debar childhood from this joy, but we repeat what has already been said that we are merely presenting what we conceive to be typical experiences and their interpretation, and that we fully recognize that, in kindergartens connected with public schools, modifications demanded by the public mind must be made promptly and cheerfully.

at the *Mother Play* picture of the Church; hanging upon the walls of the kindergarten a fine photograph of some great Gothic cathedral; noticing once more nature's manifold suggestions of reviving life; repeating the play of the Butterfly, and telling the story of the "Sleeping Beauty."

At the beginning of the second week after Easter, we go with our children on a walk, and we so direct our steps that we shall see carpenters building houses, birds gathering materials to build nests, and men preparing garden beds. The suggestion which comes from this threefold experience is preparation for the protection and nurture of life.

The mother of a happy little family who often took her children for a drive was for quite a while perplexed by their constantly repeated question — Who lives in this house? At last it occurred to her to answer that in each house lived a father and mother with their children. Her own little ones never tired of hearing this answer over and over again. It seemed to give them great joy to think that the whole city was full of homes and that in each home lived a happy family. It is a feeling akin to this which we aim to develop in the kindergarten children during this spring walk. Fathers have been to the carpenter and said, Build me a home. Birds are building homes. Men are spading, hoeing, and raking the ground to make homes for the flowers.

The reaction of this experience upon the children is shown at once in their building exercises. They are eager to build homes themselves, and as they are now using the Fifth and Sixth Gifts, they can make very

satisfactory houses. Their efforts to plan good houses
are made more conscious by the play and picture of
the Carpenter, and by little talks through which they
are incited to think what a house needs in order to be
a comfortable home. Finally, as the climax of their
home-creating experience, they make and furnish a
doll house.

From interest in human homes it is easy to lead to
interest in animal homes and thus develop the second
suggestion of our spring walk. We recall the birds
busily gathering materials to build their little homes.
We bring out our collection of nests and study all the
different ways through which the parent birds have
tried to make them safe, cozy, and comfortable. We
look again at the *Mother Play* picture of the Bird's
Nest, notice where different birds have made their
homes, and ask ourselves why they chose these particular localities. Then we study once again the Pigeon-
House picture and find the homes of the serpent and
the snail, the homes of the sparrow, the pigeon and
the titmouse, the home of the child, and the church
which our little children are now ready to describe
as the home men build for God. Finally, remembering
the little children eagerly questioning who lives here,
and here, and here, we turn from the home to the
family and again search out in Froebel's suggestive
picture air families and water families, marsh families
and field families, forest families and hive families. Is
it too much to believe that, as the result of all these
concrete experiences, the world begins to seem to our
little children like one great home sheltering many
small homes, and that in tender and susceptible souls

is quickened the first far-off surmise of the Father's house of many mansions? [1]

The third incitement which came to our children on their memorable spring walk was that of garden-making. No reader who has learned the secret which our entire report has been trying to tell will need to be assured that in response to this incitement garden games are developed, actual gardens made, beautiful flowers of all kinds brought to the kindergarten, the brightly colored picture of a garden hung upon the kindergarten wall, glad songs of growing and blossoming plants learned, pictures of flowers drawn and painted, and stories told which suggest different aspects of man's relationship to the floral world. [2]

The great values of the garden as one of the educational instrumentalities of the kindergarten are that it affords occasion for the exercise of nurturing activity and responds to nurture with quick and rich reward. Children learn that unless they give their gardens constant care the plants wither and die. The earth must not be allowed to grow hard; the plants must be regularly watered; they must be protected from undue heat and cold, from destructive insects, and from crowding weeds. When carefully watered and lovingly tended, they reward the little gardener with ever fresh revelations of the mystery of development and the beauty of life. The springtime calls to the child,

---

[1] It is to be understood that all this time the games of the Carpenter, the Pigeon-House, the Bird's Nest, and the Family are being actually played.

[2] Actual gardens are not yet as common as we wish they were. But garden games, sand-table gardens, and the planting of seed in flower pots are very general.

Rejoice in an abiding and beautiful life. The great religious festival inclines his heart to love the great Giver and Sustainer of life. His own little garden says to him: Be like your Heavenly Father and care for one tiny corner of the world as he cares for the whole world and for all the worlds.

The end of the kindergarten year is approaching, and the time has come for the children to make their great excursion to a farmyard. This excursion is a climax of the many experiences through which ever since the beginning of the year the kindergarten has striven to awaken in its children some sense of themselves as nurtured beings and some impulse to share the high privilege of nurture. The following account of one such excursion comes from a Pittsburgh kindergarten.[1]

"Our excursion to a farm was one of the most delightful we have ever made.

"We went forty strong, with two of the mothers to help us get on and off the street-cars. Two other kindergartens met us at the farm, so there were altogether about a hundred children.

"The farm stood on a very high hill overlooking the river, which was spanned by many bridges. I felt the sense of freedom that comes to one on the heights, and I was glad to notice that the children felt it as I did. Said one child: 'See the butterflies, how much room they have to fly.' 'Yes,' said another, 'lots of

---

[1] This account was sent me by Miss Jessica Childs, director of the kindergarten in the Pittsburgh College for Kindergartners. I have omitted an occasional phrase or sentence.

room and lots of flowers.' Then came a chorus —
'Lots of trees; lots of chickens; lots of children; lots
of wind.'

"Our approach to the farm lay through a lane; the
pasture lots on either side. The children greeted with
delight a mare with her young colt. 'Where is the father
horse,' cried they, — and soon discovered him in a
neighboring field.

"A turn in the lane brought the farmhouse into
view. A barking dog heralded our approach.

"'The farmer's dog! he's watching the farmer's
house,' cried one of the children.

"The stable held greater revelations, for here we saw
two cows, each with her baby, as the children said.

"The 'babies' were very gentle and playful, reaching
out inquisitive noses for the children to pat.

"There was a trough in the barnyard, and on the
top of the barn a pigeon house.

"While we were looking for the pigeons, one of the
children ran to me, saying: 'I saw a little bird fly in
that hole right under the roof. He must have a nest
there.' Just then the bird flew out, 'to get some worms'
the children said.

"The chicken-house was the home of two thousand
small chickens, and the children's delight knew no
bounds when the farmer allowed them to feed the
chicks. In the chicken-yard outside were roosters,
hens, and geese.

"In the garden were beds of pansies and phlox.
'Come, see the bumblebee,' called one of the children,
while the others were content in noticing the colors
of the flowers and burying their faces in them.

"Noontime came all too soon, and regretfully we turned our faces homeward. The sun was very bright and the children noticed the shadows. 'Now we can make some shadow-rabbits,' said one child; while another cried: 'Yes, and mine is going all the way home with me; he can go as fast as I can.'

"Seeing some mules hitched to a wagon which was being filled with bricks, one of the children said: 'See how still they stand; they have to be patient and wait just as we do.' 'Yes,' answered another, 'but they can run and so can we.' There followed a series of remarks in which the children noted similarities and dissimilarities, between themselves and the animals.

"'We can jump and the rabbit can jump.' 'A caterpillar can only crawl, but a butterfly has wings to fly. Why can't we fly? — we're bigger than butterflies.'

"We reached the kindergarten tired, hungry, and happy, and sat down to rest for a few minutes while the piano played softly.

"After we had sung good-bye, I said, 'Tell me what you are going to do the minute you get home?'

"'Tell mother all about it,' said every one of the children."

For many days after this thrilling experience its influence was clearly discernible in the free creations of the children.[1] "Clay, paper, paints, and crayon,"

[1] On the third day after this excursion the director told the children that any one who had a pet animal might bring it to the kindergarten the next morning. I give her own account of the response. "When my ears were greeted with 'maa-maa' as I neared the kindergarten I knew the pets had come. I began to wonder whether I had been rash in inviting them all at once. We had two doves; three

writes the director, "seemed to hold animals waiting
to be released. In the free cutting were reproduced
the farmer's house, the pigeon-house, the dog-house,
then the dog himself and many little chickens. When
paints and paint brushes were distributed, the children
cried with one voice: 'Let's paint a barnyard.' Then
they all made fences with gates and afterwards painted
animals inside.[1]

kittens; a rabbit, a parrot, and a goat. The latter we thought it
best to tie in the yard and we spent our recess admiring him. He
was very tame and sat up and begged for food. The children shared
their lunch with him. The kittens slept in their basket after they
had been given some milk; the doves cooed in their cage, while the
parrot enlivened the morning with shouts of 'Polly wants a cracker.'
The rabbit has been presented to the kindergarten."

[1] Miss Child's account of a conversation on the *Mother Play*
picture of the Two Gates will explain why the children began by
painting fences with gates: —

We looked at the picture of the Garden Gate and the following
points were brought out in the discussion of its details: The gate was
closed to keep out chickens and dogs. The garden belonged to the
two children and they had taken good care of it. The little girl was
putting the flower inside the fence so that it would n't get broken.
It was a beautiful garden. The fountain helped to make it beautiful
and cool.

"I know what the fountain says," cried one child: 'Drip drop,
drip drop.'"

"There must be fishes in it," said another.

"The birds fly into the garden to get a drink."

"The butterflies and the bees come in right over the fence."

Next we looked at the picture of the Farmyard. Here is a gate,
too, but it is open.

"Johnny will get it shut in time."

"There are no flowers here, but there are animals here."

"Should they be here?"

"Yes: this is the place for them."

"Were the flowers where they belonged?"

"Are the animals where they belong?"

"Do they each need to be taken care of?"

"A modeling exercise contributed to the reactions from the barnyard, horses, pigs, cows, chickens, a pond with ducks swimming, a trough, a pump, and finally a small boy who the children said was 'Johnny shut the gate.' In free drawing many barnyard animals were reproduced. The drawings of one child were especially interesting because they showed how greatly he had been impressed with the characteristic peculiarity of each animal. The ram drawn by this little boy had very large spiral horns worked out in detail, while the rest of the body was merely an indefinite mass with four lines for legs. The sheep was drawn with a greatly exaggerated covering of wool; while the cow was an almost exact duplicate of the sheep in general contour, but was differentiated by the absence of wool and the addition of a very large udder."

Then followed these comments: —
"The mother cow takes care of the baby calf."
"The mother horse takes care of the baby colt."
"The mother hen takes care of the chickens."
"The farmer takes care of them all."
"Do mother plants have anything to take care of?" said I.
"The seed babies," said one child.
"How does she do it?"
Then the children told me over again what we had discovered when we were studying seeds — how they were wrapped up to keep them dry and warm, etc., etc.
"Mother takes care of our baby," said one child.
"What have we to take care of?" I asked.
"Our gardens," said one.
"Our bunny," cried another.
"Ourselves," said Elizabeth, who is possessed of a restive spirit and to whom self-control has meant a struggle.
Thus ended our discussion, and I felt that the little nurtured beings who came to us in the fall had felt the quickening touch of the year's experiences and were themselves becoming nurturers.

"The influence of the farmyard upon the minds of the kindergarten children was shown not only in their free creations, but in the stories they asked to have retold and the plays and songs selected for repetition. The stories of "Ludwig and Marleen" and "Thumbelina" were called for, the former being described as the story of the boy who bound up the foot of the fox, and the latter, the story of the little girl who took a thorn out of the bird's foot. Another story chosen was "Peter, Paul, and Espen," which pictures Nature revealing herself as ally to the man whose ear is open to her call. Finally, the children wanted to hear again about the little Christ-Baby cradled in the hay. On the circle the games of the Farmer and Grass-mowing, learned in the fall, were revived and the games of the Barnyard and Garden played daily with increasing zest. The Light-Songs and the song of the Church were called for, as was also the song of the Christ-Baby, which had not been sung since February. After singing this last song, one of the children ran across the room to the Madonna picture, saying: 'See the Christ-Baby in his mother's arms!' " [1]

No kindergartner who follows with discerning sympathy the unfolding life of her little community can doubt that towards the end of the year a total series of experiences converges in the dawning ideal of nurture. The children do really begin to know themselves as nurtured beings. They do really begin to have prescient faith in a nurturing God and joy in the consciousness of an abiding and progressive life. It has been with the hope that this convergence of experience

[1] Miss Child's Report.

might suggest itself through the reactions of the children in an actual kindergarten upon their last excursion that we have permitted ourselves to relate what may seem trivial and uninteresting details. Will our readers kindly remember that little children can do only little things and give slight intimations of the trend of their feeling and thought.

The kindergarten has been defined as an institution which from the plays of childhood breaks a path of approach toward all human values. The aim of our discussion of the program up to its present point has been to suggest the approaches toward religion, ethics, language, literature, music, the dance, and the drama. It is believed that the approaches toward religion and ethics have been indicated in sufficient detail to make comment unnecessary and that a brief statement will suffice to clarify the evolution of the remaining values.

It is quite generally recognized by intelligent primary teachers that children promoted from the kindergarten have both larger and more precise vocabularies than children entering school directly from the home. It would be strange, indeed, were this not so, because in the kindergarten words are learned in connection with the acts, objects, qualities, and relations to which they refer. Every representative game defines a number of verbs by acting them and a number of objects by showing their use. In good kindergartens the actual objects whose use is represented are shown to the children and many of them later made by the children. When it is impossible to show the actual object, a picture takes its place. Seeing, using, and making objects, children become familiar with their qualities, and therefore learn readily the adjectives which name these qualities.

For many years kindergarten children enriched and clarified their vocabularies, but did not learn to express themselves in complete sentences. Even to-day their speech is defective in this respect. But kindergartners are becoming alive to the importance of being precise and concise in their own speech, and as they learn to use words few and fit, children learn to form complete sentences. It is because the speech of adults is prolix, ambiguous, and circumlocutory that children are arrested in the use of single words. In the tumult of sound that assails their ears they can distinguish only a few clear meanings.

In addition to the development of language through representative and creative exercises must be mentioned the influence upon speech of the stories to which the children listen and the poems they learn. Stories are carefully selected with reference both to their content and their literary form. The vexation of spirit shown by children, when changes are made either in the words of a story or in the order of its events, is teaching kindergartners to follow the example of the great story-tellers of primitive ages. The constant repetition of stories in the same fitly chosen words amplifies and clarifies the speech of eager auditors. Poems committed to memory enhance still further the power of linguistic expression. It is true that we do not as yet possess many of the poems which the life of the kindergarten demands for its self-expression. We cannot say to ourselves, Go to: we will make a book of songs and sonnets. We cannot at will make ourselves poets, and we await the genius who shall adequately translate the heart of things to the heart of childhood. There has, however, been a cheering advance in the simplicity and beauty of our songs, and when we contrast the present poetic wealth of the kindergarten with the dearth of pioneer days we are filled with hope for the future.

For many years large numbers of kindergartners have given much time to the study of Homer, Dante, Shakespeare, and Goethe, the Bible, and the Greek Tragedians. Through this study they have learned to feel the charm of literary expression and to see with their own eyes how literature interprets the meanings of nature and of human life. They have also learned to distinguish between local and temporal literature and world literature. They have come to realize that there is a world literature for childhood as well as for maturity and have been incited to study fairy tales, primitive myths, and national and religious legends. The practical result has been a greatly increased ability to recognize what types of character and situation should be presented to little children and an approximate attainment of that distinction of speech which proceeds from distinction of thought. Therefore, the stories now told in large numbers of kindergartens do really perform the several functions of literature by helping to create forcible, delicate, and discriminating speech; by defining those ranges of thought and feeling which are accessible to childish imagination; by suggesting the evolution of action out of feeling and thought, and by illustrating the deeds which may and may not be done.

Passing from the values of language and literature
to that of music, it must be regretfully confessed that
the kindergarten is very far from realizing its own
musical ideal. As Froebel conceived the kindergarten
game it was a motor expression translating itself into
thought by words and into feeling by music. In the
actual kindergarten, words, melodies, and motor expression often attack each other instead of supporting each
other. Furthermore, much of our music is poor; much
of it is not adapted to children. In too many kindergartens this defective music is badly played and
badly sung. We confess our faults and our sins are ever
before us. But once again we cannot at will make ourselves musicians and musical composers. We can only
continue to announce our ideal until the announce-
ment shall call forth a musical genius who will make it
possible for us to do that which we desire. The necessity of the moment is that graduate kindergartners
should study music, as many of them have already
studied literature, and should learn to select from the
constantly accumulating store of songs and games
those having musical value. The elimination of music
which is tinged with mawkish emotion is greatly to be
desired. In telling stories we have learned to tell what
heroes do and to avoid dissertations on how they feel
and what they think. Our poems of nature and human
life portray deeds and events. Our hymns are eliminating exhortations to love God, and inspiring love
by suggesting his character through appealing images.
When children look at the sun they do not need to be
told that it is bright, and when they feel its genial rays
they do not need to be told that it is warm. Still less

do they require to be told that they ought to like light
and warmth. So whether we wish to call forth in children response to nature, man, or God, our one principle is to portray deeds and let feelings take care of
themselves. The music interpretive of such songs and
games should be as joyous as childhood, as noble as
the ideal, as simple as the images under which childhood
apprehends the ideal. Above all it should be inspired
by ethical purity and should avoid both sensuous tick-
ling of the nerves and "the railroad gallop style which
makes the nerves vibrate with undue excitement."

The ideal of Froebel with regard to the evolution of
values will not be realized in music until, in addition to
supplying good melodies, we help children to discriminate rhythms and tones and to use them creatively.
In the discrimination and creative use of rhythms a
fair beginning has been made, but practically nothing
has as yet been achieved in the discrimination and
creative use of tones.

The attentive reader of this report will have observed that the heart-centre of all the activities thus
far described is the kindergarten game, and will also
have recognized that this game approaches the value
of art as embodied in the forms of the dance and the
drama. The characteristic feature of the kindergarten
game is that it translates into symbolic motor expression the valid and typical experiences of childhood in
all countries and in all ages, and therefore tends to
develop normal and joyous emotions.

Recent studies of folk-dances have indirectly illuminated kindergarten games. "In these dances," writes
Dr. Gulick, "any or all of the chief events of human

experience were told not merely in words, but were accompanied by gesture and bodily expression."[1] They were acted stories of sowing and reaping, of war and the chase, of love and marriage, of worship and sacrifice. Through this motor rehearsal of typical experience the experience itself was assimilated and intensified. Rhythmic representation of sowing, reaping, and weaving liberated the livelier emotions incidental to these economic activities; hunters and warriors grew acquainted with themselves through dramatizing their deeds; the dance portraying pursuit of the maid, and symbolically suggesting her coy retreats and veiled advances, was the first recital of the old love story told anew in the novel of yesterday; and finally, genuflection and bodily prostration quickened the sentiment of worship, and religious legend translated into act reacted to enliven the faith of the actors. So, for the kindergarten child to fly is to begin to feel free; to march is to begin to feel self-restraining; to cuddle a doll is to get ready to cuddle a baby; and to bend the knees and fold the hands is to quicken the spirit of reverence and devotion. The kindergarten game agrees with the folk-dance in developing thinking and feeling out of motor activity. It differs from the folk-dance by declining to rehearse adult experience in adult form. It is a story acted, told, and sung of the typical experiences of childhood itself and of adult experience as reflected in the child mind.[2]

It cannot be too often repeated that the final aim

[1] Dr. Luther Halsey Gulick, *Folk and National Dances*, p. 10.

[2] The value of the folk-dance for the youth of the country can scarcely be overstated.

of the kindergarten is to help children to create a miniature world and through this creation to interpret the larger world in which they find themselves. We have seen that the kindergarten games create in imagination a picture of institutional ideals, call forth an emotional response to these ideals, and portray those phenomena of nature which analogically interpret human affections and aspirations. We are now to see that the plays with the kindergarten gifts correspond with those forms of human activity whose aims are the transformation of nature through the industries, the transfiguration of nature through the fine arts, and the theoretic interpretation of nature through mathematics and science.

The traditional method of using the kindergarten gifts calls for the three kinds of exercises formerly described as making forms of life, beauty, and knowledge. Translating these obsolescent names into contemporary terminology, we may say that the traditional method calls for construction, representation, design, and the discovery of mathematical relations and implications. Under the term constructive activities we include exercises with the building gifts, together with peas-work and paper, clay, and sand modeling in so far as their products are objects of utility.[1] Under the term representation we include all exercises wherein one object stands for another in virtue of an analogical tie, and all picture-making, whether with masses, lines, or points.

---

[1] As technical activities, sewing and weaving may also be included under this head. In the kindergarten, however, the emphasis of these occupations is upon representation and design.

CONSTRUCTIVE EXERCISES

The nearer agreements among kindergartners relate to exercises with the building gifts; hence no extended description of our play with these gifts is necessary. In common with other kindergartners we encourage the making and grouping of furniture for bedchambers, dining-rooms, kitchens, laundries, schoolrooms, and kindergartens; the construction of objects belonging to the yard or farm; the building of dwelling-houses, stores, factories, libraries, art galleries, churches, and public edifices of all kinds; the erection of bridges and the grouping of buildings into villages and cities. We incite the children to discover for themselves how to make all these objects. With the Third and Fourth Gifts we encourage the transformation of one object into another. With the Fifth and Sixth Gifts, while not excluding transformation, we place our emphasis upon the improvement of the single object. We avoid dictation, and use chiefly the methods of imitation and suggestion. We incite children to pile blocks in order that their various possibilities may be discovered and their architectural values discerned. Finally, we encourage the discovery and repetition of architectural units of design.

It is superfluous to do more than suggest the fact that building exercises offer many connections with games, stories, and pictures, and that we avail ourselves of these natural connections in the organization of our program.

With regard to other forms of constructive activity, it is sufficient to say that peas-work is almost exclusively restricted to the development of simple objects from the linear outlines of plane and solid geometric forms; that exercises with sand and clay conform to the general practice; that in paper modeling we place our emphasis upon processes, rather than products, and that our aim is to encourage original invention and transformation. For older children we approve of the exercises suggested by Froebel, which, in addition to their constructive value, are concrete applications of mathematics.

REPRESENTATION

Symbolic representation is adapted only to the younger children in the kindergarten, and we deplore that extension of the analogizing act which so often produces arrest of development. In picture-making our effort is to avoid monotonous repetition of the same forms with different media of expression, and in the use of any particular medium to encourage representation of the objects to which it is best adapted. For example, we limit our tablet pictures almost entirely to houses, furniture, bridges, boats, engines, and different kinds of vehicles; we confine stick exercises to the representation of direction and to the outlines of rectilinear objects; and our ring pictures are chiefly waves, vines, leaves, flowers, and fruits. We recognize that the richest media of representation are paper, crayons, and paint, but we believe that the very limitations of such materials as tablets, slats, sticks, rings, and lentils, concentrate attention upon facts which are ignored in the use of more plastic instrumentalities and tend to develop that conscious power which is always achieved through restraint.

It is manifest that both constructive and representative exercises point towards the great value of industry, and it is interesting to remind ourselves that the obvious contribution of the kindergarten to this particular value was one of the chief arguments urged for its introduction into the public school system. In his monograph entitled *Early History of the Kindergarten in St. Louis*, Dr. Harris writes as follows: —

"If the school is to prepare especially for the arts and trades, it is the kindergarten which is to accomplish the object, for the training of the muscles, if it is to be a training for special skill in manipulation, must be begun in early youth. As age advances, it becomes more difficult to acquire new phases of manual dexterity. Two weeks' practice of holding objects in his right hand will make the infant in his first year right-handed for life. The muscles yet in a pulpy consistency are very easily set in any fixed direction. The child trained for one year in Froebel's gifts and occupations will acquire a skillful use of his hand and the habit of accurate measurement of the eye, which will be his possession for life.

"Not only is this training of great importance by reason of the fact that most children must depend largely upon manual skill for their future livelihood, but from a broader point of view, we must value skill as the great potency which is emancipating the human race from drudgery by the aid of machinery. Inventions will free man from thraldom to time and space.

"By reason of the fact already adverted to, that a short training of certain muscles of the infant will be followed by the continued growth of the same muscles through his after life, it is clear how it is that the two

years of the child's life (his fifth and sixth), or even one
year, or a half-year in the kindergarten will start into
development activities of muscle and brain which will
secure deftness and delicacy of industrial power in all
after life. The rationale of this is found in the fact that
it is a pleasure to use muscles already inured to use;
in fact a much-used muscle demands a daily exercise
as much as the stomach demands food. But an unused
muscle, or the mere rudiment of a muscle that has
never been used, gives pain on its first exercise. Its
contraction is accompanied with laceration of tissue
and followed by lameness, or by distress on using it
again. Hence it happens that the body shrinks from
employing an unused muscle, but, on the contrary,
demands the frequent exercise of muscles already
trained to use. Hence, in a thousand ways unconscious
to ourselves, we manage to exercise daily whatever
muscles we have already trained and thus keep in
practice physical aptitudes for skill in any direction."

As pointed out in the passage cited, the kindergarten
gives a general training for industrial pursuits rather
than a specific training for particular industries. It
does, indeed, introduce children to the primitive arts
of agriculture, pottery, sewing, and weaving, but its
direct contributions to the development of industry
are an aroused interest in constructive activity and "a
skilful use of the hand and the habit of accurate measurement of the eye." In addition to this technical
training the kindergarten creates through its industrial
games a genuine reverence for the ideal immanent in
the great institution of civil society, which, as pointed
out in the second section of this report, is "a more or

less conscious effort to complete the desire for development in nature by helping nature to fulfil its mission as servitor of man."

DESIGN

There is no divergence of opinion among kindergartners as to the importance of approaching the great value of industry through wisely directed play, but there is marked divergence of opinion as to the relative stress to be placed upon exercises pointing respectively towards the practical and the fine arts. The most interesting fact of contemporary kindergarten history, however, is the very general awakening of kindergartners to an appreciation of the fine arts; and the consequent fading away of one line of scission between representatives of the Froebelian institution. As a result of this awakening appreciation, exercises in rhythmic and symmetric arrangement have become universal in kindergartens, and very intelligent activity is displayed in the creation of methods whose aim is to help children to discover architectural, plastic, graphic, and pictorial possibilities. Stimuli of various kinds are provided, experiment is encouraged; social coöperation is invoked in aid of individual effort; units of design are discovered and combined; the consciousness of space-relations is developed; children are encouraged to scrutinize and improve the forms they have made, and — *mirabile dictu* — it is granted that the kindergartner herself may take a place among the incitements of environment. With regard to the use of geometric elements in the development of art values, no general consensus of opinion has been reached. The signers of this report, however, are unanimous in the conviction that since proportion inheres in and is most simply created with geometric elements, practice in the grouping and spacing of different lines and in the symmetric cutting of the various polygons is an indispensable phase of the method of initiation into the arts of space. We approve of the grouping and spacing of concrete objects when children have developed sufficient skill to draw or cut these objects themselves, but we think that allowing children to arrange objects cut or drawn by the kindergartner betrays them into expecting too large results from too little effort, and we are furthermore convinced that in arrangements of concrete objects, proportion is less easily discernible than in the arrangement of geometric elements.

In general, our chief points of difference from some representatives of the kindergarten with regard to design are a more pronounced evolutionary accent and the conviction that children should be made aware of certain normative standards.

THE APPROACH TOWARDS MATHEMATICS

Kindergarten gifts are not only playthings through whose intelligent use an approach may be made towards the practical and fine arts. They are most evidently intended by their creator to make also an approach towards mathematics. This fact is too patent to have escaped even the most superficial observation. No child can play constantly with spheres, cubes, cylinders, circles, squares, oblongs, and other geometric solids and planes without creating in himself a tendency to classify presented objects under these archetypal forms; neither can he constantly apply numerical relations without creating in himself a tendency to observe them. His play with the kindergarten gifts, therefore, weaves in his mind a series of "apperceptive nets" with which he catches and holds presented objects.

The history of the kindergarten makes evident the fact that there has often been a deplorably exaggerated emphasis upon form and number. When a child describes a dog as a large cylinder in a lying position and supported by four upright cylinders; when looking at a beautiful picture he notices only that its frame is oblong; or when, instead of listening to an interesting story, he counts the buttons on the narrator's dress, it is manifest that a distinct arrest in mental development has been made by some exponent of the "developing method" of education. It was only natural that such arresting work should call forth both a theoretic and practical protest, and that large numbers of present-day kindergartners should insist that the stimulus of the material itself is the only mathematical incitement needed and that it is an educational error to direct attention either to geometric archetypes or numerical relations. Stated in the terminology of the kindergarten, this point of view demands the elimination of that type of exercise described by Froebel as making forms of knowledge.

The French have a proverb to the effect that it is foolish to throw out the child with the water in which it has been washed. Were we to throw out of the kindergarten all the forms of activity which have been

perverted by exaggeration, we should leave ourselves
nothing to do. Were we to refuse appeal to all the
native tendencies of childhood to which some kindergartners have appealed in ridiculous ways, we should
cut ourselves off from every path by which a child's
interests may be reached and his activity aroused.
We do not reject animism because some ignorant kindergartner describes a pea as having cheeks and then
tells her children to run a stick through them. We do
not discard symbolism because of such absurd perversions as drawing an apple and telling children it
stands for all the fruits of the Thanksgiving season.
We do not give up the ideal of inner connectedness
because numbers of kindergartners make arbitrary
connections. Neither shall we give up forms of knowledge because numbers of kindergartners have unduly
emphasized geometric forms and numerical relations.

The true way of escape from arresting methods is to
create kindergartners consciously aware of the different educational values and their relative importance.
It is because many essential things are left undone
that there is time for less important things to be over-
done. In any good kindergarten time should be consciously divided between eleven forms of activity
graded in the order of their value. These exercises are
Pure Movement and Dance Games, Representative
Games, Learning of Songs and Poems, Looking at
Pictures, Listening to Stories, Excursions, Garden
Work, Care of Animals, Representation of three kinds
— with solid material, with planes and with lines. Is
it not self-evident that an intelligent division of time
between these several forms of activity will not only

preclude undue emphasis upon form and number, but will tend to eliminate all the other one-sided extremes into which the kindergarten has been betrayed by the defects of its representatives?

Since the Froebelian approach toward the value of mathematics is less generally understood than the approaches toward the practical and fine arts, it may be well to mention some of the typical exercises through which this approach is made. In the kindergarten little children spin the sphere, cube, and cylinder of the Second Gift so as to exhibit a panoramic procession and metamorphosis of forms. They blow soap-bubbles and by the help of circular wires change iridescent spheres into cylinders. They pound clay spheres on opposite sides and produce cubes. They divide spheres, cubes, and cylinders of correspondent diameters by the same principal axial cuts. They make with clay, cardboard, and sticks connected by softened peas, the series of forms from the triangular pyramid to the cone and from the triangular prism to the cylinder. They connect the square with the circle through play with sticks and with the jointed slats. They reproduce in clay the series of the solid gifts, and by cutting them become aware of the relations of their component parts. With the Third, Fourth, Fifth, Sixth, and Seventh Gifts they illustrate fractional relations, square root and cube root. They learn to recognize the same square and cubic contents in different forms. They make many significant perceptible ratios between forms. They derive planes, lines, and points from the solid and build up the solid from points, lines, and planes. Could we keep our children longer, they would evolve not only the circle, but a number of different curves from their tangents. They would make analyses of clay spheres, cylinders, and cones correspondent to the analyses of the cube offered in our existent building gifts. They would receive Froebel's completed Second Gift and derive the tetrahedron, octohedron, rhombic dodecahedron, and three transitional forms from the cube. Finally, they would make the Seventh Gift cut, and, after learning through experience how the tetrahedra it yields are produced, would be given numbers of these tetrahedra to combine into different forms and to use in making metamorphoses of form. For, as Froebel himself writes: "The keystone of kindergarten employment is the transformation of solid bodies and consequently the knowledge of the relations of the different geometric solids to one another as well as their development from one another." [1]

No kindergartner who has ever helped her children to make a genetic evolution of geometric forms, who has noticed the zest with which they discover relations between these forms, who has become aware of their value in illustrating relations of number, and who has understood the necessity of furnishing a perceptible basis for the idea of ratio, will doubt that Froebel has broken a better path of approach towards mathematics than has been made by any later educator. On the other hand, it must be granted that comparatively little of the work he planned should be carried out with children under the age of six. This minimum work,

---

[1] It is hoped that our readers will observe that in all the exercises referred to, children either use things, make things, cut things, or combine things. Every exercise is a deed or series of deeds.

however, is important, because without it a nascent interest in mathematical relations may be atrophied by disuse.

The first merit of the Froebelian approach to mathematics is that through it children are incited to discover mathematical relations. The second is that it creates a dynamic and evolutionary conception of mathematics. The third is that the several concepts of form, number, and ratio are conceived and treated in their organic unity. The fourth is that since the discoveries made are typical facts, they are ancestral thoughts and constantly beget a progeny of new discoveries.

The prejudice which so many persons feel against giving kindergarten children concrete mathematical experiences arises from failure to distinguish between the very different ideas of giving elementary lessons in mathematics and quickening interest in mathematical relations. It cannot be too strongly insisted that these two ideas are not only different but antagonistic. There can. scarcely be a more effective check upon mathematical interest than lessons in arithmetic or object lessons on geometric forms. The kindergarten stands for the conviction that early attitude is far more important than early teaching, and its play with type forms as an approach to mathematics is precisely analogous to the care of pet animals as an approach to zoölogy, or garden work and gathering wild flowers as approaches to botany.

The following narrative of an accidental experience of childhood and its results illustrates precisely the aim and method of the kindergarten: —

"The majority of professional teachers, at present,

on their own confession, have no idea *on what depends the receptivity of the child* when the teaching age for a subject has begun. Parents also are still so unawake to this that they confuse *preparation for a subject with premature teaching of a subject;* and do great harm by such premature teaching. Many teachers strongly deprecate amateurish attempts to instruct children before the proper time and in this I entirely agree with them. A concrete instance may help to make clear in what preparation for a subject consists. In my young days cards of different shapes were sold in pairs in fancy shops for making needle-books and pin-cushions. The cards were intended to be painted on; and there was a row of holes round the edge by which twin cards were to be sewn together. As I could not paint, it got itself somehow suggested to me that I might decorate the cards by lacing silk threads across the blank spaces by means of the holes. When I was tired of so lacing that the threads crossed in the centre and covered the whole card, it occurred to me to vary the amusement by passing the thread from each hole to one not exactly opposite to it, thus leaving a space in the middle. I can feel now the delight with which I discovered that the little blank space so left in the middle of the cards was bounded by a symmetrical curve made up of a tiny bit of each of my straight silk lines; that its shape depended upon without being the same as the outline of the card and that I could modify it by altering the distance of the down-stitch from the up-stitch immediately preceding. As the practical art of sewing perforated cards was already quite familiar to me, my brain was free to receive as a *seed* the discovery I had made and to let it grow naturally, all the more because no one spoke to me then of tangents or tried to teach me any algebraic geometry until some years had elapsed. Therefore, when I did begin to learn artificially about tangents, the teacher was not obliged to put cuttings into raw soil; *he found ready a good strong wild stock of living interest* in the relation between a curve and the straight lines which generate it on to which he was able to graft the new knowledge. The teacher came, not as an outsider thrusting on me the knowledge of something unfamiliar and strange, but as a brother-seer, more advanced than myself, who could show me how to make further progress on a path which I had already entered with delight. *On such accidents as this of my card sewing depends I think much of those special receptivities for certain subjects quite distinct from great power which puzzle psychologists. When we understand better how they originate they will no longer depend upon accident and we shall more often be able to produce them at will."* [1]

"In a concrete experience," writes Froebel, "three things are always present: the particular fact, its universal application, and the relationship of both to the person who has the experience." [2]

The kindergartner who understands these words will never teach mathematics, but neither will she desist from the attempt to quicken interest in mathematical relations and awaken mathematical imagination. [3]

---

[1] M. E. Boole, *Preparation of the Child for Science,* pp. 91–93. (Italics mine.)

[2] *Mottoes and Commentaries,* p. 122.

[3] Some contemporary writers describe concrete experiences of typical facts as "material for unconscious cerebration," as "fertili-

THE APPROACH TOWARD SCIENCE

The main purpose of our discussion of the kindergarten program has been to suggest the approach it makes from the concrete experiences of childhood toward the values of life. One great value — the value of science — remains to be considered, and the point we desire to stress is that kindergarten children approach this value most directly through the mathematical stimulus of the Froebelian gifts. As a single illustration of such approach, let us consider the questions a child may be incited to ask and answer through his play with the Third and Fourth Gifts. Why can the bricks stand, sit, and lie, while the cubes can take only one position? Why is it so much easier to knock over a brick than a cube? Why, when bricks are set in a row and one is struck, do all tumble, while eight cubes in a row stand solid against the most vigorous attack? Why do the bricks of the Fourth Gift make so much better walls and floors than the cubes of the Third Gift? Why can the child build with them so much better steps? Why can he inclose such large yards and windows, and yards and windows of so many shapes? Why can he pile his cubes only in five ways, while he can pile his bricks in forty ways? Why is it possible with his bricks to make so many delightful experiments in balance and equilibrium, and why do they yield such a variety of symmetric forms? Great is the joy of the embryo experimenter when he

zation of the unconscious mind," as a "crystallizing thread around which later experiences may group themselves." The process is the same, however described, but Froebel's description, which implies a minimum degree of consciousness, is the most accurate.

discovers that one fact answers all these questions. His cubes stand firmly and do so little, because their length, breadth, and thickness are equal; his bricks are so easily overturned and do so much, because they are twice as long as they are broad and twice as broad as they are thick.

We do not ignore the path of approach towards science opened through constructive exercises, neither do we undervalue the reaction upon the mind of the simpler relations to which attention may be called during excursions into nature and in connection with garden work and the care of pet animals. It is well for a child to know that his kitten has large pupils because it is a night-prowler; that the Christmas tree is evergreen because it has a resinous sap; that the thorn of the rose and the prickles of the gooseberry are weapons of defense against animal attack; that the dandelion tufts he loves to blow and the burdocks which stick to his clothes are devices adopted by plants for the dissemination of their seeds. The suggestion of these and similar relations will do something to kindle interest in seeking relations. Nevertheless the fact remains that science means the *classification of facts and the discovery of their relations and sequences, and that no interest in explained relations, however lively, implies development of the scientific attitude of mind.*

In brief epitome of the final section of our report we repeat that the kindergarten program arises as a spontaneous evolution out of the life of the kindergarten community. The object of life in this embryo community is the social creation of a play-world. The reaction of this play-world upon its creators helps them to make an ideal interpretation of the larger world into which they are born.[1]

All great human values are approximate definitions of the human spirit. Since children participate in this spirit they tend to re-create human values. The kindergarten aims to abet this process of creation and to help children to do better what they themselves are trying to do.

It is as native to mind to scrutinize its deeds as to create these deeds. Therefore, the genetic-developing method calls upon children not only to act, but to observe the result and process of activity. Through such scrutiny, mind takes possession of itself. It would be a parody of the Froebelian method should there be any attempt to anticipate in consciousness an unattained level of experience. It is an omission of one of the most distinctive features of the method when actual experience is not observed, interpreted, and assimilated. It would seem, indeed, that only through such observation is life transmuted into experience.

If Froebel is wrong in holding that upon every level of experience human beings should act, should notice their action and its result, and through such scrutiny take possession of themselves and incite themselves to mount to a higher plane of life, then the kindergarten as he conceived it is an educational blunder. If, on the other hand, it may be that Froebel is right, then, verily, there is "a new thing under the sun," the excluding extremes of educational absolutism and educa-

[1] For a definition of what is meant by an ideal interpretation of the world, see *Educational Issues in the Kindergarten*, p. 63.

tional anarchy have been mediated, and the little child made a happy copartner in the process of his own normal development.

We accept the genetic method as our working hypothesis for education. The world has not succeeded so well with the plans previously tried as to discourage us from experiment. We cannot shut our eyes to the fact that all around us are men and women who are slaves to the moral evils they were not taught in childhood to face and also slaves to the intellectual prejudices which have accumulated in their minds through the subconscious convergence and coalescence of uninterpreted experiences. Froebel at least dreamed of an education which from the beginning should aim at conscious insight and free self-direction. We are willing to give our lives to the effort to prove this dream true.

The kindergarten is the educational phase of a great "time movement" whose character is defining itself through many different expressions. Humanity is stirred in its inmost depths by a new divination of its own freedom. The great mass of men obscurely feel that they should have larger opportunity to grow into freedom, and threaten society by an inarticulate demand for their birthright. The favored minority tremble with the suspicion that they can no longer keep their own manhood if they deny their brethren the privilege of becoming men. The church announces that nothing but a fiercer flame of religious life can make possible clearer vision of Eternal Reality. Literature and art are once more enthroning and crowning the human will. Great statesmen descry from afar the vision of maternal governments which shall nurture in their citizens the ideals of freedom. The one great message of the Time-Spirit is, Become, O man, the truth you would see, and thereby achieve the freedom which is your dower from God. Echoing this message the kindergarten whispers, Educate your little children through the deed which sees into and through itself, and thereby help them to mount over stepping-stones of ever-dying selves to living selfhood.

SUSAN E. BLOW.	CAROLINE M. C. HART.
MARIA KRAUS-BOELTÉ.[1]	LAURA FISHER.
ADA MAREAN HUGHES.[1]	MARIAN B. B. LANGZETTEL.
ALICE E. FITTS.[2]	HARRIET NIEL.
MARY C. McCULLOCH.	FANNIEBELLE CURTIS.

[1] While agreeing in the main with Miss Blow's report, I find a difference in point of view with regard to a detailed program planned for the year, and also with regard to the general arrangement and decoration and opening of the kindergarten.

[2] The contents of this report I endorse as Froebelian theory. This method of application of these theories in the kindergarten, I differ from. I believe that each kindergartner should make her own program, and that this program should be adapted to individual conditions.

SECOND REPORT

PATTY SMITH HILL

PART I

THE PRINCIPLES UNDERLYING THE SELECTION AND ORGANIZATION OF THE SUBJECT-MATTER OF THE KINDERGARTEN PROGRAM

ANY conception of the kindergarten as an organic part of education presupposes a faith, more or less conscious, in the universality and validity of the laws which underlie both the higher and the lower education.

When teachers of all grades shall accept the universal validity of so fundamental a law as self-activity, the differences found in the curricula of kindergarten, primary, and elementary education will not be due, as formerly, to the acceptance of Froebelian theories of development in the lower grades and to Herbartian theories in the higher grades. The day has passed when kindergartners can afford to offer as an argument against a theory its Herbartian origin. On the other hand, the fact that primary and elementary teachers have so largely accepted the fundamental principles of Froebel, is sufficient guarantee of their breadth of view.

Now that self-activity is so universally recognized as the basic law of growth in all education, we have as a result an intelligent effort to study each stage of development in order to discover those aspects of a common subject-matter which will stimulate normal self-effort.

The group of kindergartners who unite in presenting this report conceive of the kindergarten program as a flexible plan of action, which plan affords the teacher the opportunity of selecting and organizing those native activities, interests, and experiences common to all children together with the subject-matter which feeds them. This flexible plan should admit those aims and purposes of the child which have educational significance, as well as those which have been contributed by the wider experience of the teacher.

The problems of primary importance in the kindergarten are the same as those in all education; namely, *what* shall we teach — and *how* shall we teach it? The former problem gives rise to the need of selecting the right materials or subject-matter; the latter, to the importance of right method in presentation and execution.

Since Dr. Dewey wrote his *Pedagogical Creed*, and *The Child and the Curriculum*, it is well-nigh commonplace in modern educational theory to state that the process of education to which the kindergarten program and curricula of education correspond has two distinctive aspects which may be differentiated — the psychological and the sociological. The psychological aspect presents the claim of the individual — the right of the child to be studied in order that the teacher may discover the methods which must be pursued in putting at the child's disposal opportunities for the fullest development of all his native powers in and through social situations. The sociological aspect presents the rightful claim of society to an education which will develop in the members social consciousness and readiness for social service. This is but a legitimate return demanded by society for its bequests — tested and tried values, and richest experiences, to each new generation. The mutual rights of the individual and of society demand that society realize its obligation to educate every child ; hence our recognition of the necessity for compulsory education. The protection and development of society, however, demand that the process by which the child is educated bring to his consciousness an ever-deepening sense of his obligation to social service.

While these distinctive aspects are recognized, they cannot be separated, inasmuch as they are part of one process, and are related as "what" and "how," as ends and means, or as aim and instrumentality.

When this theory is applied to the study of the curriculum and to the methods of education, we have two interrelated factors; on the one hand, we have as motive power those early manifestations of self-activity contributed by the child in the form of instincts and impulses or native tendencies ; on the other hand, we have the subject-matter or materials of the course of study contributed by the experience of past and of present civilization, which serves as stimulus to the self-activity of the child.

When self-activity comes into contact with the material of civilization, a process of interaction is set up in which the child may be led to appreciate and re-create, in his own immature, crude way, the so-called achievements of civilization. In this process of action and reaction between self-activity and materials, carried on under the guidance of a teacher who has a knowledge of both, Froebel hoped to harmonize his twofold ideal of education as a process by which the self both achieves and inherits the experience of the race. If it is granted that education is a self-active process in which the individual must on a small scale re-win as well as inherit the experience achieved by the race, then materials become an actual necessity. In this way they become an organic part of education, serving as stimulus to the powers resident in the child, and also as the stuff out of which the self realizes or actualizes its aims and purposes. Thus materials become what Froebel calls a "counterpart" to the child, activity and materials being inseparable aspects of one and the same process, each being incomplete and inconceivable without the other.

This conception of the relation between the self-activity of the child and the materials of the curriculum would seem to define the teacher as one who stands between, serving as mediator, interpreter, or guide. She, with her knowledge of the creative impulses of the child, and with her insight into the educational values embodied in the materials, selects and presents to him that subject-matter for which he is ready. By her insight into the reaction of each of these upon the other, she brings to the consciousness of the child those values which adult guidance alone can adequately reveal to him.

In this sense the teacher becomes a guardian of the child and of the experience of the race, a trustee of society. The teacher, then, is the social agent selected by society to transmit its noblest traditions, and to train immature members to appreciate, respect, and

preserve the permanent bequests from the past, with
the hope that the child will in time contribute his
share in creating an ever-new and nobler civilization.

This view of the course of study grows out of the
acceptance of three fundamental theories regarding
the nature of mind, and the relation of the child-mind
and subject-matter to the civilization of the past and
of the future: first, mind must be defined in terms of
activity — an activity involving all the varied impulses which make it possible for the self to appreciate,
know, and control; second, subject-matter must be
interpreted as human achievement — as the tested
and tried results of past struggles in man's adaptation
to, and control over, an environment natural and
social; third, it must be recognized that the same creative spirit which has achieved the great arts, sciences,
religions, and institutions of the highest civilization of
the past and of the present, has its dim beginnings in
the work and play of the child. The subject-matter
of the curriculum, or the achievements of civilization
in which it has its origin, makes its own appeal to
these immature but native tendencies in the child
which are, however unconsciously and inadequately,
reaching out for and aiming toward similar achievements. Could we know just what aspects of subject-
matter the child is ready for, the discipline of the school
would be reduced to a minimum, because the child
would be held by the materials and by the problems
presented by the teacher rather than by the teacher
herself.

The simplest and sanest basis of organization for the
subject-matter of a course of study seems to grow out

of the theory that it originates in, and grows out of, social life. Here each study is treated as one differentiated aspect of social experience, which has emerged out of an original unity in social life to which the curriculum itself corresponds.

The most fundamental problems in the planning of a kindergarten program, or course of study, may be stated as follows: —

I. The selection of the impulses, instincts, and interests which are developing at this period of the child's growth, and which make for the highest good of the child and society when provided with educative stimuli or material.

II. The selection of the best subject-matter or materials for the creative impulses of the child to act upon in the self-active process through which he comes to appreciate and re-create the achievements of civilization.

III. The organization, correlation, or arrangement of the subject-matter or materials in a unity such as makes for the economy and simplification of the whole. This unity must be secured without sacrificing the individual nature or achievement of any one of the impulses entering into the organization.

Before we can progress further it is necessary to treat each of these problems more fully.

I

The first problem presents the need of two studies. In the first place, it demands a study of the child himself in order to discover which instincts or impulses are growing most rapidly at any stage of development and making the most insistent demand for food and exercise. The necessity for this study grows out of what Dr. James terms the "law of transitoriness in instincts." [1] "Many instincts ripen at a certain age and then fade away. A consequence of this law is that if during the time of such an instinct's vivacity objects adequate to arouse it are met with, a habit of acting on them is formed, which remains when the original instinct has passed away. In all pedagogy the great thing is to strike the iron while it is hot." Or, again, "In children we observe a ripening of impulses and interests in a certain determinate order. Later, the interest in any one of these things may wholly fade away. The hour may not last long, and while it continues you may safely let all the child's other occupations take a second place." [2]

The second aspect of this problem demands keen discrimination in studying the relation of the lower stages in the development of an instinct in relation to its higher manifestation. While the philosophy of idealism which Froebel represents, acknowledges the evolutionary process as a fundamental factor in education, it continually asserts its belief that the true nature of any impulse on its lower levels of development can be evaluated only in terms of its highest realization.

Many instincts of recognized importance in their maturer stages give little promise of this significance in the crudity of their early expression. Because of this, instincts which later are of great value to society

[1] James, *Psychology*, pp. 402-404.
[2] James, *Talks to Teachers*, p. 61.

are often overlooked in their crude forms of expression in child life. An ability to discern promise in these transitory instincts, which often fade for want of food and exercise, would insure their preservation for the present development of the child and the future welfare of society.

II

Any attempt to solve the second problem in the construction of a course of study demands not only a consideration of the materials of civilization, but involves the still more subtle question — *what* aspect of these materials will meet the needs of children at different stages of development. One must know not only materials in general, but, also, what in particular should be selected to present to children at a given age or grade.

Those materials must be presented which best stimulate the impulses developing at the time. The process by which the child comes to assimilate the educational values embodied in materials is a self-active one in which, in a small way, he comes to reinvent or rediscover these values won by past civilizations. The dynamic or experimental method must be preserved throughout. Even though the mode of expression may be crude, it must represent the high-water mark of the child's ability at any given stage.

The subject-matter presented should grow out of the child's personal experience, or in some way function in it, if he is to gain that insight which is necessary for the reconstruction of the experiences of the past.

If it is granted that the subject-matter of the kindergarten should grow out of, and interpret, the experiences of the children, this would seem to suggest the necessity for variation of both subject-matter and method in meeting the needs of children living in different natural and social situations.

The function of environment in the process of building up experience would demand a scientific and philosophical treatment far beyond the scope of a report of this nature; but as many of the differences in both theory and practice of the kindergarten arise from conscious, or unconscious, differences regarding this particular aspect of philosophy, it must at least be touched upon. Few are conscious of the theory of knowledge which underlies their practice, though all are consciously, or unconsciously, acting upon the method suggested by a philosophy of mysticism, rationalism, empiricism, or pragmatism as a knowledge process.

It must be admitted that the function of environment has been ignored by some educators and overemphasized by others. Few have seen that, while environment is an important factor in the making of experience, it is neither independent of nor identical with it.

From one point of view, environment may be studied as a stimulus to mind, stirring the creative impulses to act upon it in a process of adaptation to and control over it. In this process of interaction both the self and the situation undergo a change; the environment not only serving to stimulate the mind by setting up an obstruction or problem which demands adaptation as solution, but serving also as the means of realization.

Thus environment provides the very stuff which stimulates the self to reconstruct its own thought, and to alter the face of the external world.

If it is acknowledged that environment is at least a factor of importance in the experience process, and that not only the self but environment changes, one would seem to have an argument in favor of a careful study of the rôle played by these varying environments in the experience of different children.

While the majority of kindergartners agree in the theoretical statement that the program is based upon the experiences of children, — that it is these experiences which are to be selected, interpreted, and organized, — few seem to act consistently upon the possibilities and limitations of environment in illuminating, modifying, and rectifying these experiences.

Out of the different attitudes of kindergartners regarding the function of environment in broadening, deepening, completing, or reconstructing the experiences of children living under varied conditions, grow the much-discussed problems as to the uses of somewhat fixed or uniform programs.

The varied individualities, temperaments, training, and experience of the teachers as well as those of the children would seem to require the opportunity to vary programs and courses of study, if the teachers are to do living, vital work in the classroom.

Common sense would seem to demand that any course of study which is supposed to meet the actual, as well as the theoretical, needs of particular groups of children should embody the convictions of both the supervisor and the classroom teacher.

School administration under a democratic government seems to demand a study of those conditions which make freedom go hand in hand with guidance. Democratic control in schools should provide for a coöperation between supervisors and classroom teachers, sufficiently flexible to leave ample opportunity for the individual initiative, conviction, and sense of responsibility on the part of each, without endangering the welfare of the children or of society.

In democratic administration the straight and narrow path between uniform and individual programs and courses of study must be solved in relation to the protection of the mutual rights and privileges of (1) the classroom teacher and her children; (2) the supervising officers and the teachers under supervision; (3) the boards of education or superintendents, and the parents and the community to which they are responsible.

With the teachers and children the problem seems to present questions such as these: How may the individuality, personality, originality, and initiative of the children be preserved in the teacher's attempt to organize the whole through the contributions of both children and teachers? How can she use the initiative of each individual so as to enrich the group, and stimulate in each a desire to contribute his best to the making of the course of study for the whole?

In the case of the supervising officers and teachers the problem seems to be the preservation of the individuality, personality, freedom, and development of the classroom teachers through their attempt to provide programs and courses of study for the protection

of the children. How may courses of study be
planned in which both the rank-and-file teacher and
the supervising officers have contributed their common
and peculiar experiences, their individual initiative,
their personal convictions, and their sense of responsibility to the boards of education, to the parents, and
to the community?

Some of these problems will be considered: —

1. *The principles of democracy as applied to the relations
   of teachers and children.*

If, as is generally conceded, the early manifestations
of self-activity take the form of native impulses or
instincts, we can readily see that the application of
democratic principles to early education demands
that these contributions of the child be utilized by the
teacher in the course of study. Until these impulses
begin to react upon the materials of the environment
in the process of building up ideas and knowledge of
the meaning of life, they are blind tendencies to do, or,
as Professor James puts it, "Instinct is usually defined
as the faculty of acting in such a way as to produce
certain ends without foresight of the ends."[1] At first
the child contributes the activities only, the mother or
the teacher contributes the foresight of the ends these
are destined to attain. Although some extreme adherents to a sort of "overwrought idealism" may regard
these impulsive activities of too humble origin to be
considered, nevertheless, they seem to many the only
points of departure in any democratic conception of a
self-active process of education.

However blind the child may be to the ends which

---

[1] *Psychology, Briefer Course,* p. 391.

these instinctive activities are destined to attain, the
teacher who is conversant with the fundamental principles underlying modern psychology and pedagogy
knows that these activities are indications of awakening powers and interests of great value in the building
of a curriculum.

Though instinctive activities may serve as the
starting-point and motive power in early education,
yet the child, as he comes to realize through experience
the ends toward which he is working, and learns to
adapt means to the attainment of these ends, is gradually freed from the domination of instinct. This emancipation from instinct is due to the fact that the knowledge gained through the early performance of these
instinctive activities awakens reason and reflection.
When the child is able to reflect upon his past activities, and through reason and reflection experiments in
order to find better ways and means to reconstruct,
these instinctive activities are giving place to the control of ideas and thought. Thus while originating in
the blind impulses to act, they attain their real significance only when dominated by reason and reflection.
As differences of opinion on this point affect the practical procedure of the kindergarten materially, the
point seems worthy of illustration. The dissimilarity
in practice is the result of the theories regarding the
psychological distinction between work and play, and
the function of each in the kindergarten. Those who
look upon play as activity which is pursued with no
interest in nor vision of ends, believe that kindergarten
children are necessarily robbed of their native spontaneity and freedom when they participate in activi-

ties directed toward an end. Those holding to this conviction would prescribe more of the traditional occupations which have been handed down from the days of Froebel, such as sewing lines in cardboard, weaving paper mats, or the folding and cutting of paper in sequences. It is held by some advocates of this theory and practice that the child at this age has no desire to sew, weave, or fold as a means of accomplishing an end. The processes of sewing, weaving, and folding are supposed to be sufficiently absorbing in and of themselves, so that the result attained is of slight moment.

An opposing view is held by those coöperating in presenting this report. While the younger children may be absorbed in activity for its own sake, we are firmly convinced that the older ones are not only interested in these processes, but are capable of using some of them as a means to a more real end to which they apply themselves with spontaneity and freedom. This is not only true when the technique is partially under control, but we hold that the end may serve in this process as a motive or stimulus in gaining mastery of the processes involved.

If the problem or end presented by the teacher is one which the child can readily grasp, and if its solution in any way furthers his play and social life, he is not only interested in the activity involved, but is absorbed in discovering ways and means to realize the end toward which he is working. For example, with sufficiently large and durable material he may weave a simple doll's hat or rug, or fold and cut a crude kite, both of which will function in his play life, instead of weaving paper mats and folding and cutting 'a form resembling a kite to paste in an occupation book to be taken home at the end of] the term or year.

In a study of the traditional occupations of the early kindergartens, and those introduced later under the rather misleading name "constructive occupations," Dr. Dewey draws this conclusion: "Upon the whole, constructive or 'built-up' work (with, of course, the proper alternative of song, story, and game which may be connected, so far as is desirable, with the ideas involved in the construction) seems better fitted than anything else to secure these two factors — *initiation in the child's own impulse and termination upon a higher plane*. It brings the child in contact with a great variety of material; it supplies a motive for using these materials in real ways instead of going through exercises having no meaning except a remote symbolic one; it calls into play alertness of the senses, and acuteness of observation; it demands clear-cut imagery of the ends to be accomplished, and requires ingenuity and invention in planning; it makes necessary concentrated attention and personal responsibility in execution. Unless the child can get away from it (that is, the model) to his own imagery when it comes to execution, he is rendered servile and dependent, not developed. . . . From the psychological standpoint it may safely be said that when a teacher has to rely upon a series of dictated directions, it is just because the child has no image of his own of what is to be done or why it is to be done. Instead, therefore, of gaining power of control, by conforming to directions, he is really losing it, — made dependent upon an external source."[1] Or again, "No one seriously questions that, with an adult, power and control are obtained through the realization of personal ends and problems, through personal selection of means and materials which are relevant, and through personal adaptation and application of what is thus selected, together with whatever of experimentation and of testing is involved in the effort. Practically every one of these conditions of increase of power for the adult is denied for the child. For him problems and aims are determined by another mind. For him material which is relevant and irrelevant is selected in advance by another mind, and, upon the whole, there is such an attempt made to teach him a ready-made method for applying his material to the solution of his problems, or the reaching of his ends, that the factor of experimentation is at the minimum. With the adult we unquestioningly assume that an attitude of personal inquiry, based on the possession of a problem which interests and absorbs, is a necessary precondition of mental growth. With the child we assume that the precondition is rather the willing condition to submit to any problem and material presented from without. *Alertness* is our ideal in one case, docility in the other."[2] Often the end, aim, or problem which is in the teacher's mind only, might be easily and profitably shared with the child, though not initiated by him, if the teacher realized the attitude of inquiry and eagerness to find means of solution which the child's possession of the aim or end would stimulate in him.

[1] Dewey, *The Schoolmaster and the Child*, pp. 58–61.
[2] Dewey, *Psychology and Social Practice*, pp. 13–14.

Thus if the occupations described above involve a simple technique, and the end is childlike and not too remote, they stimulate interest and effort so that, though initiated in the play impulse, they develop into the beginnings of creative work, art, and industry on a higher level.

Dr. Cole, in his study of Herbart and Froebel, states clearly this principle of initiation through impulse and emergence in values of the curriculum in these words: "Freedom in education seems to mean that instincts and impulses are to be utilized, not eliminated. For these are the obvious contributions of the self to the educative process. If they be not respected, or in some way maintained, it is difficult to see how there should be talk of freedom. Yet it is one thing to respect instincts and impulses, and another to admire them as they blindly perform an unasserted work. Then instincts and impulses may be thought of, not as opposed to ends, ideals, or values so much as the possibilities and cravings for these very realizations and satisfactions. The educational situation ought then to be not impulses vs. the curriculum, but impulses for it." [1]

The inability of the child to start from any point other than where he is, makes the use of his experience with all its narrow limitations not only advisable but inevitable. What else can we start with in any true process of development? Where the child is, is the only point of departure for the development of the ideal experience which should be. Children do not enter the kindergarten as "idealess," "purposeless," or "experienceless" as some would have us believe. Pre-

[1] Cole, *Herbart and Froebel*, p. 83.

kindergarten experience has, through the child's activities pouring out upon his environment, built up desires, ideas, and purposes, however incorrect or partial these may be.

Any attempt to disregard "His little Past" as a starting-point because of the poverty and narrowness of its range, in order to substitute some remote, vicarious experience selected for its supposed ideality, is unconsciously autocratic, for the following reasons: In any educational institution laying claim to democracy the child would seem to have four inalienable rights: (a) The right to express his own ideas and experiences in order to have them rectified, interpreted, or utilized for the development of himself and for the social group; (b) the right to have his own limited, narrow, and personal experience extended through those contributed by other children in the group; (c) the right to participate in the wider experience and vision of the teacher; (d) the right to come into direct contact with the experience of the race as embodied or preserved in its literature, arts, songs, games, industries, laws, and institutions.

Any teacher who is not willing to use the broken bits of experience contributed by individual children, and her own experience as a means of clearing, rectifying, completing, interpreting, and relating the whole, has failed to grasp Froebel's great social law of "Gliedganzes," in which each child is related as member, and as whole, to a larger whole.

The difficulty seems to be due to the tendency to treat both environment and experience as static; a deeper study of the needs of the child would seem to

indicate the necessity for deepening and extending
these. A good part of kindergarten education should
be devoted to the gaining of new experience through
first-hand contact with nature, and with human activities — domestic, industrial, æsthetic, and religious.
We are often guilty of singing about these, dramatizing them, relating stories of them, or expressing them
through hand work, when what is needed is not the
expression of these but the actual experience itself.
More excursions and gardens, more experiments in
using, seeing, and participation in the use of tools of
human activity would lay the basis for spontaneous
songs, dramatizations, and expressions of these, together with a finer appreciation of the vicarious experience brought to the child through stories, song, and
verse.

Granted that the warp of the program must be the
nearest approach to the common experiences of the
children drawn from the significant factors in their
common environment, yet the woof must be furnished
by the introduction of new experiences which will
fashion the new and the old into an organized whole.
A discriminating study of the experiences already in
the possession of the children would seem to point to
the necessity of introducing new elements in order to
relate or extend the old ones. Nor does this introduction of the new imply any necessity of presenting the
remote, chosen on the basis of its supposed superiority
in stirring the imagination. On the contrary, the unknown or unfamiliar should be chosen only upon condition that it furnish the missing link in completing and
giving new meaning to the known and familiar. A lack

such as this often exists within the most familiar experiences of childhood; these are frequently neither appreciated nor understood because they are unrelated; the skillful use of some unfamiliar factor may become the means of linking together, interpreting, and unifying the whole process. Even here the unknown is not the end sought; it is only a means to a higher end to be found in the illumination and unification it brings to bear upon the disconnected experiences of the child's past.

On the other hand, when we have wrung from the child's past all the problems it offers in meaning and control, the new function of the known and realized will be to serve as leverage for gaining some deeper insight into, and control over, the new, the untried, the unknown.

We grown people forget that subject-matter which seems dull and commonplace to us, because it represents processes familiar to us and under our control, may be full of significance to the child, stirring a deep sense of wonder when it offers new opportunities for experiment in discovering meanings and solutions. For this reason, we are astonished to find that a round of action, monotonous to the adult, may offer a whole unexplored world of romance and adventure to the child.

As the actual experiences of no two children can possibly be the same, even in one home or in one kindergarten, the skillful teacher not only weaves the unknown as an interpretative factor into the disconnected elements of the familiar, but also uses the known as a point of departure toward the unknown, the unfamiliar, and the unmastered. She also guides the children in all their associations so that the particular experience of any member of the group, whether child or adult, may be contributed to link together and make more complete the experience of all the others, until a certain degree of unity is attained. In this way the experience of yesterday may be reconstructed in the light of that of to-day, and this new illumination makes it possible not only to interpret the old by the new, but the new by means of the old.

It is interesting to recall the fact that this problem presented itself to Froebel many times. A few quotations here may illustrate this point and serve in making clear his position on this subject. He says: "The second remark is that objects are here brought before the child, which indeed the playing adult has seen, but which as yet the playing child has not seen at all. Though this is not to be scrupulously avoided, as little is it to be thoughtlessly carried too far; kept within limits, it justifies itself to any simple, straightforward mind. Man has a peculiar presaging power of imagination. [Therefore] objects not yet seen in life by the child may be introduced to him through word and plaything that represent this object, but with the following restrictions."[1] Again he writes, "This is quite natural, for the child's world, from the remembrance of which come his formations and his conceptions, is at first principally confined to house and room, table, bench, and bed. The child moves from the house and its living rooms, through kitchen and cellar, through yard and garden, to the wider space

[1] Froebel, *Pedagogics of the Kindergarten*, p. 49.

and activity of the street and market, and this expansion of life is clearly reflected in the development of his productions. His representations proceed from his nearest experiences, and are intimately connected with them. The child is not to be forcibly torn away from his inner world and his environment. But the mother or kindergartner has many opportunities of correcting the child's perceptions by his representations; and the amendment will be gladly accepted by *the child, if only they lie within the circle of his experiences and ideas.* As these building gifts afford a means of clearing the perceptions of the child, they give occasion for extending these perceptions, and for representing in their essential parts, objects of which the child has only heard."[1]

Froebel's belief that the spontaneous expressions and productions of the child grow mainly out of his immediate experiences in and about the home and neighborhood is evident in the following quotation: "Now, in the family, the child sees the parents and other members of the family at work producing, doing something; the same he notices with adults generally in life and in those active interests with which his family is concerned. Consequently the child at this stage would like himself to *represent what he sees.* He would like to represent — and tries to do so — all he sees his parents and other adults do and represent in work, all of which he sees represented by human power and human skill."[2]

[1] Froebel, *Pedagogics of the Kindergarten*, pp. 221, 222. (Italics not author's.)

[2] Froebel, *Education of Man*, p. 98. (Italics not author's.)

While home and neighborhood activities and life are rapidly changing from this ideal simplicity in process and product to the mechanical devices of modern industry, — which obscure and complicate the machinery of the simpler and more obvious domestic and industrial processes of an earlier day, — the psychological principle underlying this description of the activities of the child in relation to those in the home life of Froebel's day still holds good. The principle involved is indicated in these words, " *The child would like to represent what he sees.*" This is true yesterday, to-day, and forever.

This principle represents a problem increasingly difficult to apply with intelligence and wisdom because the surroundings of little children grow more and more complex and obscure in both meaning and technique as civilization advances. Now that the simple candle and lamp have given place to the hidden mysteries of gas and electricity, the broom of straw to the carpet sweeper and vacuum cleaner, the knocker to the electric bell, the open fire to the radiator, one can but wonder how this problem is to be solved in days to come. How may the teacher preserve a sane balance in making use of the tendency of the child to reproduce the complex forms of civilization by which he is surrounded without any understanding of their hidden processes, and the possible necessity of introducing into the school the simpler processes of an earlier, more primitive, and remote civilization to illumine them?

The subject-matter of the kindergarten program must represent the dual value of child and race experience. With the younger children a form of unity, omitting processes or involving exceedingly simple ones, seems to be all that is required; but with older children, in either kindergarten or in primary, the processes lying back of the product seem to have a fascination which should be met by experiment in securing them. Professor Sully says, regarding children's questions, "From the first, however, the 'why' and its congeners have reference to the causal idea, to something which has brought the new and strange into existence and made it what it is. In truth, this reference to origin, to bringing about or making, is exceedingly prominent in children's questionings. Nothing is more interesting to a child than the production of things. This inquiry into origin and mode of production starts with the amiable presupposition that all things have been hand-produced after the manner of household possessions. The world is a sort of big house where everything has been made by somebody, or at least fetched from somewhere."[1]

2. *The principles of democracy as applied to the relations between the supervising officer and the teachers under supervision.*

If we expect teachers to regard the individuality, personality, and initiative of children as one of the chief factors in the enrichment of the social groups in their care, it would seem that the same attitude should be manifested in the relations of the supervisor to the teachers themselves. The classroom teachers have a right to expect the supervising officers to manifest the same respect for the teachers' freedom, the same zeal in providing conditions which offer development,

[1] Sully, *Studies of Childhood*, pp. 78, 79.

health, and happiness for all under their supervision, that they expect these teachers to exemplify in their relations with the children in their care. If the classroom teachers have no part to play in the making of programs and courses of study, how can they be expected to encourage children to think with freedom, to offer their initiative, their solutions to group problems? How can they allow children freedom when a prescribed result is demanded of them? How can any *deep sense of responsibility* for either the course of study itself or for the method of carrying it out be developed if classroom teachers have no voice, no choice, no responsibility in the creation of the course of study? However, while there seems to be such difference of opinion regarding the use of *somewhat* uniform courses of study for the protection of the children, even with deep conviction one cannot afford to be dogmatic until experiments have been tried with both methods, and the results compared. Quotations for and against a somewhat uniform program or course of study will be given to illustrate the wide differences of opinion held by able authorities.

The most noted kindergarten authority in favor of using a *somewhat* uniform kindergarten program is Miss Blow. When Courthope Bowen, of England, criticized the kindergartens of other countries for using the identical experiences, plays, and games of Froebel's *Mother-Play* book, his criticism was answered in these words: "In opposition to this view, I hold that Froebel's games dramatize ideal experiences which all children may and ought to have, and that consequently they should be played by children of all nations, and all conditions of life."[1] An opposing point of view is well expressed by Mr. James L. Hughes in these words: "What kindergartners need is not a unified program, but specific outlines of the work that should be accomplished in the kindergarten, and directive laws for making programs."

That the same problem is under discussion in elementary supervision is confirmed by the following quotation: Dr. Frank McMurry says: "One of the leading duties of higher officers is to establish a feeling of great freedom among teachers. Superintendents, supervisors, and principals bear the same relation to classroom teachers, touching the development of the personality and individuality of the latter, as these bear to their pupils. A somewhat elaborate plan for the preservation of the teacher's freedom must be formed, corresponding to the elaborate theory that guides the teacher in her development of the individuality of pupils. In regard to the curriculum, the subject-matter should be outlined for large units of time, or by terms, rather than by days, or weeks, or even months. It should be outlined by large topics with comparatively little detail, accompanied with a very clear statement as to the degree of freedom the teacher is to enjoy in eliminating and supplementing, and choosing equivalents and substitutes. The higher officers of the school should show the freedom that is to be enjoyed in this field at least as forcibly as they show the restriction."

While the members of this group would unanimously agree that to leave programs to the unguided initiative

[1] Blow, *Symbolic Education*, p. 169.

and judgment of the individual kindergartner would be an equally serious error, they do believe that there is here again a *via media* which avoids the grave consequences resulting from holding extreme views in favor of either theory.

III

The third problem in the construction of a course of study demands a thorough consideration of the principles involved in the coördination or correlation of the impulses and materials entering into its organization.

The variety of impulses and materials involved in the construction of a modern course of study demands an organization which makes for economy of effort and the elimination of waste. In some way the experience and knowledge, won through the activity of one impulse, should be related to that achieved by another.

Correlation grew into a conscious problem in the elementary school when the course of study became enriched through the rapid introduction of a variety of subjects, such as nature study, manual training, art, etc. The relation of the three Rs was a simple matter compared with the complexity and overcrowding which resulted when the so-called "fads and frills of the new education" were introduced.

As each new subject which was admitted into the curriculum was evaluated according to its ability to meet the needs of the developing individual and social life, it was felt that simplicity could not be secured through the elimination of any of the subjects themselves. A proposal to eliminate any one of these invariably met with a storm of protest from enthusiasts.

If no one of the subjects could be withdrawn without individual and social loss, there was but one remaining method by which simplification could be accomplished and this was soon discovered. It was observed that when any two subjects were related in an organic way there was immediate gain in the reduction of friction and complexity. The more the studies reinforced each other, while still preserving their individuality, the greater the simplification of the whole. Many serious blunders were made in trying to treat the course of study as an organic unity.

If the course of study may be compared to an organism of which the different subjects are the organs, one might carry the comparison further by saying that correlation grew out of the necessity of treating the subjects from the physiological rather than from the anatomical point of view.

This organization or correlation of impulses with their corresponding materials has two aspects. First, each impulse must be seen as a developing activity, as a process beginning with crude results in its first efforts to respond to the stimulus of materials especially adapted to its development in early life. More and more we are coming to realize that a wide knowledge of materials themselves — materials in matured forms — is necessary to guide wisely and economically the first attempts of the child to express his impulses through the medium of materials.

These more ideal goals or higher levels of achievement serve as standards toward which impulses must be guided even in their crudest beginnings. An aim like this demands of the teacher not only a knowledge of beginnings, and standards or ideal ends, but that knowledge of the developing child which will make it possible for the teacher to know just what kind of material and what mode of expression represents the maximum efficiency of the child at any given stage of growth.

The second aspect of the problem of correlation requires a diligent search for a natural basis of unity to be found in and among the varied native impulses and the materials which they require for growth. In other words, there is not only a natural tendency for the impulses in their lower stages to reach upward or toward their more ideal ends, but for one impulse to reinforce or function in the achievements of another.

The problem, then, is to find some natural basis of unity in and among the native tendencies with their corresponding materials or subjects, which, while leaving ample room for the predisposition of one impulse to reinforce another, shall be so elastic and flexible as to provide the fullest and freest development possible to all the individual impulses entering into the organization. If the attainments of any one impulse are unduly sacrificed to any other, or to the whole, the true principle of correlation, or organization, is violated.

If the unripe fruits of creativity in the early life of the child are not cultivated in the light of the promise of full-grown possibilities in later life, there is necessarily wasted energy, dissipated effort, and arrested development. If, on the other hand, the creative impulses are not studied in the psychological relation (the physiological *versus* the anatomical), that is, in their normal interaction, we have as a result an isolated sequence of achievements.

Here we have a sequence in technique secured at the cost of the content or meaning which the experience won by one impulse expresses through the activities of another. For instance, the experience a child gains from an excursion to the garden, park, or blacksmith shop tends to pour itself out through the medium of language, drawing, or dramatization. In this expression the logical technique or grammar of expression is subordinated to the mode of telling. This principle seems to be violated in the use of the sequences in the technique and logical development of material exemplified in the so-called "schools of work" or "occupations" passed on by tradition from the days of Froebel. For example, no child would spontaneously isolate the technique of drawing from social meaning in any fashion such as the Froebelian school of drawing would seem to prescribe. The impulse to draw is used by the child, *in the main*, as a medium for telling the social experience gained in life. This is not peculiar to this mode of expression, but rather seems to be a principle controlling development through all modes of expression. While the child has a native love of arrangement, to separate content from form, as is frequently done in the use of the gifts and occupations of the kindergarten, seems to be a violation not only of Froebel's law of organic unity, but of the normal relation between idea and technique.

This separation of content and technique has arisen

through what appears to be a dualistic interpretation
of the place and function of the sciences and humanities in the development of the individual and of society.
While it is granted that, as certain subjects in the
curriculum ally themselves more easily and naturally
with one group of subjects than with others, this must
be respected, it must also be remembered that they are
one in their common *origin* and *aim*. In other words,
they arose in social life, and differentiated in obedience
to the law of division of labor in meeting varying aspects of social experiences. While all subjects must
be studied in the light of their common *social origin
and aim*, it is equally important that they be carefully
examined in the light of their *individual differences* in
meeting human need through obedience to the law of
division of labor. In this sense one fails to secure the
finest results from either the sciences or humanities if
these are treated as identical in their contribution to
social necessity. While it is accepted that all studies
are one in their social origin and aim, the contribution
to social life differs with each, if it is to meet the special
human need which gave rise to it. While we must avoid
the pitfalls which inevitably beset the pathway when
one pursues the dangerous method of arguing from
social origins and racial modes of thinking to those followed by the individual child of to-day in an altogether different social and natural situation, there still
seems to be an element of danger in the theory that
the subjects of the curriculum are "mutually repellent."
When Miss Blow draws our attention to the fact that
Herbart saw the subjects of the course of study fall
"into two main lines, the one for understanding, the

other for feeling and imagination," she says, "In this division he clearly recognizes an important difference between scientific and humane subjects. Defining this difference more closely, we become aware of a momentous contrast between physical nature and human nature, and realize that science and the humanities must differ in their aim and method, in the forms of mental activity to which they appeal, in the convictions to which they give birth, in the practical solutions of social problems which they suggest, and in the 'emotional undertones which they create.'" [1]

Any mode of correlation which fails to discover the peculiar contribution of each subject to social life will result in an attempt to force some or all of the different creative activities to achieve the same end. This would sacrifice the individuality and development of the varied impulses, and distort the products they are destined to achieve and contribute to the school and society. The kindergarten has made many mistakes in its efforts to correlate the subject-matter of the program. One group of kindergartners, treating the gifts and occupations as one aspect of science (science being interpreted as the medium through which man has gained control over physical nature), has isolated these from the songs, games, and stories which are related to a "pattern experience" selected from Froebel's *Mother-Play* Book.

It is difficult to say where the most serious blunders have been made, by conservatives or progressives in the kindergarten, or the elementary school. In the early attempts to correlate the gifts and occupations, the

[1] Blow, *Educational Issues in the Kindergarten*, p. 20.

form produced in the gifts was reproduced in the
occupation in a more "permanent" form, the only
difference in result being due to the characteristics of
the two materials. In this way the correlation was
made through the common medium of form. For example, if the tablets were used at the gift period,
parquetry repeated the geometric form for an occupation. Later in kindergarten history, kindergartners
endeavored to correct this external conception of correlation, and as usual the reform movement fell into an
error, as evident from another point of view as the one
it sought to rectify. In the attempt to reform a correlation based on geometrical relationships between the
gifts and occupations, the reformers sought correlation
through the repetition of the same "subject," "idea," or
"topic." This was made central and repeated through
as many channels of expression as possible. For example, if one made a house with the blocks, it must be
followed by a drawing, a parquetry or cardboard
house. This mistaken notion of correlation resulted in
a dreary round of activities in which the teacher
endeavored to repeat through morning talk, games,
stories, songs, gifts, and occupations, the same "idea,"
"subject," "topic," or "thought" for the day. Miss
Blow in the following passage ably criticizes this
method, which really used materials to *illustrate ideas
in the teacher's mind*, rather than as a means of expressing and clarifying the ideas in the child's mind, which
he is spontaneously endeavoring to bring to consciousness through play. "What becomes of that cardinal
principle of progressive pedagogy that 'in the beginning is the act,' if children may not act until their

minds have been filled by the kindergartner with a thought content?"[1]

A criticism which might be added is that this is not an expression of experience which the children have gained from their social environment and are attempting to clarify and make their own through play, but an illustration of a vicarious experience or idea in the mind of the teacher, or secured from literature, which is forced into as many modes of expression as possible. These offenses against the true principle of organization were common to both the kindergarten and the school at this period, though it must be acknowledged that the elementary school has solved the problem more successfully than the kindergarten has.

One cause of the difficulty grew out of an inability to trace the materials back to a *past* common origin in social necessity, and to their *present* need in the social life of the child and adult society. The subjects were viewed as separate entities, and instead of studying the actual relations existing between them in past and present civilization and that of the social experience of the child of to-day, they were placed in artificial connections and "tied together" by some ingenious, unnatural device discovered by the teacher. This artificial unity often made use of the most extraneous, far-fetched, and even ludicrous relationships. As soon as we see the instincts of the child and the race *in* subject-matter, viewing it as the record of these at work upon an environment natural and social, these mistakes disappear.

The trend of thought in modern elementary educa-

[1] Blow, *Educational Issues in the Kindergarten*, p. 8.

tion is to treat the different studies and materials of the course of study as parts of an original unity to be found in the social life in which they not only came into existence, but in which they came to differentiate because of some function which they fulfilled in society.

This earlier problem of correlation falls into the background, or rather seems to take care of itself, when the unity of the curriculum is found in the unity of human experience, or the unity of social life which the curriculum represents. As Dr. Dewey expresses it, "Each study stands for one differentiated phase of social life, and the problem of correlation is to make studies act and react upon each other in the same way in school that the processes for which they stand do in actual life. . . . Conceive it [the curriculum] as imbedded in social life — taken out of its social setting for the sake of going back into it — by making life richer, more sympathetic, and more comprehensive." Thus, one might add, the problem seems largely reversed by modern educational thought. The old problem of correlation — how can we unify or correlate studies which originally exist as separate entities — has given place to the new problem — how do the separate studies differentiate out of an original unity in social life, and how may we preserve, in the curriculum and the school, both the mode of *differentiation and the unification* found in the social life which they represent?

The mistakes made by the kindergarten, in treating the impulses and materials as unrelated both to each other and to the social life out of which they have emerged, resulted in isolated, meaningless sequences of form, without social content or function — each step bearing a relation in *form* and *process*, or technique, to that which preceded and that which followed, but holding no relationship to the achievements and interpretations of the other impulses, or to the function of each in social life; while in the equally unfortunate mistake made in attempting to find the relation between the impulses themselves and their function in achieving and interpreting human experience, we have such evidences of correlation carried to the extreme, as is so well criticized by Miss Blow in her chapter on the "Concentric Program." [1]

While it is acknowledged, however, that the "Concentric Program" had faults as serious as the isolation of subject-matter which it made an attempt to remedy, it was a most effective stepping-stone in bringing meaning and thought into the technique and instrumentalities of the kindergarten and the primary school.

If the kindergarten program may be compared to an organism where the life of the whole depends upon the contribution of each member and the interaction between the individual members, we have a complex organization which would make it impossible to withdraw the contribution of any one of the parts without serious loss to all the others and the organism as a whole. When this principle of organization is applied to the kindergarten, it would seem to indicate that all the constituent impulses, with their corresponding materials which enter into its organization, should in turn receive their emphasis and their fullest development, being at the same time enriched and reinforced by experience gained through all of the others. The necessity for

[1] Blow, *Educational Issues in the Kindergarten.*

continuity — for increasing complexity in content, technique, and form — is the sequence which we should strive to preserve.

All early attempts to secure a steady progress in technique, whether in reading, writing, mathematics, manual training, gifts, or occupations, substituted the logical for the psychological. Professor Leonard Wahlstrom thus describes the mistake made when introducing manual training into the schools: "When manual training first found a place in the school, it was the physical side which predominated, in definite courses of models and exercises." W. A. Baldwin classifies the use of materials and manual training in the schools under three types. The first he describes as, "schools where an elaborate, well-defined course of study is marked out in a perfectly logical fashion with its regular set objects to be made. The place of each piece of work in such a course of study is determined by its relation to what follows, so that the difficulties of technique may be gradually approached. The followers of Froebel have gotten manual training of this type. To my mind nothing can be further from the real spirit of Froebel."

Is not that progress or continuity, in both appreciation and control, — for which sequence in its best sense stands, — equally important in the use of songs, games, and stories as in the gifts and occupations? While the necessity for sequence or progress in these materials is much less apparent, is it any the less important, because more difficult to discover and realize? It is readily conceded that it is far easier to correlate songs, stories, and games without any *apparent* sacrifice in the progress and development of each, to the others, and

to the whole; but would not a deeper insight into the
problem of true organization or correlation reveal the
same, though more subtle and hidden necessity for
sequence or continuity of development in technique
in these? The time has passed when we can hope to
have slovenly thinking solve so delicate a problem.

Thoughtful kindergartners must discriminate between the external correlation of impulses and materials based upon ingenious relations revolving around
some center arbitrarily selected by the teacher, and the
true unity existing among the impulses and their corresponding materials *as found in child nature and in
life*. In such an organization of materials as the latter,
the unity is true to life because each impulse is contributing to the whole through preserving its own individuality and development. These are related in a
larger unity, which is made up of a variety of impulses
and materials, in which no one attempts to repeat the
achievements of the other, but accomplishes for the
whole what no other could contribute. Thus nature
work may naturally reinforce or function in the art-
work or occupations, while contributing something
essentially different; or, the occupation may contribute to the game or the pageant in which it finds its
motive or function; for example, kites for experiment
with the wind in nature study, flags for marching, May
baskets for the celebration of May Day, etc.

We have in all courses of study an attempt to stimulate some form of related thinking, though the type
of correlation varies according to the theory of the
thinker who plans it. In a study of this problem, made
by Dr. Judd, he points out two typical methods. He

describes at length the logical relationships of facts and
principles as they exist within the subject itself, and
contrasts with these the examples found in the applications of these in social life. Both, he claims, are the
results of related thinking and correlation, though
adherents of the latter method, he tells us, fail to see it
as such. "The interesting fact about many discussions
of correlation is that the obvious lines of correlation
just described are ignored. To many thinkers correlation of number facts means the taking of these facts
out of their arithmetical connection and the placing of
them in some other connection. Thus the fraction $\frac{1}{2}$ is
part of a number scheme. It may be also a part of a
cooking lesson, as when one wishes to divide a cupful
or a quart into equal parts. Many thinkers would
regard it as a true example of correlation to bring the
fraction $\frac{1}{2}$ into the cooking lesson, but would fail to
recognize that there is just as much correlation in
relating $\frac{1}{2}$ to $\frac{1}{4}$ or $\frac{1}{8}$. . . . For the purpose of defining
the two types of connection which have been under
discussion in the foregoing examples, let us speak of
longitudinal correlations and transverse correlations.
The following diagram will illustrate what is meant by
the terms longitudinal and transverse.

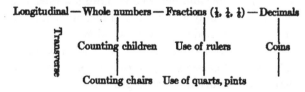

With the distinction between longitudinal correlations
and transverse correlations clearly in mind, it will

readily be seen that the longitudinal connections are much more systematic and orderly while the transverse connections are illustrative and concrete." [1]

While the kindergartners coöperating in this report recognize the value of both modes of correlation, we would emphasize our faith in the fact that with the younger children we believe that the social associations predominate. The child lives in an environment in which the relations are largely social. He sees and feels personally regarding these facts, and he comes to see them abstractly and logically after he has become somewhat familiar with them in their social connections.

The straight and narrow path which excludes neither of these modes of relating experience, while throwing the emphasis upon that which offers the best key to child thought, is difficult, indeed, to find. Serious consequences follow the total exclusion of either. For example, if programs and courses of study are based upon the longitudinal type of correlation exclusively, we have as a result an accumulation of knowledge based upon more or less abstract qualities and logical relations within the subject itself, plus a technique acquired by a method absolutely contrary to the more normal process which life offers for the acquisition of these. Here the child has secured both knowledge and technique, not only without social meaning, but if the experiments in modern psychology along the line of the doctrine of "formal discipline" be at all trustworthy, we have slight basis for any faith in his ability to apply these in the solution of social problems.

[1] Judd, "Types of Correlation," *Elementary School Teacher*, September, 1911.

On the other hand, if the transverse mode of correlation is used at the cost of the longitudinal, some of the following errors seem inevitable. In the first place, either a poor selection of materials may be presented, in songs, games, stories, et cetera, chosen because they illustrate or correlate with the thought or topic chosen for the day; or, if good materials are selected, their excuse for use is found in some'far-fetched, extraneous, or ridiculous relation to the subject, which is invented by the ingenious teacher because of her blindness to the true relations existing in human experience.

Another consequence of the exclusive use of transverse connections is found in the tendency to ignore the problem of how to secure a gradual growth in expression, or a steady progress in mastery of technique. The so-called "sequences" in all of the earlier uses of the gifts and occupations were efforts to solve this problem of growth in skill. Unfortunate as these isolated, meaningless exercises in skill were, they were no more unfortunate than some of the efforts made by the reformers' who frequently ignored the problem altogether. In these attempts at reform the problems presented were, in the majority of cases, suggested by some thought associated with the "topic" for the day. The technique or control of materials involved in solving the problem often presented a difficulty too arduous and complex for mastery to-day, or too easily mastered to-morrow to call forth the child's best effort.

In the mistakes made by both types of correlation, the free, spontaneous expression of the child may be inhibited. Both impose adult modes of thinking upon him. In one case it is the imposition of an abstract logical technique which kills the spontaneous expression; in the other, it is the imposition of an idea or subject which the teacher has forced upon the child through some artificial mode of expression.

The golden mean, the *via media*, which seeks to find the degree to which both of these types of thinking are characteristic of the child mind, is not only the test of a good course of study, but of the highest of all arts — the art of teaching.

In conclusion, it may be said that neither transverse nor longitudinal connections, neither isolation nor unification, should serve as a *single* aim in the construction of a program or course of study, but rather both differentiation and unification when seen as two stages in the one process of development through which the mind passes, — first, in an attempt to break up the naïve and unconscious unity in which the child finds the materials of social life; and second, the desire to consciously rebuild or reconstruct the original unity in which the constituent materials of the course of study exist in social experience.

Just as the mind plies between the processes of analysis and synthesis, deduction and induction, so it finds the necessity for both differentiation and unification in its efforts to define and control human experience.

The kindergarten program will grow in value as our vision of life and our insight into the meaning of education deepen and broaden. It will be altered from year to year by reflection upon what we have attempted, and what we have accomplished. Out of this will come a new vision, a higher standard which will enable us to reconstruct and create newer and more ideal courses of study for the children of the future.

If the school, the college, and the university are still pursuing their quest for more ideal curricula from year to year, the kindergarten, too, must endeavor to "better its best" if it is to survive and to contribute its quota to the whole.

PART II

ILLUSTRATIONS IN PRACTICE

In this section an attempt will be made to illuminate the preceding section on theory with a non-technical statement of the practice of which it is an application.

In the preceding section three fundamental problems are given as of prime importance in the planning of a kindergarten program, or a course of study. I. The selection of the native tendencies of childhood which make for the development of the individual and the advancement of civilization. II. The selection of the best subject-matter or materials for the creative impulses to act upon and react toward. III. The organization, arrangement, or correlation of subject-matter or materials in such a unity as makes for economy and simplicity, while leaving ample opportunity for the fullest development and richest achievements of all the impulses entering into the organization.

As the last problem was more fully illustrated than were the first and second, an attempt will be made to present some of the most evident native tendencies or impulses which should be selected in the organization of a program or course of study, together with the subject-matter or materials which the kindergarten, the school, and social life offer for their development.

This is not intended to serve as an exhaustive list of

instincts, social needs, and materials, but rather as a
suggestive one which may stimulate study and criticism.

Native tendencies, impulses or social need of children to be met in planning a course of study.	Materials or subject-matter, provided by the kindergarten, the school, and society to meet these.
To make, construct, or control.	Gifts, occupations, manual training, and industry.
To nurture, protect, and control.	Care of plants, animals, dolls, younger children, and room.
To investigate, explore, and find out. (This also a motive and method which enters into the exercise of all impulses.)	Nature study, science, excursion, commerce, and industry.
To tell or communicate.	Conversation, gesture, dramatization, song, writing.
To adorn, decorate, arrange, or beautify.	Art, design, dance.
To transmit, record, interpret, and make permanent valuable experiences.	Literature, song, art, history.
To coöperate and compete with other selves.	Dramatic games and dances, games of skill, work, festivals and ceremonials.
To measure, calculate, compute, and make accurate.	Mathematics, standards of weight, measurement, counting, etc.
To wonder, aspire, worship, or commune.	Religion or worship.
To coöperate, formulate, and preserve social experience.	Laws and institutions.

While all these are but different aspects of self-
activity, creating its own ways and means of satisfying human need, those which seem to be central are

the relation of man to nature, to his fellow man, and
to God. These are the three great elemental experiences of man — the central factors in human life —
all the so-called subjects in the course of study or
program, being ways and means by which these are
investigated, elucidated, computed, communicated,
interpreted, recorded, regulated, controlled, and preserved. If this is accepted, it follows that the function
of each subject in the program or curriculum *must* be
studied in the light of its individual or peculiar contribution to human experience through some one of these
channels.

The relation of man to man is the one in which the
child is first interested — the one which may most
easily be brought to his consciousness. As civilization
advances, the child's adaptations to nature are more
and more made for him by adult society. It is adult
society which looks in advance of the actual need for
food, clothing, shelter, fuel, etcetera, and provides these
for its helpless, immature members. While it is believed that the child is in close relation to God from
the first, he is unconscious of this, and gradually
grows into a realization of the unseen tie through the
more tangible relation with man and nature.

NATURE STUDY

The child makes many, if not most, of his adaptations to humanity for himself, and learns in the first
few months of his baby existence whether he is to control or to be controlled by adult society. He adapts
himself accordingly. Nature is in the *background* of
his consciousness, and it soon becomes a setting for

human activity which is for him the matter of supreme moment. To primitive man it was the source of supply for food, clothing, fuel, shelter, tools, and weapons, but to win these he early learned that in order to gain control over nature he must first adapt himself to nature. It aroused curiosity and provoked the investigation and research of science, commerce, and industry; it inspired the wonder, awe, aspiration, and reverence of religion; it stimulated the fancy, and the imagination of literature, and the love of beauty in art. But the child of to-day has few opportunities to adapt himself to nature, as civilization steps in and makes this adaptation for him.

As the race came to nature consciousness through first-hand contact with nature in its relation to human needs, whether domestic, industrial, æsthetic, or religious, so the child must come to consciousness of needs in his life which nature alone can supply.

Nature-subjects must be selected in relation to human needs, through direct contact with it, through the method of experiment. Little children need nature experience and nature wonder and *nature play* as a basis for later *nature study*, and *nature work*.

If this principle is applied in practice, it rules out of the program and course of study much of the unrelated nature work now being used in the kindergarten and primary school. The central interest in child life is not what nature is doing, but what man is doing.

The sun, moon, and stars, the wind, rain, and snow are very personal matters to the young child, and this personal relation should be respected and utilized as the basis for the more impersonal approach to science pure and simple in later education. If the kindergartner would see to it that children are given every opportunity possible to come into contact with natural objects and forces indoors, in garden-work, and excursions, and through nature-play or experiment, nature study and nature-work would follow more naturally in the grades.

Those aspects of nature which, while stirring the child's imagination, are yet beyond his ability to approach through the experimental method, should be left to the realm of wonder and fancy. Wonder and fancy may be as important as the method of experiment in the beginnings of nature experiences.

LITERATURE

As literature arose in the desire to interpret, communicate, and record some actual or fanciful experience which was considered too important for the race to lose, it would seem that with little children it must interpret some experience of their own, or furnish some desirable experience calculated to supplement group life in an ideal way.

"Literature is born when it becomes possible for men to see that their experiences have a value which goes beyond their momentary occurrence, and the momentary practical fruits resulting from them. It is the expression of man's consciousness of the more permanent and enduring values of his experience. Literature is to be regarded as a means of interpreting one's own experience through the reflection back into it of the best expressions of such experience proceeding from others, but it is not to be treated as a substitute for this experience." If this statement of the origin and function of literature is accepted, the story should on the whole follow and interpret the experience rather than precede and foreshadow it.

While this principle seems to limit the use of literature, it is large enough to include some realistic stories, some wonder and fairy tales, some poems and rhymes; but it would tend to reduce the multiplicity of stories told in the kindergarten and primary school, because of their supposed value in stirring the imagination.

We would suggest fewer stories, more closely related to, and interpretative of, child life and child problems, well told, and so frequently told that the child comes to possess them, not only in the content but in the literary form.

GAMES

Games offer the very best opportunities for social coöperation and wholesome social competition.

The two main divisions into which they seem naturally to fall are the games of skill, and dramatic games, including the simple and ideal forms of the folk-game and the folk-dance.

The games of skill include such spontaneous activities as running, jumping, skipping, leaping, throwing, and tossing, and often require some tool or toy as the means of building up technique; for example, balls, rings, tops, marbles, ropes, etcetera. Such games are especially valuable from the standpoint of health, physical vigor, and dexterity.

The dramatic games in the main rehearse or portray human activities. They interpret human relationships and culminate in the drama. There are some exceptions to this, such as the spontaneous dramatizations of birds, horses, and engines.

The formulated games should be evolved from, and organized out of, the spontaneous expressions of human activities in somewhat unorganized play, and, as far as possible, should be preceded by the actual experience of which they are dramatizations. Again we would prescribe fewer and simpler games, played·more frequently, and with increasing control over the technique involved, rather than the multiplicity now in use in many kindergartens.

MUSIC AND SONGS

There is an increasing demand for shorter and simpler songs for the kindergarten. A child's song should be a musical embodiment of a desirable mood, which poetically interprets and colors the child's view of some ideal experience. In instrumental music, we would urge a higher standard of selection, greater simplicity, and a reduction of the amount.

There is undoubtedly much over-stimulation of children in the kindergartens through the almost incessant use of song and piano to accompany every activity. When this stimulation is withdrawn, as it necessarily will be when the child enters the primary school, he must suffer as one inevitably does when suddenly deprived of a stimulus which has been used to excess.

We would again suggest simpler songs, fewer, shorter, better selected, and better sung, as the foundation for later musical education. The song is another mode of interpreting experience, and should, on the whole, follow or accompany the experience, helping

the child to a new and more ideal vision of that which
he has experienced in life. The function of art here as
elsewhere might be expressed in the words of Browning, —

> "We're made so that we love
> First when we see them painted
> Things we have passed perhaps a hundred times
> Nor cared to see."

GIFTS AND OCCUPATIONS

These are looked upon as selected educative materials with which the children are to play and work. They
have great social as well as scientific and mathematical
values, and are to be used not merely as a means of
gaining a conquest over materials through a knowledge
of their qualities and relations, but as a means of
stimulating social comparison and social coöperation
in work and play. They are closely related to human
experience, and, from our point of view, are no more
to be isolated from this than the songs, games, or
stories. Just as industry and art grew out of social
experience and were ways and means of satisfying
human needs, so the gifts and occupations to which
they correspond are to be kept in close relation to the
social needs of which children are or may become
conscious.

While we believe that on the whole Froebel selected
wisely and well, we do not stand for any closed circle
of materials such as that represented by the Froebelian
gifts and occupations alone.

While we agree in the main with Miss Blow in her
denunciation of the so-called "Concentric Program,"
we cannot accept this statement: —

"Wherever traditional school aims and concentric methods have prevailed, it has been found necessary to eliminate many of Froebel's gifts and occupations, exclude numbers of his games, and discard some of his most characteristic types of exercises. The result of such eliminations, exclusions, and rejections is that the kindergarten loses its distinctive merit and the Froebelian instrumentalities cease to be an organic whole through the active use of whose related elements the child organizes his own thought, feeling, and will."[1] Nor do we believe the exact mathematical relations in these materials, as a whole, of such importance that the elimination of one or more would rob the child of the value of the whole, because the "charmed circle" of relationships was broken.

A combination of wisely selected materials from any worthy source, which meets the different needs of the child at this stage of his development, would be approved by this group of kindergartners. For example, some of the Montessori materials seem admirably adapted to the needs of the youngest children. When the child is at that stage of development where manipulation of materials is more important than adaptation of materials to embody and clarify the meanings found in social life, the larger Montessori materials might prove more developing than some of the Froebelian gifts. The fact that their possibilities are so limited — that with many of them there is only one thing to be done — makes them fascinating to children of pre-kindergarten age and to the very youngest children in the kindergarten. The one problem set is a very

[1] Blow, *Educational Issues in the Kindergarten*, p. 9.

concrete one, and the child can discover his own error without the aid of the teacher; but as children develop into the ideational stage, where materials are subordinated to social meanings and uses, they need the freer and more imaginative materials provided by Froebel, with their many possibilities and endless variations. It would be an addition to every kindergarten to be equipped with the stair, swing, and rope ladder suggested by Dr. Montessori. The methods she suggests for providing freedom in selection of materials, and greater opportunity for the individuality of children to manifest itself, is worthy of our most serious study. There has undoubtedly been too great emphasis placed upon uniform results in the kindergarten, and the kindergarten has an opportunity to learn the danger lurking in uniformity from the study of this Montessori method.

A significant experiment would be to select the best material from both Montessori and Froebel, in a combination which would include the larger and more simple though limited materials of Montessori for the younger children, with the freer, more imaginative, and more artistic materials of Froebel for the older ones.

We value the mathematical basis of Froebel's materials as a substratum of experience leaving a sediment of great value for later consciousness; but we would make little effort to bring this to the consciousness of the child except in so far as he spontaneously reaches out for it, or as it furthers his construction, or fills some function in his work and play. As mathematical values are consciously or unconsciously embodied in all good building materials and constructions, so the child's play materials and constructions must, if true to the requirements of life, have these inherent values; but he must come to consciousness of these through their organic relation to function, or in so far as the recognition of this relation enables him to produce the form desired. The correct geometric terms may be used as naturally as the name of other familiar objects and of people, and will in time be used by the children.

Our emphasis would be placed on the building gifts and such occupations as drawing, painting, modeling, crayoning, cutting and folding, weaving with coarse and durable materials, and some sewing, if sufficiently large and creative. In fact, all those gifts and occupations which point to the typical and valuable arts and industries would be selected and emphasized.

We believe that the technique of control should be kept in close relationship to the thought, idea, or experience being realized through the materials. Due attention should be given to continuity or the gradual development of skill involved in the problems met in play and work; but the logic of the materials, or the grammar of technique and control (the old idea of sequence), should not be isolated from the content and meaning involved in the social experience being realized by the children in their constructions. Through the so-called life form the child is trying to bring to consciousness social problems and meanings, and for this reason our emphasis would fall on these, though not to the exclusion of the beauty forms. Adequate opportunity must be left for the child's native interest in decoration, arrangement, and symmetry, to which the beauty forms are supposed to correspond. These, however, would be kept in close relation to life forms, being used *in the main* to decorate objects of social service, or as units of decoration themselves embodying social meaning or content. We would endeavor to preserve the close relation between art and social life so characteristic of primitive and child art.

CONVERSATION

As conversation is such a valuable medium of expression, we deplore the tendency of kindergartens to become so large that the interchange between child and children, and children and teachers, characteristic of real conversation, is becoming more and more impossible.

As conversation is not only a medium of expression for ideas, but a most important factor in the process of their formation, therefore it is most unfortunate for the development of children that the kindergartens in our public schools tend to offer decreasing opportunities for conversation of this intimate character. As children at the kindergarten period are "talkers" rather than listeners, and as conversation is a necessity in the formulation of thought through linguistic activity, we urge young kindergartners to practice the art of developing thought through this mode for the interchange of ideas and experience.

We also urge school boards to reduce the number of children in the kindergartens, so that conversation, which corresponds to the ideal form of recitation in higher grades, may be made possible.

CULTURE AND INDUSTRY

We would plead for a deeper study of the cultural values in domestic and industrial activities. In the trade, vocational, technical, and industrial education, so necessary in a democratic nation where large proportions of the citizens must participate in trade and manufacture, children need to be equipped not only with technical skill, but with a scientific, æsthetic, and social vision of the part they are to contribute through these avenues to social welfare. For this reason in the trade and industrial education of the higher grades we would urge the accompanying studies of science and art. While working toward industrial ends, the method of experiment must be preserved, together with the spirit of art and play, which make for the freedom of the self and that joy in doing which alone will prevent the introduction of the evils of child labor into the school.

The child must participate in the plan, *must* be an inventor as well as one who executes plans made by others. We must avoid the unfortunate division now existing in industry which regards those who plan, who create and invent, as necessarily separated in kind and grade from the "hands" who execute only. In a democracy we must come more and more to Browning's view, "All service ranks the same with God."

We would make a plea for the ideal interpretation of the domestic and industrial activities in conversation or in the songs, games, and materials in the kindergarten. Froebel has set the example in his little play "The Target," and in his high appreciation of work and art.

As the health of the child is of supreme importance at the kindergarten period, every precaution should be taken not only to prevent disease, but to contribute to the growth and general development of this period.

The responsibility of educating the child at the kindergarten age is borne in upon us when we have words of such serious import as these from one of the great hygiene experts of our day: Dr. Burnham says, "The young child is specially liable to infection. Nothing offers great resistance, neither the epithelial barriers nor the blood nor the tissues; hence we should expect that germ diseases would be especially prevalent and especially fatal in the early years. This is precisely what happens. To quote a few of the old statistics; in Munich, between the years 1888 and 1895, 28,988 cases of measles occurred, and of these 1077 proved fatal. Of cases that occurred in the first year of life, in round numbers 21 per cent proved fatal; of those between the years two to five, 5 per cent, and of those between the years six and ten, 0.4 per cent. That is, if an epidemic of measles occurs in the kindergarten the chances are that four or five children in a *hundred* cases will die. If you can postpone the epidemic until the age of the primary school, the chances are that only four out of a *thousand* cases will die."[1]

While children of all grades have a right to the best hygienic conditions possible to provide, according to

[1] Burnham "Hygiene of the Kindergarten," *Proceedings of the N. E. A.*, 1904.

this authority we are under peculiar obligation to procure the best for the child at the kindergarten and primary period. Unclean floors with their dust, providing a deadly means of distributing germs, affect the child most disastrously at this age, not only because at this period of his development he comes into more frequent contact with the floor, but because his low stature forces him to live in and breathe this dust-laden atmosphere. Provided the floor is clean and free from drafts, the child doubles the exercise he ordinarily secures by working at the table, if he can do his work on the floor. However, the ordinary cleaning of the average kindergarten makes such use of the floor a positive menace to the child's health.

The child's legitimate demands for opportunities to run, jump, climb, throw, and play vigorously, due to the development of the fundamental muscles, would seem to be sufficient argument for school boards to provide large rooms in order to give the proper amount of exercise and air.

We would urge right seating of the kindergarten children with regard to light, height of table and chairs; separate drinking cups, tissue paper towels, and sanitary toilet arrangements. The importance of frequent medical inspection cannot be too strongly emphasized, especially during periods of contagion, when so much is at issue.

We would make a plea for the large materials. The fact that "children love little blocks" and materials sufficiently small to throw the strain upon the small muscles of eye and hand is no excuse, when such an expert as Dr. Judd gives us this warning: "One of the most noticeable facts about the child's diffuse movements is the fact that these movements are excessive, especially the movement of the finer muscles. Somewhere or other the false notion has entered into our pedagogy that the child's fine muscles do not develop until later than the large muscles. How can we believe such a false statement when we see a young infant clutching with its little fingers and exhibiting in this grip one of its strongest movements? How can one believe this dogma when he sees the boys and girls in the first grade doing all the work that they do with the fine muscles — literally overdoing this work in a very noticeable degree? The fact is, the finer muscles are in full operation very early in life. Indeed, they are the muscles which in diffuse movements are most apt to be called into action. It requires a less powerful excitation from the nervous centers to set the fine muscles into action. They contract at the slightest stimulation. These are the muscles which always grow tense first in later life when the brain becomes over-excited. In emotional excitement, for example, it is the fine muscles of the face and hand that are first affected. This limitation in nature's provision for free movement *is the first point at which the teacher's rational mode of developing the child must come in to supplement nature's provisions. The teacher should see to it that if diffusion tends to emphasize the small muscles, teaching should emphasize in due measure the large muscles. It is well to devise some other method of supplementing nature and calling the large muscles into play.* Large arm exercises are the most available devices for attaining this end."[1] One of the best qualities of the Montessori material is that some of them are large. Dr. Burnham, in describing the ideal kindergarten of the future says, "The kindergarten material is all large; fine work is not done."

In so far as is possible the use of playgrounds, parks, and yards should be encouraged for a part of each day's work, or for the whole of it during certain periods of the year. Garden-work, so strongly emphasized by Froebel, has often been overlooked by teachers who have ample opportunities for securing it.

Open-air schools, and frequent excursions in climates which make these possible and advisable should be fostered and supported.

More attention should be given to the study of the fatigue and over-stimulation heightened by an unwise arrangement and alternation of periods of activity and rest in the time schedule. Children are frequently permitted to select one exciting game after another, because there is a tradition to the effect that the children must *always* choose their own games.

METHOD OF CONDUCTING TRAINING CLASSES

At this period when there is such diversity of opinion regarding the principles and methods underlying infant education in Germany, Switzerland, England, France, Italy, and America, it would seem advisable to consider the question of conducting our training classes on the basis of inquiry and investigation. It must be conceded that it is an open question as to how far the young women in our normal classes shall be

[1] Judd, *Genetic Psychology*, pp. 222–225. (Italics not the author's.)

trained to consider the differing viewpoints which confront them as practical problems when they leave the training classes.

It seems advisable to members of this group to present some of these opposing views in the training school, leaving the student free to think for herself and come to some conclusions which possibly may not agree in detail with those of her training teacher.

The method of authority has been used to such an extent in the past that to agree with Froebel and with the teachings of one's *Alma Mater* have been the test of loyalty. As a result, in many cases students go out from training classes utterly unprepared for the decided differences of opinion which they are more than likely to meet; or, if they are prepared in advance for this, it not unfrequently happens that they have been so prejudiced against opposing views, that their minds are closed to any opportunity to learn from a co-worker or supervisor who presents a new, or conflicting conception.

The practical situation with which students are confronted immediately upon graduation would seem to warrant an attempt to develop in students while undergoing training an attitude of respect toward difference of opinion, which would help them to meet gracefully and graciously a supervisor or co-worker holding a different point of view.

The morality of inquiry, the wider horizon made possible by intellectual hospitality, would seem to leave ample scope for grounding students in what the training teacher considers fundamental, while guaranteeing a freedom from prejudice. This method gives principles by which the young kindergartner may test any new ideas presented. It frees her from the test of tradition and mere personal opinion, and leads to true freedom and progress.

Thus the pathway of the supervisor, the supervised, and the co-worker would be made not only easier, but happier, and the opportunities for growth and service would be greatly enhanced.

> PATTY SMITH HILL, *Chairman*.
> CAROLINE T. HAVEN.[1]
> MARY BOOMER PAGE.
> JENNIE B. MERRILL.
> ALICE H. PUTNAM.
> NINA VANDERWALKER.

[1] Deceased.

THIRD REPORT

ELIZABETH HARRISON

I. TYPE OF PROGRAM PREFERRED

"THE details of the program should be based on the best that civilization of the past and present have to bestow."

This would include the activities which have aided in the development of the spiritual life of man; such as his establishment of the institutions of the family, society, and church; his mastery over the material world which has provided him with food, clothing, and shelter; his discovery of the laws of nature and their uniformity of processes which have developed science; and his creation of the world of art which has enabled him to express his highest nature in forms of beauty as seen in sculpture, architecture, and paintings; in dancing, music, and poetry. This is the "reservoir" from which the kindergartner should draw her supplies.

II. PRINCIPLES UNDERLYING PROGRAM-MAKING

(a) Man, being a child of God, has an infinite nature. We aim in education for the realization of this nature.

(b) Comprehending man's finite limitations we recognize that his endowment must be "self-creation," that only through progressive self-expression can he come to a realization of himself.

Therefore, the important part of program-making is the recognition of this by the teacher and the making of opportunities for the child in self-expression, or creative work.

(c) The discovery of the law of human development has been the endeavor of all thoughtful men, in all ages, and in every advancing stage of human activity it has come nearer being understood and made use of.

The application of this law to education was first made distinctly and definitely to be applied by Froebel, as is shown by his creation of the kindergarten gifts, occupations, and games, all of which were planned by him to be used according to this law.

His explanation of the same is seen in his pedagogical writings. He has, also, shown in the *Education of Man*, how this same law of development may be applied to all stages of education. This law, in its essence or immediate thought-perception, is shown as "The Law of Opposites and their Connection." In its pedagogical or sense-perceived process it is known as "Evolution or Sequence." Both of these processes, the mediate and the mediated, should be given to the child as the law by which he is to use his material, for the reason that through them is first foreshadowed the "Unity that Lives and Reigns in All Things," a gradual comprehension of which is the aim of the kindergarten.

We believe in the kindergarten not alone as it was first evolved and planned by Frederich Froebel, but *as it has since developed*, and *as it promises to develop*, whenever the change or expansion is in conformity with this law of development and not merely capricious change or experimental work.

III. PROCESS OF PROGRAM-MAKING

WITH REFERENCE, FIRST, TO THE CHILD

1. Kind of Child.
- a. Nationality.
- b. Class.
- c. Age.
- d. Approximation to Normal.
- e. Accidental Handicap.
- f. Environment.
- g. Degree of Development both Material and Social.

All of these considerations will necessarily have to modify the program made.

2. The materials must be simple enough for the child to master, yet be difficult enough to demand an effort on his part. They must also have increasing possibilities.

3. There should be sufficient material for each child to use individually, and also in coöperation with a group of children, but no waste of materials.

4. Each kind of material presented to the child should represent a whole in itself, yet be related to a larger whole.

5. All exercises must take the form of play, yet contain that which will stimulate educative effort on the part of the child.

6. The child's work must be an expression of his own, yet he is best led to free self-expression through (1) experimental or "undirected" use of the material; and (2) through guided or "directed" use of it in order that he may use it in the best way and learn both its

limit and its possibilities; then (3) his creative or
"self-directed" use of it.

7. Incidental materials may be used, but should
always be subordinated to the higher aim so as not to
interrupt the educational aim of the program.

8. Each child must be regarded in relation to the
length of the periods of work and of play, and, while
not allowed too great length to a period, he should
have sufficient time given to him for the comprehension and completion of his task. Frequent repetition
of one activity should be given, and repetition of one
material, enough to insure a mastery of materials and
an understanding of the principles or process involved.

WITH REFERENCE, SECOND, TO THE TEACHER

The teacher should know the ideals of human institutions, as upon them is based all ethical advancement
of the human race.

She should have gained the insight given in Froebel's
Mother Play book, in order that she may understand
Froebel's educational aim.

She should know why Froebel altered the folk-
games when he made the kindergarten games.

She should understand the typical process and form
of the organization of the work which Froebel has
given to the child in the gift and occupation, in order
that she may use new materials in the same way.

She should comprehend that what she brings to the
child is important, as this awakens and guides his
power so that he will relate himself aright to humanity
and to nature.

She should realize that the material selected by

Froebel and the use of the same frees the child in such a way that he may use his creative power as it is based on the recorded development of the race, not on capricious choice.

She should learn to distinguish between the use of the material which helps and that which hinders the child in the mastery of nature and self-expression.

She should have sufficient understanding of the various forms of art to appreciate what is art in the child's work, and what part it plays in his development.

She should have such a knowledge of literature as will enable her to distinguish between temporary and permanent values of the same in her use of it in the kindergarten, in stories, poems, and songs.

She should be interested in the general welfare of the educational institution with which the kindergarten is connected and respect its laws.

She should be able to see the child's standpoint.

She should understand the nature of play and its purpose in kindergarten, and should know how to play.

She should have a time schedule for regular work, in order that time may be well used and changes be rightly calculated, but this time schedule should not be inflexible if the needs of her children demand a change or variation.

ELIZABETH HARRISON.
MARIA KRAUS-BOELTÉ.[1]
LUCY WHEELOCK.

[1] I endorse Miss Harrison's report as truly Froebelian and progressive, particularly in what is said of the schedule, to which I especially agree.

𝕮𝖍𝖊 𝕽𝖎𝖛𝖊𝖗𝖘𝖎𝖉𝖊 𝕻𝖗𝖊𝖘𝖘
CAMBRIDGE · MASSACHUSETTS
U . S . A

The HOUGHTON MIFFLIN PROFESSIONAL LIBRARY

For Teachers and Students of Education

THEORY AND PRINCIPLES OF EDUCATION

AMERICAN EDUCATION
By ANDREW S. DRAPER, Commissioner of Education of the State of New York. With an Introduction by NICHOLAS MURRAY BUTLER, President of Columbia University. $2.00, *net*. Postpaid.

GROWTH AND EDUCATION
By JOHN M. TYLER, Professor of Biology in Amherst College. $1.50, *net*. Postpaid.

SOCIAL DEVELOPMENT AND EDUCATION
By M. VINCENT O'SHEA, Professor of Education in the University of Wisconsin. $2.00, *net*. Postpaid.

THE PRINCIPLES OF EDUCATION
By WILLIAM C. RUEDIGER, Ph.D., Assistant Professor of Educational Psychology in the Teachers College of the George Washington University. $1.25, *net*. Postpaid.

THE INDIVIDUAL IN THE MAKING
By EDWIN A. KIRKPATRICK, Teacher of Psychology, Child Study and School Laws, State Normal School, Fitchburg, Mass. $1.25, *net*. Postpaid.

A THEORY OF MOTIVES, IDEALS, AND VALUES IN EDUCATION
By WILLIAM E. CHANCELLOR, Superintendent of Schools, Norwalk, Conn. $1.75, *net*. Postpaid.

EDUCATION AND THE LARGER LIFE
By C. HANFORD HENDERSON. $1.30, *net*. Postage 13 cents.

HOW TO STUDY AND TEACHING HOW TO STUDY
By FRANK MCMURRY, Professor of Elementary Education in Teachers College, Columbia University. $1.25, *net*. Postpaid.

CPSIA information can be obtained at www.ICGtesting.com
Printed in the USA
LVOW01s0157200913

353309LV00009B/399/P